SOCIAL WORK
AND CRIMINAL LAW
IN SCOTLAND

SOCIAL WORK
AND CRIMINAL LAW
IN SCOTLAND

by
George Moore and Chris Wood

ABERDEEN UNIVERSITY PRESS

First published 1981
Aberdeen University Press
A member of the Pergamon Group

British Library Cataloguing in Publication Data
Moore, George
Social work and criminal law in Scotland.
1. Criminal law—Scotland
I. Title   II. Wood, Chris J.
344.1105'024362   KDC913

ISBN 0-08-025731-3

PRINTED IN GREAT BRITAIN
THE UNIVERSITY PRESS, ABERDEEN

CONTENTS

PREFACE

The purpose of this book is to provide information and guidance about those aspects of the judicial and penal systems and the measures relating to child offenders which affect social workers and those who, from other reference points and disciplines, require a source book on these matters. It encompasses coverage of the legislation, and has been prepared to take account of the Criminal Justice (Scotland) Act, 1980, though in advance of implementation of the Act. It also deals with aspects of practice and procedure which require to be understood and appreciated, and includes material providing a range of specimen documentation not otherwise available. In the nature of things the text cannot be binding but the work does seek to persuade. It acknowledges a wide range of considerations outside its scope. The knowledge and understanding it aims to provide are a necessary adjunct to professional skills.

G.M.
C.J.W.

December, 1980

ACKNOWLEDGMENTS

We are indebted to a number of people without whose help this work would not have been possible. To Sheriff G. B. C. Nicholson for his comprehensive advice and guidance, both in regard to purely legal aspects and to matters of approach and interpretation. To Sheriff J. L. M. Mitchell for his interest and encouragement and for the suggested wording of probation requirements. Sheriff J. Aikman Smith, for many years a staunch supporter and advocate of a strong social work presence in the courts, encouraged and sustained us through the more difficult passages; his thorough reading of the first draft enabled the work to go forward into its present form.

Our thanks are due to Scottish Office officials who kindly read and commented on an earlier version and to Colin MacLean of Aberdeen University Press whose interest survived the many vicissitudes of Scottish Criminal Justice legislation in the late 70s. Without the active assistance of the Publications Committee of Jordanhill College the production of this work would have been infinitely more difficult and we would like to record our appreciation of their timely and generous aid.

To H.M. Stationery Office for permission to use material under Crown copyright, particularly the statutory references and the quoted material from the Departmental publications acknowledged in the text.

Finally to our typists, especially to Mrs. Isabel Grant who brought the work to its final form, our sincere thanks for their patience and tolerance.

INTRODUCTION

by Sheriff J. Aikman Smith

Society must protect itself against the wrongdoer. It must show its disapproval of crime. But we take it as axiomatic that a society whose morality acknowledges the worth and dignity of each of its members must seek, in fulfilling these objects, the minimum interference with life and liberty that is consistent with them.

This statement of principle explains, in a very few words, why it is that the courts need social workers.

There cannot be a caring society without law and order. The criminal courts exist to protect society from crime. They deal only with crimes which have already been committed, but in the exercise of their sentencing powers they have an essential role in the prevention of crimes which may occur in the future.

The effects of a high rate of crime must be obvious to all social workers. The most numerous victims of the types of crime which are most prevalent, violence, dishonesty and vandalism, are found amongst the least privileged section of the community.

Law-abiding citizens look naturally to the courts for protection, and in popular view judicial severity is plainly the best means of keeping crime within tolerable limits. The courts certainly cannot be seen to condone anti-social behaviour and there are many cases where, because of the nature of the crime or the character of the offender, severe measures are necessary. But the crime rate is essentially the reflection of prevailing moral and social values, and these cannot be changed by a simple policy of punitive or retributive sentencing.

If the courts are to use their sentencing powers constructively and humanely, so that the best interests of society are served, they must have officers to investigate and report impartially on the circumstances of the offenders appearing before them; judges must have the information which will help them to assess the probable consequences of the sentence they are thinking of imposing.

Scottish prisons, notoriously, have now become so overcrowded that they can offer only limited prospects of improving the attitude and habits of those who are sent there. Monetary penalties too often result in hardship for the innocent and provide no support for offenders who may wish to lead a law-abiding life in future. Both imprisonment and fines create new family and social problems of the type with which social workers are constantly occupied, problems which sow the seeds of future delinquency.

The courts have a duty to express the public disapproval of crime. Unfortunately, in the absence of better alternatives, they are, all too frequently, forced to adopt measures which, on a rational view, are unlikely to be at all effective for the protection of the community. Probation methods, at present languishing in Scotland, if properly understood, developed and practised, offer in many circumstances the best hope of avoiding the counter productive consequences of prison sentences and fines.

It is only in quite recent years that professional social workers have become significantly involved in the service of the adult criminal courts in Scotland. For practical purposes the development began with the Criminal Justice (Scotland) Act 1949 which made it necessary that every court should have the services of probation officers; this Act initiated the system of social enquiry reporting and it gave clear authority and encouragement for the use of probation as a disposal in cases involving adult offenders. As a result of the Act, the probation service rapidly expanded. Between 1950 and 1968 the number of whole time probation officers in Scotland grew from about seventy to about three hundred, and, as the service grew in size, efficiency and experience, it acquired increased statutory responsibilities in regard to adult first offenders, aftercare, fines supervision and parole.

The evolution of a professional social work service, exclusively concerned with work amongst offenders, was welcomed by the courts, and particularly by the Sheriff Courts where most of the work of probation officers lay. Mutual confidence and understanding developed between Sheriffs and probation officers through frequent personal contacts. Most Sheriffs came to regard the reports of probation officers as reliable, and indeed essential, aids to constructive sentencing, frequently requesting such reports in cases where there was no statutory requirement to do so. The number of probation orders made on adult offenders steadily increased, often in cases which would formerly have attracted prison sentences. The courts became increasingly 'probation-minded'.

The nature and functions of probation and of the probation service in England and Wales, and also in Scotland, were examined by the Morison Committee which reported in 1962. This Committee defined probation as "the submission of an offender while at liberty to a specified period of supervision by a social case-worker who is an officer of the Court: during this period the offender remains liable, if not of good conduct, to be otherwise dealt with by the court." In regard to the distinctive functional role of the probation officer, the Committee had this to say: "while as a case-worker the probation officer's prime concern is with the well-being of an individual, he is also the agent of a system concerned with the protection of society and as such must, to a degree which varies from case to case, and during the course of supervision, seek to regulate the probationer's behaviour. He must also be prepared, when necessary, to assert the interests of society by initiating proceedings for breach of the requirements of the probation order."

The Social Work (Scotland) Act 1968 disbanded the Scottish probation service and abolished the title of 'probation officer'. However, as the succeeding chapters show, all the statutory functions of the service for the courts (and the penal system) continue. Local Authority social workers have inherited all the responsibilities, and also the role, of the former probation officers.

The considerations which led to the absorption of probation officers into the new local authority Social Work Departments, as expressed in the 1966 White Paper

'Social Work in the Community' (which foreshadowed the Social Work (Scotland) Act),
were the desirability of avoiding a multiplicity of services carrying out essentially similar work in the same community, or even in the same family; and the
view that the main duty of the probation officer(personal social work with the
offender and his family in the community) is basically similar to that of other
social workers. His function of assessment, though for the assistance of the
court, is part of the social worker's essential skills. The authors of the White
Paper in expressing their opinion that the body of expertise necessary to all
social workers is substantially the same also observed that specialised knowledge
and experience are often necessary. This observation, has, perhaps, received too
little attention in the organisation of social work for the courts and the penal
system.

As social work has so far been practised under the 1968 Act, for most social
workers court duties form only a part of a work load which is mainly concerned
with the care of children in need, the aged, the handicapped, the homeless and
others in troubles basically not of their own making. The pressure of such varied
work loads allows them few of the opportunities which were open to probation
officers to become familiar with what happens in criminal courts, to meet the
judges, and to learn from personal observation how anxious the sentencing problems
can be for judges daily confronted with the evidence of a constantly increasing
volume of anti-social behaviour, and its effects on the victims.

It is true that many of the offenders with whom the courts have to deal have
themselves suffered disadvantages of the sort that are familiar to social workers,
and undoubtedly in the field of adult delinquency the social worker has scope for
the use of all his basic professional skills. In the service of the courts,
however, social work takes on an orientation of its own to which the social
worker has to adjust. His mandate and his terms of reference call for a specialist approach. In no other field is the social worker acting directly under the
authority of a criminal court, or charged with duties specifically directed
towards the protection of the community from crime.

The criminal law is concerned to preserve the freedom of citizens to live their
lives according to their own wishes as long as, in doing so, they do not damage
the rights of others. In a free society, personal privacy must be jealously
guarded; there must be good reasons before compulsory intervention into a
citizen's affairs can be justified.

The individual with whom the social worker is authorised by the court to deal
is an individual who (although he may be to some degree psychologically or
psychiatrically disturbed) is legally sane and fit to plead. The reason, and
it is the only reason, which entitles the court itself to intervene in his
affairs, or entitles a social worker on the court's instructions to intervene,
is that he has admitted, or been found guilty of, some contravention of the
criminal law for which he is liable to be penalised.

The term 'client', ubiquitous in social work, can be misleading in the context
of work for the courts. The offender on whom the court directs a social enquiry
report to be prepared is in no sense a client of the social worker. The report
must be prepared with professional objectivity; if the social worker has a client
at all, the client is the judge who has called for the social worker's assistance.
In supervising an offender who has been placed on probation by the court the
social worker is not only concerned with the interests of the probationer; the
social worker is responsible also to the court for insisting that the conditions
of the court's order be observed and for reporting breaches of the order if they
occur.

The courts cannot make probation orders unless they are satisfied that the interests of the community will be properly safeguarded. It is understandable that a social worker, accustomed to regarding the well-being of the individual in his charge as his prime concern, may find difficulty in adjusting to the duty of acting as an agent of a system concerned with the protection of society. Court duties can give rise to a sense of divided loyalties, but in the nature of probation work this must be so.

In many cases, probation orders are made because the court regards the offender as more in need of help than of control. In such cases the social worker's task is clearly to advise, assist and befriend the offender, and conflicting loyalties rarely arise.

The real challenge for court social workers lies with those offenders, and they are numerous, whose conduct shows that they present a potential future danger to the welfare of others. In dealing with offenders of this type, the court can only contemplate probation if it is satisfied that the supervising social worker will exercise firm control. Probation must not appear to such offenders, or to the observant and critical public, as a 'let-off'. The order is likely to contain requirements in regard to such matters as restitution or unpaid work or place of residence which the offender sees as punitive and which he has only agreed to accept under duress. The social worker entrusted with this kind of case needs all his or her professional skill and strength of personality to overcome the resentment of authority which such offenders often initially exhibit, if the mutual confidence which is necessary for successful casework is to be established.

It is seldom, if ever, that the court will make a probation order in this type of case unless it has been encouraged to do so by what has been said in a social enquiry report. When the court chooses probation it does so in the hope that with skilled, professional help the offender will learn to lead a law-abiding life in future; this, if it can be achieved, will be in the best interests of the offender himself, since no one can live happily if he is continually in conflict with the law. The authority which the social worker derives from the court, wisely used, can make a valuable, and even essential, contribution of the offender's rehabilitation.

Overcrowded prisons are an affront to the concept of the caring society which the system inaugurated by the Social Work (Scotland) Act is designed to foster. They are also an enormous expense to the taxpayer. In recent years, the use which the courts have been able to make of probation has been steadily declining, while custodial sentences have increased. Considerations both of humanity and of economy call for the revival of confidence in probation as a realistic alternative in the difficult cases where the choice between custodial and non-custodial treatment is narrow.

The purpose of all the legislation which requires local authorities to provide social work services for the courts has been to minimise the number of offenders who have been kept locked up in custody. The courts, for their part, so far as it consists with their over-riding duty to discourage criminal activity, are ready to make use of non-custodial methods; the extent to which they will be able to do so, however, must depend on the sufficiency and reliability of the social work assistance which local authorities are prepared to provide.

The chapters which follow have been written for social workers by colleagues with specialist training and experience in work for the courts, in the hope that they will provide guidance in an unfamiliar, but surely challenging and rewarding, field of duty. They also make plain how extensive are the obligations which Parliament has placed on local authorities.

PART ONE: COURTS: PRACTICES AND PROCEDURES

Chapter 1

The Prosecution of Crime and the Criminal Courts

The Prosecution System in Scotland

The prosecution of crime is the responsibility of the Lord Advocate, whose powers
are exercised through the Crown Office in Edinburgh. He is assisted by the
Solicitor-General and ten Advocates Depute. These law officers are known collect-
ively as Crown Counsel. The Lord Advocate and Solicitor-General are both political
appointments and are members of the Government of the day.

Throughout Scotland the local officers of the Lord Advocate are the Procurators
Fiscal. It is to the Procurator Fiscal that the Police report all alleged crimes
and offences. Since the 19th century the whole system of prosecution in Scotland
has been under central control: private prosecution is all but unknown, and there
is no system of police prosecution comparable to that of England and Wales.

The word "crime" is used to refer to breaches of common law, for example, theft,
fraud, assault. The word "offence" strictly refers to breaches of particular
statutes, for example, a contravention of section 99(b) of the Road Traffic Act,
1972, which creates the offence of driving while disqualified. It is important
to note that particular instances of otherwise ordinary crimes may have been made
the subject of a special statute, and that such a statute may give a court greater
powers than would have been available at common law: for example, theft of mails
is governed by the Post Office Acts: and assaults on police officers by the Police
(Scotland) Acts. In general though it is a hallmark of the Scottish legal system
that there is much less statute law than in England and Wales, and this feature
can be regarded as making for greater flexibility in prosecution.

There are two methods of procedure for the prosecution of crime, once a Fiscal has
decided that there is a prima facie case, and that the circumstances justify the
mounting of a prosecution. The methods of procedure are known as solemn procedure,
and summary procedure, and we shall consider these in detail below. In a few
instances the relevant law may govern which of these methods of procedure shall be
used. Otherwise the choice lies with the prosecuting authorities, and for the
most part their discretion is considerable. Especially it should be noted that
many frequent and familiar crimes and offences can be prosecuted by either method:
the Fiscal has to exercise choice and discretion in each case according both to
the intrinsic circumstances surrounding it, and with regard to his duty of
representing the public interest.

The Criminal Courts

Whilst there are two methods of procedure, solemn and summary, for the prosecution
of crime, there are three levels of Criminal Court, and thus a recognition of the
type of procedure being employed by each is crucial to an understanding of the
overall system. The choice of prosecution method will depend in part on the powers
of the various courts at each level. The High Court hears cases only on solemn
procedure. The Sheriff Court can hear cases on solemn procedure, but its powers
of imprisonment when hearing such cases are restricted to a maximum of 2 years: it
can however send a case on solemn procedure to the High Court for disposal if it
thinks its own powers inadequate. The Sheriff Court also hears cases on summary
procedure, but in any such case its powers of imprisonment are generally restricted
to a maximum of 6 months, and its maximum fine to £1,000. The District Court only
hears cases on summary procedure, and its maximum penalties are 60 days imprisonment, and £200 fine. One consequence of these arrangements is that the Sheriff
Court hears cases by both methods of procedure and deals with the bulk of criminal
matters in Scotland. With the exception of the Sheriff Court's power to remit a
case already on solemn procedure to the High Court for disposal, there is in
general no other power for lower courts to remit to higher courts for a greater
sentence, whereas this is an important feature of arrangements in England and Wales.
District Courts cannot remit cases to Sheriff Courts with a view to a prison
sentence of more than 60 days; a Sheriff Court hearing a case on summary procedure
cannot transform it into one on solemn procedure, and proceed to give a sentence
in excess of 6 months imprisonment: all this serves to underline the importance
and significance of the choice of method and court initially made by the prosecuting authorities. We deal in detail with the two methods of procedure, solemn and
summary, below but will first consider the powers of the various courts in greater
detail. It is also important to note that the Sheriff and High Courts both deal
with a whole range of civil and other matters - for example, adoptions, proofs for
the Childrens Hearing, Fatal Accident Inquiries, and so on - which fall outwith the
scope of this book: This means that the judges in these courts do not only deal
with criminal cases, and that in any court building the people present may not
necessarily be involved or interested in criminal cases.

The High Court of Justiciary. The High Court of Justiciary is the supreme court
in criminal matters. It consists of the Lord Justice General, the Lord Justice
Clerk, and nineteen Lord Commissioners of Justiciary. When dealing with cases a
High Court Judge usually sits alone, but in matters of importance two or three may
sit together. If the public interest demands it, the presiding Judge may seek the
opinion of the whole High Court bench.

The consequences of the system of prosecution are that the High Court deals only
with the most serious cases. It has exclusive jurisdiction in cases of murder,
rape and treason. Those offences which cause deep public concern, e.g. bank
robberies, serious assaults, will be tried in this court. The court will also
sentence those offenders remitted from the Sheriff Court, where a sentence of more
than two years imprisonment is considered appropriate by the Sheriff concerned.

The pronouncements of High Court Judges when passing sentence concerning the
relative seriousness or prevalence of certain types of offence influence the
practice of lower courts. The High Court also has the power to pass *Acts of
Adjournal*, to regulate the workings of those courts:- for example, the format of
a Probation Order is specified in an Act of Adjournal.

The High Court hears all criminal appeals: when sitting as an appelate Court it is
constituted by at least three judges. It hears appeals against conviction (i.e. a
dispute concerning the facts or the application of law in a trial), or against
sentence. It also deals with *bail appeals* - a dispute concerning the detention of

a person in custody by a lower court. Only one Judge hears bail appeals.

Two further facts are worthy of note:-

> The High Court can, on appeal, *increase* an original sentence.
> There is no appeal from the High Court.
>
> The court functions in four 'circuits'. Sittings are held:
>
> - in Edinburgh
>
> - in Glasgow, Stirling and Oban   (West circuit)
>
> - in Aberdeen, Dundee and Perth   (North circuit)
>
> - in Dumfries, Jedburgh and Ayr   (South circuit)

When acting as an Appeal Court, the sittings of the High Court always take place in Edinburgh.

The Sheriff Court.   Scotland is divided into six Sheriffdoms, each with a Sheriff Principal and a varying number of Sheriffs. Each Sheriffdom is further divided into a number of Sheriff Court Districts, which are not necessarily co-terminous with Local Government Districts. The Sheriff Principal may appoint a number of honorary Sheriffs, who have the same powers as a Sheriff, and exercise jurisdiction in the absence of other Sheriffs. Sheriffs are appointed by the Crown from among the legal profession, and enjoy considerable independence under the law. In criminal matters the powers of a Sheriff Principal are the same as any of his Sheriffs. The Sheriff Court can hear cases both by solemn and by summary procedure. It deals with the bulk of criminal prosecutions.

> Solemn Procedure.
>
> The sentencing powers of the Sheriff Court hearing cases on solemn procedure are:-
>
> 1. Custodial sentence of up to and including 2 years. Special considerations apply before any young offender can be sentenced to a period of custody, and to the types of custodial sentences which can be imposed.
>
> 2. Remit to the High Court for disposal - if longer sentence thought appropriate.
>
> 3. Unlimited fines.
>
> 4. Community Service Order - provided an approved scheme exists in the area where the offender resides or is to reside.
>
> 5. Probation - including requirements for unpaid work if made available by the community service scheme in the area where the offender resides or is to reside.
>
> 6. Deferred sentence.
>
> 7. Admonition.

8. Absolute discharge.

9. Caution.

10. Compensation Order (unlimited amount).

11. Hospital or Guardianship Order.

12. Detention of children for up to 2 years under section
    44 of the Criminal Justice (Scotland) Act, 1980 or
    remit to High Court.

13. Remit to Children's Panel for disposal in any case
    involving a child.

Summary Procedure.

The sentencing powers of the Sheriff Court hearing cases
on summary procedure are:-

1. Custodial sentence of not more than 3 months.

2. Custodial sentence of not more than 6 months, PROVIDING:-

    (a) the offender is convicted for a second or subsequent
         offence of dishonesty,

or (b) the offender is convicted for a second or subsequent
         offence involving the appropriation of money,

or (c) the offender is convicted for a second or subsequent
         offence of personal violence,

and (d) the offender is appearing for a second or subsequent
         offence of *attempting* to commit any of the above.

         None of these alternatives are mutually exclusive
         of the rest.

3. Young offenders are subject to special considerations
    as far as the imposition of any custodial sentence is
    concerned. The Sheriff Summary Court can sentence
    young offenders to:-

    (a) Detention Centre Training, except that the duration
         of this sentence may not exceed 3 months unless the
         conditions noted at No.2 above are fulfilled.

    (b) Determinate periods of detention in a Young Offenders"
         Institution, subject to the considerations noted
         above at 1 and 2.

4. Fines not exceeding £1,000.

5. Community Service Order - provided an approved scheme
    exists in the area where the offender resides or is to
    reside.

6. Probation - including requirements for unpaid work if these are made available by the Community Service scheme in the area where the offender resides or is to reside.

7. Deferred Sentence.

8. Admonition.

9. Absolute Discharge.

10. Caution.

11. Compensation Order, up to a maximum of £1,000.

12. Hospital or Guardianship Order.

13. Residential Training for children, up to a maximum of 2 years.

14. Remit to Children's Panel for Disposal, in a case involving a child.

The Sheriff Clerk and the various members of staff within the Sheriff Court are civil servants. The Sheriff is afforded the respect due to the dignity of his office under the Crown, which is one of great antiquity and prestige.

The District Court. District Courts came into being on 16th May, 1975 following the enactment of the District Courts Act, 1975. The District Court serves an area defined as a District by the Local Government (Scotland) Act, 1975. There are 56 such areas in Scotland, and each has its own District Court, except one Island area where there would have been insufficient business. The District Courts replaced a variety of courts of summary jurisdiction which had previously existed, and they reflect an amalgam of different aspects of their predecessors.

The District Court only hears cases on summary procedure. Its maximum powers are 60 days imprisonment, or £200 fines. The sentencing powers of the District Court also include:-

1. Detention Centre Training) provided that reports have been
2. Young Offenders' Institution) obtained and that the sentence does
   for young offenders.) not exceed 60 days.

3. Probation.

4. Community Service Order - but only if a scheme in the offender's area of residence has been made available to the District Court, and this is fairly rare as yet.

5. Admonition.

6. Caution - up to a maximum of £200

7. Absolute Discharge.

8. Compensation Order - up to a maximum of £200.

It can be noted that the following disposals are not available to the District Court:-

Hospital or Guardianship Orders.

Orders for the Residential Training of children as they have no jurisdiction in respect of children.

Whilst the maximum penalties open to the District Court are of the magnitude indicated, some of the statutory offences with which they deal may carry much lower maximum penalties - for example, the offence of plain drunkenness (contravention of section 70 of the Licensing (Scotland) Act, 1903), even though the 1980 Criminal Justice (Scotland) Act, has now raised that maximum to a fine of £25. The jurisdiction of the District Court also covers a range of social nuisance offences whose contents are defined in local statutes, and whose precise detail thus differs from area to area: for example, the Edinburgh Corporation Orders of 1967 proscribe matters such as loitering, vagrancy, begging, and similar matters; the District Court will also deal with local matters such as car parking, one-way streets, 'bus lanes and so on. However the general criminal jurisdiction of District Courts has recently been significantly enlarged by the Criminal Justice (Scotland) Act, 1980: Section 7 of that Act lifts certain restrictions on the type of criminal case which can be dealt with in District Courts. Previously the District Courts could only deal with cases inferring dishonest appropriation of property - i.e. their reset, fraud or wilful imposition, breach of trust or embezzlement - where the amount involved did not exceed £25: that amount has now been raised to £200. Also it could only deal with such cases where the person was a first offender, but that restriction has also been lifted by section 7. It remains to be seen how Procurators Fiscal will use these new powers in terms of the cases they decide to deal with in District Courts. It is worthy of note that while District Courts now have a potentially much more significant area of criminal jurisdiction, and have powers of imprisonment, they are precluded by the same section 7 from dealing with any road traffic cases in which disqualification from driving is a possibility.

The judges in the District Court are known as Justices or Magistrates, and are addressed in court as "Your Honour". It is competent for a lay Magistrate to sit alone in the District Court, but the preference is for a multiple bench. Section 14 of the District Courts Act empowers the Secretary of State to order a period of training for Justices, but his role in their selection is a complex and finely balanced one. Each District Council will have a Justices Committee, which regulates the running of the court.

In Glasgow, the district Court is presided over by a professional, fulltime, salaried, stipendiary Magistrate. The jurisdiction and powers of this court are equivalent to those of the Sheriff hearing cases on summary procedure.

The Clerk of Court and his staff are all employees of the District Council. The court is entitled to the full range of services in regard to probation and after-care which Regional Councils are obliged to provide under section 27 of the Social Work (Scotland) Act, 1968: these include the attendance of officers of the Director of Social Work at the court as may be necessary.

The methods of prosecution.

Solemn Procedure

The Indictment. No case can go forward on solemn procedure without the authority

and approval of Crown Counsel, who in turn decide whether such a case shall be
heard in the Sheriff or in the High Court. The charge(s) in any case on solemn
procedure will be contained in a document known as an *indictment*. Confusion can
arise over the meaning of the phrase "indictable offences," particularly as it is
frequently used in discussions of criminal statistics: a very wide range of crimes
and offences can be tried "on indictment," - i.e. in Scotland by solemn procedure
- but each and every instance of such offences need not so be tried. The indictment is a full written statement of the charge(s) that an accused will have to
face at his trial in any case on solemn procedure. The indictment proceeds in the
name of the Lord Advocate as being authorised and initiated by him. The part of
it which contains the ground of the charge(s) is known as the *libel*. An indictment
will further include a list both of the material evidence, known as the *production*
in the case of documentary items, and *labels* in the case of non-documentary items:
and also of the names and addresses of prosecution witnesses: at a trial the
prosecution cannot make use of any material or person not so listed. The prosecution of a case on solemn procedure in the Sheriff Court will usually be undertaken
by the Procurator Fiscal, although the Lord Advocate or one of his Deputes could
so prosecute: in the High Court the prosecution is normally undertaken by one of
the Advocates Depute, although occasionally the Solicitor General or Lord Advocate
may appear in person to prosecute.

The Petition. Because solemn procedure involves the approval and authority of
Crown Counsel, its use requires that the Procurator Fiscal report the case to the
Crown Office before the indictment can be prepared and issued: thus a series of
preliminary stages occur during which the case is investigated by the Procurator
Fiscal, and the accused *committed for trial* for prosecution by solemn procedure.
Where police or other evidence suggests there is prima facie case for the use of
this method, - whether because of the intrinsic nature or seriousness of the
offence; or because of the accused's record; or because of his involvement with
other older or more serious offenders; or for whatever reason the Fiscal adopts in
the public interest - the accused will first of all be charged on *petition*. The
charge(s) at this stage are formally laid by the Procurator Fiscal in the petition,
and a series of enquiries and consultations instigated by him follow. During this
part of the process the accused appears before the Sheriff Court, even if it is
known that he must ultimately go before the High Court, but he is dealt with in a
closed court, or before the Sheriff in the privacy of his chambers.

Judicial Examination. The 1980 Criminal Justice (Scotland) Act has made significant changes to proceedings at this preliminary examination stage in cases on
solemn procedure. It has revised in part an earlier practice of judicial examination, whereas until the Act's enactment proceedings at this point were almost
entirely a matter of formalities and usually fairly brief. The law previously
stated that at this stage the accused need not "emit a declaration", and almost
invariably an accused who appeared "on petition" gave no plea to the charge and
made no declaration. Subsequently he was either "fully committed" for trial, or
"committed for further examination", with the major point at issue being whether
or not he remained in custody, or was released on bail.

Now the 1980 Act has amended section 20 of the Criminal Procedure (Scotland) Act,
1975 by introducing a further section 20A which gives the Procurator Fiscal the
right to question an accused, "insofar as such questioning is directed towards
eliciting any explanation, denial, justification or comment which the accused may
have as regards matters averred in the charge" subject to certain safeguards in
that the questioning is directed towards a determination in respect of e.g. alibi,
incrimination, consent of an alleged victim and also in respect of any alleged
confession or admission to or in the hearing of a police officer, providing that
the accused has received a written record of any such statement made. A number
of important procedural points are made (S.S.2) respecting the form of such

questions and the whole is subject to prescription by Act of Adjournal.

This revival of judicial examination largely results from the recommendations of the Thomson Committee on Criminal Procedure, and is in large part designed to avoid unnecessary investigation by the Fiscal, and needlessly delayed trials.

Committal for Trial

Either at the first appearance on petition for examination, or after a period for further examination, the accused will be "committed for trial". Thereafter the Fiscal will investigate the case, including seeing the witnesses and taking their "precognitions" as may be necessary, and thereafter submit a full report to the Crown Office. If the Crown Office accepts that the case should proceed, an indictment will be prepared and served on the accused, showing at which court and on what date he must appear for trial. Alternatively the Crown Office may instruct the Procurator Fiscal to take the case on summary procedure, for which he then needs no further authority; or it may even instruct that no proceedings be taken, in which event the accused would be informed, and, if he had been detained in custody after committal for trial, would immediately be liberated.

Until the enactment of the 1980 Act, an indictment would indicate two diets on which the case would be called: the first was a "pleading" diet, and always took place in the Sheriff Court, and at it any legal arguments about issues such as the relevance or competence of the indictment, notices of special defences, alibis and so on, were signified. The second diet was the "trial" diet, and might be in either the Sheriff or the High Court, as shown on the indictment. Section 12 of the Act has abolished the mandatory first diet, and schedule 4 of the Act now sets out the arrangements. The indictment now contains notice of only one diet, but the diet must be at least 29 clear days after the service of the indictment. If the defence wish to pursue issues such as relevancy and similar matters, notice can be given and a diet to consider the issues, to be known as a "preliminary" diet, established. At a preliminary diet, the trial diet may be postponed by the court for up to 3 weeks, but at the conclusion of a preliminary diet, the accused will be required to state how he pleads.

The position of accused committed for trial on solemn procedure is protected by an important provision known colloquially as the "110 day rule", which is regarded as a notable feature of the Scottish legal system. The detail of this provision is now redefined by section 14 of the 1980 Act. Section 14 amends section 101 of the 1975 Criminal Procedure (Scotland) Act, which previously governed the position. The section now provides that any accused shall not be tried on indictment unless the trial commences within 12 months of his first appearance on petition, with this mainly affecting persons who are liberated on bail at the examination or committal stages; this section does not apply if the accused fails to appear and a warrant has to be taken for his arrest. The section goes on to state that an accused who is detained may not be detained after committal for more than –

> "(a) 80 days, unless within that period the indictment is
>   served on him, which failing he shall be liberated
>   forthwith; or
>
> (b)   110 days, unless the trial of the case is commenced
>   within that period, which failing he shall be liberated
>   forthwith and thereafter no proceedings shall be competent
>   against him in respect of that offence."

There are various miscellaneous provisions for this period to be extended in certain unforeseen circumstances.

Shortened Procedure

The law also contains a procedure whereby an accused may hasten the hearing of his case if he intends to plead "guilty". This general possibility has existed for some time in Scottish law, but is colloquially known as "section 102" procedure, as the power is currently located at section 102 of the Criminal Procedure (Scotland) Act, 1975. That section makes it possible for an accused to intimate in writing to the Crown Agent an intention to plead guilty to the offence charged in the petition, and a desire to have his case disposed of at once, and thereafter for him to be served with an indictment which lacked any list of witnesses or productions. Under the 1975 Act any such case had to be heard initially in the Sheriff Court, but section 16 of the 1980 Act has now made a slight amendment to section 102 of the 1975 Act to permit that the accompanying notice to appear at court may specify either the Sheriff or the High Court. If the accused at a section 102 diet then pleads Not Guilty, or makes a guilty plea to only part of the charge such that this is not acceptable to the Prosecutor, the diet is "deserted pro loco et tempore", and the accused still stands committed for trial on solemn procedure.

Trial

An accused who pleads "not guilty" to an indictment will be tried by the Sheriff or by the Judge of the High Court sitting with a jury. In Scotland a jury consists of fifteen persons, and may return a simple majority verdict. The jury's job is to decide questions of fact: the judge's task is to direct the trial and rule on questions of law. A jury may return one of three verdicts - guilty; not guilty; or not proven: only the first involves the possibility of the court proceeding to sentence. It is further open to the jury to find an accused guilty of a lesser or alternative charge; or to find him guilty of only one or more of a total number of charges contained in an indictment. It should be noted that in Scotland an accused has no right to a jury trial, but will only be so tried if the case is on solemn procedure. Also in cases on solemn procedure unless the prosecutor moves the court to do so the latter cannot proceed to conviction and sentence.

<u>Summary Procedure</u>.   Either the Sheriff or the District Court may hear cases on
summary procedure.   There are restrictions on the types and/or severity of cases
which the District Courts may hear, reflecting their generally lower maximum
sentencing powers, and additionally the Lord Advocate may from time to time issue
instructions to procurators fiscal about the general distribution of cases between
these two courts: otherwise, unless a specific statute determines the choice, the
discretion lies with the procurator fiscal.   Cases can be brought on summary procedure without reference by a fiscal to the Lord Advocate but it can also happen
that a case may eventually go forward on summary procedure, after originally
starting life as one on solemn procedure, as a result of specific instructions to
that effect from Crown Office.   In general, however, there are no preliminary
court proceedings in cases of summary procedure comparable with those of the examination stage in solemn procedure.

The charge(s) in any case on summary procedure are contained in a document known as
a *complaint:*   a complaint proceeds in the name of the local procurator fiscal, not
of the Lord Advocate.   If any of the charges in the complaint is an offence created
by statute, as opposed to a common law crime, the accused will receive along with
his copy of the complaint, *a notice of penalty* showing the maximum penalty
which is available to the court.   Where applicable the accused will also receive
a *schedule of previous convictions* which it is alleged apply to him.   These are
normally considered only after he either pleads or is found guilty: if he has
pled guilty by letter, it is assumed that he accepts they apply to him, unless he
indicates to the contrary; otherwise he is specifically asked in court to agree
that they do apply to him, and thus has specific opportunity to indicate any
dispute as to the schedule's contents.

An accused who is detained in custody after his arrest, and is charged on summary
procedure, will appear before the court on the "next lawful day."   Otherwise an
accused will be cited to appear by the fiscal and the diet on which he is due to
appear will be shown on the citation.   Unless either the prosecutor or the defence
moves to the contrary,   i.e. to continue the case "without plea" for some specific
reason which then has to be given, debated, and either acceded to or refused by
the court, a plea is taken at this first hearing.   If that plea is one of "guilty",
no trial of the evidence is required, and the prosecutor gives such account as he
feels is necessary to fill out the details of the charge.   He does not need to
'move' for sentence in cases on summary procedure, and, after hearing any
mitigation by the accused or his agent, the court is then in a position to proceed
to sentence.   If the plea is one of 'not guilty', or if the plea tendered is not
acceptable to the fiscal, a further diet is almost invariably required for the
trial to take place, and the immediate question for the court is that of on what
terms the accused will be released.   In the event of a not guilty plea in cases on
summary procedure, there is no trial by jury: the case is determined by the
Sheriff or the Magistrate(s) sitting without a jury, and the decision as to both
facts and the law is theirs alone.   The same verdicts are available - guilty, not
guilty, and not proven - but there is no right of an accused person in Scotland to
elect for or insist on a trial by jury.

The Criminal Justice (Scotland) Act, 1980 has made an innovation to summary procedure by the introduction of an "intermediate diet."   Section 15 of that Act
introduces a new section, 337A, to the Criminal Procedure (Scotland) Act, 1975
defining this new diet.   Its introduction represents a response to the related
problems of the long delay between plea and trial in the busier courts, and the
number of trials which subsequently prove to be unnecessary because the accused
changes his plea to guilty on the day of the trial.   Section 15 of the 1980 Act
defines section 337A of the 1975 Act thus:-

              (1)   The courts may, at any time, as respects a case which
                     is adjourned for trial, fix a diet (to be know as an

intermediate diet) for the purpose of ascertaining -

a) the state of preparation of the prosecutor and of the accused with respect to their cases; and

b) whether the accused intends to adhere to the plea of not guilty.

(2) At an intermediate diet, the court may ask the prosecutor and the accused any question for the purposes mentioned in subsection (1) above.

(3) The accused shall attend an intermediate diet of which he has received intimation or to which he has been cited.

(4) A plea of guilty may be tendered at the intermediate diet.

Specimen Documentation

In the nature of things a number of documents are in common use in Court settings. Some of these may reach Social Workers direct, e.g. lists of previous convictions. Others, such as those which follow will not. It is, however, important for Social Workers to appreciate the forms used and the respective context in which each is appropriate, so that in communication with Court officials, police and accused persons, the individual Social Worker is able to display a level of knowledge commensurate with the specific situations about which he or she is required to make professional inputs. It is useful and advisable, to be able to discuss these matters meaningfully, rather than to attempt to deal with situations in a vacuum which does little to serve the respective interests of court and accused, both of which benefit from purposeful Social Work interests in the concerns which bring them into face to face contact.

Broadly the documentation may be divided into

(1) Petition

and (2) Indictment

which are associated with matters processed at solemn procedure level

and (3) Complaint which is used in summary proceedings

and such warrants as may be issued to secure the attendance of the person concerned.

An important document is the notice of previous conviction which is served on persons facing criminal charges.

Petition

UNTO THE HONOURABLE THE SHERIFF OF THE LOTHIAN AND BORDERS EDINBURGH

1 December 1979.

The Petition of GEORGE SMITH

Procurator Fiscal of Court of BLACKTOWN   for the Public Interest:

HUMBLY SHEWETH,

That from information received by the Petitioner, it appears, and he accordingly charges, that STEVEN JAMES (born 30.10.40), 49 Phillip Street, Blacktown – at present in custody – you did on 30th November, 1979 in the premises at 50 Jericho Lane, Blacktown, assault Michael Redpath, hit him on the head with a broken glass whereby he sustained multiple lacerations, jump on him, kick him, and repeatedly hit him about the body with your fists, all to his severe injury.

Signed ....
Procurator Fiscal Depute.

In order, therefore, that the said Accused may be dealt with according to Law,

May it please your Lordship to grant Warrant to Officers of Law to search for and apprehend the said Accused

STEVEN JAMES

and meantime, if necessary, to detail him in a police station, house, or other convenient place and to bring him for examination respecting the premises; and thereafter grant Warrant to imprison him within the Prison of EDINBURGH therein to be detained for further examination or until liberated in due course of Law: Further, to grant Warrant to search the person, repositories, and domicile of the said Accused, and the house or premises in which he may be found, and to secure, for the purpose of precognition and evidence, all writs, evidence, and articles found therein tending to establish guilt or participation in the crime foresaid, and for that purpose to make patent all shut and lockfast places; and also to grant Warrant to cite Witnesses for procognition and to make production for the purposes foresaid of such writs, evidents, and articles pertinent to the case as are in their possession: Further, to recommend to the Judges of other Counties and Jurisdiction to grant the Warrant of Concurrence necessary for enforcing that of your Lordship within their respective territories; or to do further or otherwise as to your Lordship may seem meet.

According to Justice, &c.

Procurator Fiscal Depute.

Under the Criminal Procedure (Scotland) Act,1975

In the Sheriff Court of Seatown

The COMPLAINT of the PROCURATOR FISCAL against

Joe Smith

Date of Birth: 14.10.50

The charge against you is that

on 5th August, 1980, you did steal £5 in money the

property of F.W. BEANS and CO. from their premises in HILLHALL STREET

between the hours of 10.00 am and 2.00 pm.

Procurator-Fiscal Depute.

*Apprehension
and Search*   19   - The Court grants Warrant to
apprehend the said Accused and grants warrant to search the person,
dwellinghouse, and repositories of said Accused and any place where
they may be found and to take possession of the property mentioned
or referred to in the Complaint and all articles and documents likely
to afford evidence of   guilty or of guilty participation.

Sheriff

Indictment

        STEVEN JAMES, (born 30.10.40), prisoner in the prison of Edinburgh, you are indicted at the instance of the Right Honourable Lord MacJ......, Her Majesty's Advocate, and the Charge against you is that you did on 30th November, 1979 in the premises at 50 Jericho Lane, Blacktown, assault Michael Jones, hit him on the head with a broken glass whereby he sustained multiple lacerations, jump on him, kick him, and repeatedly hit him about the body with your fists, all to his severe injury.

List of Productions

1.   Glass

2.   Photographs of injury to Michael Jones.

List of Witnesses

1.   Michael Jones, 50 Jericho Lane, Blacktown.

2.   Philip Jones, father of Michael Jones.

3.   Wendy Jones, sister of Michael Jones.

4.   Dr. James North, M.B.

5.   Police Constable A93 Ronald Smith

6.   "   "   A320 David Campbell

        STEVEN JAMES take notice that in the event of your being committed under the indictment to which this notice is attached, it is intended to place before the Court the undernoted previous conviction applying to you.

Date	Place of Trial	Court	Offence	Sentence
18.12.78	Blacktown	District	Theft	£10 fine

Under the Criminal Procedure (Scotland) Act, 1975

_____

In the Sheriff Court of Seatown
_____

The COMPLAINT of the PROCURATOR FISCAL against

Joe Smith

Date of Birth 14.10.50

The charge against you is that on   17th September 1979

on a road, or other public place, namely Blank Square, Whitesville

you did,   drive a motor vehicle, namely Ford Cortina ABC 123

having consumed alcohol in such a quantity that the proportion thereof in your blood, as ascertained from a laboratory test for which you subsequently provided a specimen under Section 9 of the after-mentioned Act, was 200 milligrammes of alcohol in 100 millilitres of blood, which exceeded 80 milligrammes of alcohol in 100 millilitres of blood, the prescribed limit at the time you provided the specimen:

CONTRARY to Section 6(1) of the Road Traffic Act 1972.

Procurator-Fiscal Depute

Diet
5 November 1979. - The Court Assigns 18 December 1979, at 10.00 am., within the Sheriff Court-House, Seatown as a Diet in this case.

Clerk of Court.

NOTICE OF PREVIOUS CONVICTIONS APPLYING TO   JOE SMITH

In the event of your being convicted of the charge(s) in the
Complaint it is intended to place before the Court the
following previous conviction(s) applying to you.

Date	Place of Trial	Court	Offence	Sentence
5. 7.79	Inverness	Burgh	Theft	£10 fine
14.10.79	Elgin	Sheriff Summary	TOLP	S.D. 19.12.73 when £150 fine
23. 3.80	Edinburgh	High	Assault to severe injury	3 years imprisonment.

Bail It has become apparent from this discussion of the two types of procedure
that a great many cases cannot be dealt with in their entirety at one hearing.
The procedure used for ensuring an offender's appearance at subsequent hearings
or diets is his release on bail, subject to stated conditions, with his being
liable to further penalties if he either fails to appear, or breaches one of the
stated conditions. Until recently the system of bail used in Scotland involved
the offender having to find a sum of money before he could be released from
custody: it was also possible for a court to ordain an accused to appear, and
fix a penalty of up to £10 to be forfeited in the event of his non appearance.
Now the Bail (Scotland) Act, 1980 governs the interim release of offenders, and
it came into operation on 1st April, 1980. Unlike its English counterpart of
1976, it does not seek to define any "right" to bail, or the circumstances in
which custodial detention is justified; rather it legislates the procedure for
bail. In Scotland all crimes and offences are in principle bailable, except for
murder. A decision to refuse bail can be appealed to the High Court, which then
determines the issue: the latter will also consider application for bail by
offenders in the immediate wake of an appeal against conviction or sentence.

Section 1 of the Bail (Scotland) Act, 1980, makes the basic statements of principle
that "it shall not be lawful to grant bail or release for a pledge or deposit of
money," and that "release may be granted only on conditions ...". Subsection (2)
of section 1 determines that the objectives of conditions which are to be imposed
shall be four:-

(a)   that the accused appears at the appointed time at every
        diet relating to the offence,

(b)   that he does not commit an offence while on bail,

(c)   that he does not interfere with witnesses or otherwise
        obstruct the course of justice,

(d)   that he makes himself available for the purposes of
        enabling enquiries to be made or a report to be made
        to assist the court in dealing with him for the offence.

The Act neither limits nor lists the range of conditions which might be imposed
in pursuit of these objectives, but certainly residence in a bail or other hostel
might well feature.

Subsection (3) does allow that one of the conditions may be that an accused or a
cautioner on his behalf deposits a sum of money in court, but only where such a
requirement "is appropriate to the special circumstances of the case" - as opposed
to the earlier system under which this was automatic in all cases.

The Act requires that the accused shall be given a copy of the bail order, showing
these conditions and any others which may be added, and also showing an address,
known in legal terms as his "domicile of citation." The significance of this
latter is that it is the address at which any documents relating to the case may
be served on an accused, and if he changes his address while on bail he must
apply in writing to the court for the address on the bail order to be changed:
failure to do so may result in his becoming liable to the penalties for breach of
bail.

An important principle established by the Bail (Scotland) Act is that failure to
appear on the due date after being released, or failure to comply with any of
the conditions of bail, constitutes a criminal offence, and that the penalties for

it *may be added* to those for the original offence, even if the total penalty
exceeds the powers normally available to the court. The new offence is created by
section 3 of the Act, which lays down the maximum penalties as follows:-

    (a) a fine not exceeding £200; and

    (b) imprisonment for a period -

        i) where conviction is in the district court, not
            exceeding 60 days; or

       ii) where conviction is in the sheriff court or in
            the high court, not exceeding 3 months.

    On solemn procedure these maximum penalties are:-

    (a) a fine (no maximum is specified); and

    (b) imprisonment for a period not exceeding 2 years.

One matter of immediate and direct practical importance to social workers is that
the failure of a person to make himself available for a social enquiry report may
constitute an offence under this section: The procedures used by social workers,
in the compilation of reports need to allow for the fact that they may well
feature in a prosecution under this heading.

It can be noted that subsection 7 of section 3 adds this offence to the list of
those for which a person can be arrested without warrant, if the constable
suspects that the person is "likely to break any condition imposed on his bail."
Where an accused is arrested under this section he has to be brought where
practicable before the court to which his application for bail was first made,
and in this event the powers of the court are:-

    (a) to recall the order granting bail (i.e. he would go
        into custody);

    (b) release the accused under the original bail order; or

    (c) vary the order by imposing conditions designed to achieve
        the effect of the order.

However the accused has the same rights of appeal against any such decision as he
would have had against the original order of the court relating to bail.

Section 4 of the 1980 Act specifies the circumstances in which any money lodged
as a condition of bail can be ordered to be forfeited: normally compliance with
the conditions of bail enables the money to be reclaimed by the person who
deposited it. If the accused fails to appear, the prosecutor may move that the
money be forfeited, but the court may, "if it is satisfied that it is reasonable
in all the circumstances to do so" direct that the money forfeited shall be
refunded: such a decision is final and not subject to review. If the accused
fails to observe any of the conditions of bail, the money can only be forfeited
on the motion of the prosecutor if he is specifically convicted of an offence
under section 3: thus an accused who appears for his trial, but who does not
make himself available for reports, may claim his money back unless he is specifically prosecuted for that failure to make himself available. A cautioner who
lodges money on behalf of an accused as a condition of the latter's bail is
entitled to recover the money if the accused appears, but if the accused is

charged with an offence of failing to observe the conditions of bail, cannot
recover the money until -

    (a) the charge is not proceeded with; or

    (b) the accused is acquitted of the charge; or

    (c) on the accused's conviction the court decides
        not to order forfeiture of the money deposited

The Bail Act also makes specific provision about the release of persons for both
social enquiry and medical reports. To the governing sections of the 1975
Criminal Procedure (Scotland) Act which empowers courts to order such reports,
which we outline in detail subsequently, the Bail Act now expressly determines
that any such a remand shall be in custody or on bail, thus clarifying the fact
that methods of remand in use prior to the Act are now incompetent. In asserting
this, sections 5 and 6 also give the accused a right of appeal against a remand
in custody for reports, which was not previously possible: one very practical
implication of this for most report writers is that an accused, shown as being
held in custody for the purpose of a report, may have success in obtaining
release on bail, with or without any extra conditions, before the report writer
makes his first attempt to contact him for the report.

Section 7 of the Bail (Scotland) Act empowers the Police to release arrested
persons on the basis of a written undertaking, signed by the offender, that he
will appear at court when told to do so. Any refusal so to liberate an arrested
person "shall not subject the officer to any claim whatsoever." There is also
power for the Police to release persons without any such undertaking, with the
implication that the offender is believed to be likely to attend at a court in
response to any subsequent ordinary citation. While release on a written undertaking by the accused is not technically a full bail order, and it cannot include
any additional conditions other than to appear, its effects are entirely akin to
those of a bail order in that an accused is liable to almost identical penalties
as for breach of bail if he fails to appear after giving the Police a written
undertaking. Section 9 of the Act also empowers the Police to release children
who may have been arrested on the basis of a written undertaking given by the
parent or guardian, or by the child himself, but the maximum penalty for any
breach of such an undertaking is a fine not exceeding £200.

A final point about the Bail (Scotland) Act is that section 10 lifts the
requirement on criminal courts to sit on a Saturday, and in general gives Sheriffs
Principal the power to determine the court holidays, up to a maximum of 10 days,
in the various districts of his domain. Section leaves a residual power for the
business of a criminal court to be conducted on any day if necessary, but the
powers of the police to liberate arrested persons can become especially significant if the "next lawful day," in terms of the court's sittings, is in fact 4
or 5 days distant.

Examples:

A. is arrested on a Friday afternoon for stealing a motor car, but there is no
court due to sit until the following Tuesday. If the Police feel unable to
liberate him, he will spend the next 3 days in custody, without any recourse to
appeal or recompence, even if subsequently liberated by the court. The Police
may liberate him on a written undertaking to appear at the Sheriff court on the
following Tuesday: the Fiscal may decide on that morning not to proceed with the
case, and he would then be liberated from the effect of the undertaking; should
the case be due to go ahead, and A. not appear that Tuesday morning, the Police

would be entitled to arrest him without a warrant, even though he may not as yet
formally have been served with the complaint, because the Fiscal would only have
authorised it that morning, and the accused's failure to appear prevented his
being served with it. Later that Tuesday afternoon the Police succeed in
arresting A., and hold him in custody until the Sheriff Court on the Wednesday
morning: it would now be competent for the Fiscal to also charge A. with being
in breach of his written undertaking. Should A. be found guilty of both, the
Court might sentence him to 6 months imprisonment for the theft of the car, and
3 months imprisonment for the breach of the undertaking, but could order the 3
months to be served consecutively to the 6 months, making a total of 9 months,
even though normally the Sheriff Summary Court's powers are restricted to a
maximum of 6 months.

B, who is arrested along with A, is 17 years old, but is a "child" by virtue of
being under the supervision of the Children's Hearing. The Police release him
on a written undertaking signed by both B and his father to appear at the Sheriff
Court on the following Tuesday. If B fails to appear both he and his father become
liable to a fine of up to £200, in addition to whatever penalty is inflicted on B
for his part in the offence.

C, who is also arrested along with A and B, is however charged with causing death
by reckless driving and a number of consequential traffic offences, in that he
drove the stolen car and killed a pedestrian when a number of police officers
tried to stop his progress: it is accepted that A and B only participated in the
original theft, but had no idea of C's future actions. C is detained in custody
by the Police until the Tuesday morning when he appears before the Sheriff in
private on petition. Against the motion of the Fiscal, the Sheriff nonetheless
grants C bail, with extra conditions that:-

    a) he resides at a bail hostel,

    b) he lodges £100 with the court,

    c) a cautioner on his behalf also lodges £100

Both C and the cautioner lodge the money, but after 24 hours he absconds from the
hostel. Some weeks later he is arrested by the Police and brought before the
Sheriff: in the meantime, the case has been reported to the Crown Office, and an
indictment has been prepared charging him with the offence and requiring him to
appear at the High Court. The Sheriff recalls the bail order, and C goes to
prison: however he appeals against this decision and is successful, with the
High Court Judge allowing him out on the original terms. He duly turns up for
trial at the High Court.

    i)   if he is convicted, he could be sentenced by the High Court
         as follows:-

         5 years imprisonment for the death by reckless driving

         2 years imprisonment to be served consecutively for
           breach of a condition of bail, i.e. absconding from
           the hostel

         Forfeiture of his own £100, and the cautioner ordered to
           forfeit his £100 also,

    ii) if he is acquitted on the first charge, he could nonetheless
         still have been charged with an offence against section 3 of

the Bail Act, and that charge could competently
have been included in the indictment and be dealt
with by the High Court. He would thus become
liable for an unlimited fine or up to 2 years
imprisonment on that count; to the loss of his
deposit; and the cautioner to the loss of his
deposit: however it would be within the court's
powers, even though C is guilty of a section 3
offence, not to order forfeiture of the money by
either C or the cautioner, even if it imposed some
other penalty - say a fine of £100 - on C for the
breach of bail condition.

The original bail order in C's case would have looked like
this:-

UNDER THE CRIMINAL PROCEDURE (SCOTLAND) ACT 1975 AND
THE BAIL ETC (SCOTLAND) ACT 1980

Bail
Order

SHERIFF COURT   Edinburgh

ON   4th April 1980   (NB this was Good Friday)

ACCUSED   C   Date of Birth ....

ADDRESS   Bail Hostel, Stevenson Way, Edinburgh

which is the address to which any citation to appear at any diet
relating to the offence charged and any other document or
intimation may be sent.

OFFENCE   Death by Reckless Driving

                   cont. to Crim. Law Act 1977

                              s.50

The Court granted bail and imposed the following conditions
namely:-

(a)   That the Accused appears at the appointed time at
every diet, including every continuation of a diet, relating
to the offence charged of which due notice is given.

(b)   That the Accused does not commit an offence while on bail.

(c)   That the Accused does not interfere with witnesses or
otherwise obstruct the course of justice in relation to himself/
herself or any other person.

(d)   That the Accused makes himself/herself available for the
purposes of enabling inquiries or a report to be made to assist
the Court in dealing with him/her for the offence charged.

1. Insert any   (e)[1] That the Accused reside at bail hostel, Stevenson Way,
Additional   Edinburgh.
Conditions.

                 (f)   That the Accused deposits £100 into the Court.

                 (g)   That a cautioner on the accused's behalf also
                 deposits £100 into the Court.

2. Where appro- The above conditions having been accepted, the Court
priate add -   authorised the Accused's release.[2]
"on the pre-
release
condition(s)   CLERK OF COURT
being met".
                 Certificate that copy has been given to Accused.

                 I hereby certify that a copy of the foregoing Bail Order was
                 given to the said accused by me on this date.

                 Signature .... Date 4.4.80

                 Designation

Proceedings in Court: Not only are the prosecuting authorities responsible for
decisions about whether and how to prosecute offenders, but they also have to
arrange, in co-operation with the various clerks of court, for the ordering and
arrangement of court business, and for the preparation of court lists. The
prosecutor is termed the "master of the instance" and is in charge of the presentation of any case, up to and including the point at which the guilt or otherwise
of the accused is determined. During the progress of the case he may have to
decide matters such as - whether a reduced plea is acceptable; whether to ask
the court that any remand should be in custody; how much information about an
accused's personal circumstances to present to the court; whether to desert any
case; whether to move for forfeiture of items such as weapons, drugs; and so on.
We have already noted that in solemn procedure cases he also has to move for
sentence, even when the stage of conviction has been reached. From a formal point
of view, he has no direct role in the consideration of disposal, but he is entitled
to a copy of any social enquiry or other report, and he may wish to intervene if
anything said in such a report about the offence contradicts information in his
possession.

Any court building or room can be alive with a number of different people or staff,
each with a role to play in the proceedings, and with their own preoccupations and
concerns for the matter in hand. Any one official, such as fiscal or court clerk,
may have their own junior or clerical members of staff present to assist in
processing the work. Each or all may be involved in whispered or informal conver-
sations with others in an attempt to expedite the court's business. Police
officers may be present to ensure that persons in custody do not escape, or do
return to custody to receive their property before any liberation. The court
employs its own staff, such as bar officers, ushers, attendants, and others to
help ensure matters such as that witnesses are directed to the proper waiting
rooms; that jurors receive their expenses; that fines, cautions, and any bail
money can be received or even refunded if appropriate. Solicitors,with or without
their juniors, will be present for their own clients, or perhaps on a duty basis,
but their every moment spent in court is a charge either on the client, or on the
legal aid fund. Within this already thronged and complex situation, and in what
is also a public setting, with the anxiety of possible reports in the press, the
offender - with or without any entourage of his own - has to find his way about,

both literally and metaphorically, and the least service a social worker can provide is one of preparation, guidance, and interpretation in this strange environment.

Solemn Procedure

Persons who are charged on petition following their arrest, i.e. with a view to prosecution by the solemn procedure method, first appear before Sheriff either in the privacy of his chambers, or in a closed court. Members of the public are not present; neither are social workers, unless one were to be present in loco parentis of a child in respect of whom the local authority had parental rights under section 16 of the Social Work (Scotland) Act 1968. The press can only report that an accused was charged and appeared on petition, and whether or not he "made any plea or emitted any declaration."

At this first appearance for examination, two outcomes are possible:-

    i)   the prosecutor may ask the court to *"fully commit"* the accused for trial, and may make a motion as to whether that committal should be in custody. One implication of a motion to fully commit is that the fiscal considers investigations are sufficiently far advanced that he has sufficient prima facie evidence to justify the use of solemn procedure, and the prior authority of Crown Office may already have been sought. The restrictions noted above on the period of time within which any trial must begin are calculated from the moment of full committal.

    ii)   the prosecutor may ask the court to *"commit for further examination,"* and again may make a motion as to whether the committal should be in custody. If an accused is detained in custody for further examination, the maximum period of that detention is 8 days (often colloquially referred to by offenders as the "eight day lie down"), but the fiscal does have the discretion to bring an accused back to court before the 8 days have expired. The period of up to 8 days can only be used once. This short period allows for a preliminary report to be submitted to Crown Office, but at the subsequent hearing after committal for examination the fiscal must either move for full "committal," or reduce the case to a summary complaint and proceed accordingly. An accused who is released on bail for further examination does not necessarily have to make a further appearance for full committal, and the Crown Office may simply go straight ahead with the preparation of an indictment and proceed with the case on solemn procedure, or, again, instruct the fiscal to prepare and serve a summary complaint. One further possible outcome after either committal or examination is that the decision is one not to proceed with the case at all, by either method, and in that event the accused would be liberated from custody, or released from bail, as appropriate.

    There are various permutations about the respective rights of accused and prosecutor to appeal decisions about bail in these early stages of solemn procedure:-

    1)   at the stage of committal for examination, the accused may apply for bail, but if the court refuses it the

accused cannot appeal against that refusal. If the court
grants bail, the prosecutor can appeal against that decision,
with the effect that the accused remains in custody until the
appeal is heard. This factor, combined with the short period
of detention involved, often influences accused persons not to
apply for bail at this stage.

2) at the stage of full committal, irrespective of what may
have transpired at any previous stage of examination, an
accused may apply for bail, but if the court refuses to
grant bail, the accused can appeal against that decision to
the High Court. The prosecutor still has the right, if bail
is granted by the Sheriff to appeal against that decision,
but if the High Court eventually decides this appeal in favour
of the accused and then grants him bail, the prosecutor cannot
make a further appeal against that decision.

All these appearances for examination or committal take place
in private, with the consequence that the first public appearance of an accused on solemn procedure is at the trial diet
shown on the indictment with which he is subsequently served,
unless the defence wishes to use the preliminary diet. In
all cases on solemn procedure the accused must be present
in court before his case can proceed.

Summary Procedure.

In contrast the cases of people charged on summary procedure can start life in a
number of ways. An accused may come before a summary court after being kept in
police custody since his arrest, and not afforded the opportunity by them of
release under a written undertaking. Alternatively, he may appear before the
court from custody after anything up to 8 days in custody after his arrest if he
was originally charged on petition, but subsequently had the case reduced to a
summary charge. In either of these two eventualities he would have been afforded
the opprotunity of being represented by a duty solicitor under the legal aid
scheme. The third method is that he might have been released by the police,
whether on a written undertaking or not, and have subsequently been cited to
appear personally at the court: in such an event he is responsible for making his
own way to court in time for the hearing, and he may also opt to approach a
solicitor of his choice about the case, and make any necessary application for
legal aid. The fourth possibility is that he might plead guilty by letter and the
court be prepared, in view of the nature of the case, to deal with it in his
absence. Should the court decide in this instance that, in spite of a letter, it
wishes the accused to be present it would need to continue the case and order him
to be present personally at the deferred hearing: it would need to do so if it
intended to disqualify him for driving, as such a disqualification cannot be
imposed in the absence of the accused, for obvious reasons. Any accused who,
having been either cited or ordered to appear personally, fails to do so makes
himself liable to the court issuing a warrant for his arrest as a result. The
failure to appear may also render him liable to be regarded as being in comtempt
of court, for which he may receive a further penalty.

The Court Hearing

Once the court is convened, the various cases are "called" at the instance of the
prosecutor, usually by the clerk, or a Bar Officer, or by a Police Officer
assigned to court duties. Calling simply involves naming the accused person whose
case is to be heard, and if necessary shouting his name round the court precincts.

In cases on solemn procedure the calling is usually prefaced with "Her Majesty's Advocate against ....," but in summary cases the name of the accused usually suffices. Even when listed for a court hearing, it is open to a prosecutor not to "call" a case.

Once the accused is before the court, the clerk identifies him and ascertains that he is the same person whose name has been called. Following such an identification a solicitor or agent may indicate that he appears on behalf of the accused person. After identification of the accused, the complaint or indictment is put before the court, and the accused asked to plead to the charge(s) therein. As an accused on solemn procedure has the option under section 102 of the 1975 Act to intimate his intention to plead guilty, it will generally be known in advance whether a full trial will be involved, and the court business arranged accordingly. In cases on summary procedure, unless any prior letter has indicated a not guilty plea, it cannot generally be known long in advance what an accused intends to plead, and thus a plea of not guilty usually involves the fixing of a subsequent diet for a trial to take place, and the only issue at the first hearing will be that of bail or custody in the interim. In cases where a guilty plea is rendered, subsequent hearings will only become necessary if the court's disposal involves it, for example, a continuation for reports, a deferring of sentence, and so on. At the conclusion of any hearing the clerk of court will confirm by re-announcing the decision of the court, and ensure that the accused has heard and understood it.

Three other miscellaneous matters can usefully be mentioned under the heading of proceedings in court:-

It can be noted that the possibility of having offences "taken into consideration" along with a main and substantive charge, which is available in England and Wales, is not acceptable in Scotland. Any offences admitted by an accused, if they are substantiated and corroborated, have to be separately charged. It is now possible, under section 8 of the Criminal Justice (Scotland) Act, 1980 for an offender who simultaneously faces charges by both methods of procedure to have the summary charges libelled on the indictment, but without facing extra penalties on these summary charges as a result. Even so one consequence of the inability to have offences "taken into consideration" can still be that an accused may become involved in a series of different cases, each of which can have an independent "life", and which can sometimes overlap, thus affording him some opportunities to manipulate their processing through the courts.

One motion open to a prosecutor is to request that a case be "continued without plea": such a continuation, which may involve the accused being held in custody or liberated on bail in accordance with the ordinary procedure applicable to this question, cannot exceed 3 weeks duration. Such a motion can in fact often reflect matters such as - further enquiries into the charge being necessary; other cases in the near future pending against the accused; or even the need for an enquiry into the possible fitness of the accused to plead. On occasion a similar motion can be made by the defence, if special circumstances can be advanced. Whoever makes the motion, the request can be resisted, and the court may need to determine the issue before the case can proceed any further.

A further motion open to the prosecutor is to apply for a case to be "deserted". Cases may either be deserted "or loco et tempere"

i.e. in effect for the time being, but in this event the charge(s),
or similar one(s), can be reinstituted in fresh proceedings.
Alternatively the fiscal can move that a case be deserted
"simpliciter", in which event that is the end of it, as the
proceedings cannot be reinstituted.

Legal Aid in Criminal Cases

The provision of legal aid and assistance in criminal cases is now widely accepted,
and viewed as something of a normal right. Although a system of free legal aid for
the poor can be traced back to the 15th century, the basis of present provision is
the Legal Aid (Scotland) Act, 1967, as amended and qualified by the provisions of
the Legal Aid and Assistance Act, 1972, and by the Legal Aid (Scotland) Act, 1975.

The provision of legal aid derives from the principle that, in cases where in the
interests of justice legal representation should be provided, and the accused is
too poor to afford it, it should be provided from public funds. This is shown, for
example, by section 2(2) of the 1967 Act: "legal aid in criminal proceedings shall
be available to an accused person where the court is satisfied, after consideration
of his financial circumstances, that he is unable, without undue hardship to himself or his dependents, to meet the expenses of the case." It is important to note
the area of discretion of the court in relation to the considerations just noted,
as against any notions of absolute entitlement. Section 7 of the 1967 Act makes
it a function of duly authorised solicitors to provide aid in "preparing applications for legal aid, and in supplying information required in connection with the
determination of disposable income and capital." It should also be noted that
section 18 of the 1967 Act makes it an offence to knowingly make false statements
or representations in this connection, with a liability, on summary conviction, to
a fine of £100 or a sentence not exceeding 3 months imprisonment, or both.

It can be noted that criminal legal aid is not available for Hearings before a
Children's Panel. It _is_ possible to obtain legal advice and assistance about any
Children's Hearing matter, and to qualify for legal aid in regard to that advice
or assistance, but it is not possible to obtain legal aid to be legally represented
at a Children's Hearing. However, in the event of a ground of referral being referred to a court for proof, legal representation can be applied for under the
criminal legal aid scheme to cover the proof hearing: it can also be applied for
in the event of an appeal against the decision of a Children's Hearing.

The availability of legal aid varies not only in accordance with the broad considerations noted above, but also depends on the circumstances in which a case appears
before a court.

Legal aid is automatically available to all those who find themselves in custody
on a criminal charge. At every District and Sheriff Court a duty solicitor is
available to advise and represent people held in custody at their first appearance
in court. It is not always appreciated either by accused persons or by social
workers that this representation does not automatically extend to the rest of the
case, whatever the outcome. If an accused person pleads guilty at the first hearing, the duty solicitor will make a statement in mitigation, and would also attend
again in the event of the case being continued - for example, for a social enquiry
report. However, if the plea is one of not guilty, the accused person needs to
make a specific and separate application for legal aid if he wishes it during the
rest of the case, even if he is held in custody until the next hearing. Also those
accused persons who are released after apprehension and then cited to appear need
to make an application for legal aid if they wish to be represented. These applications are made to, and considered, by the court, unlike civil and other matters
where the decision about the granting of legal aid rests with a legal aid committee.

If the court refuses legal aid, that refusal cannot be appealed.

Consideration of legal aid also varies according to the type of procedure i.e. solemn or summary. In summary cases both main considerations - i.e. can the person afford it, and is representation necessary in the interests of justice - apply, and the court has to consider both. However, in cases on solemn procedure, the only question relates to the financial circumstances of the accused.

Legal aid is also available in criminal cases in the event of an accused person wishing to appeal against conviction. As always the usual financial considerations apply, but in this instance the legal aid committee (and not the court in these circumstances) has to be satisfied that there are substantial grounds for the appeal and that the granting of legal aid is reasonable.

The theme of finance is clearly a recurring one, and the Legal Aid and Assistance (Financial Considerations) Regulations govern this issue, and set out the criteria. These regulations stipulate two basic criteria:-

> a) persons whose disposable income does not exceed a stated
>   amount (and that would be one of the matters for discussion
>   with a solicitor) or
>
> b) persons in receipt, either directly or indirectly, of DHSS
>   benefits or family income supplement and

in either case, has limited disposable capital, as defined by the Regulations. In England and Wales considerations of contributions to be made by the accused also bear on this subject, but this is not the case in Scotland, where the only issue is financial eligibility. Also in England and Wales the DHSS has a duty, on the request of the courts, to investigate the financial circumstances of applicants for legal aid, but Scottish courts rely directly on the application as lodged.

Where legal aid has been granted, the person concerned is regarded as eligible in connection with any subsequent proceedings arising from the case, including guidance as to the advisability of any appeal. The potential demands on the scheme are thus considerable, and the issue of how "the interests of justice" are defined is crucial to practice. Whereas the financial criteria are regularly updated and publicly available, the "interests of justice" criterion is much more complex and a good deal less tangible.

If legal aid is granted, the applicant may nominate a solicitor of his choice to represent him, and may indicate his preference on his application. The duty solicitor scheme, however, is run on a rota basis. Each court has a list of solicitors who participate in the duty scheme, otherwise any choice depends on the preference or knowledge of the applicant.

Social workers may frequently be in contact either with duty solicitors at the early stages of a case, or subsequently with individual solicitors at stages such as the consideration of a social enquiry report. In that solicitors very clearly have an advocacy role in relation to any person that they may represent, their concerns will thus readily overlap with that part of a social worker's duty which involves the giving of advice and assistance: however, even in this context the issue of confidentiality as it affects both solicitor and social worker is one aspect of the situation, and the latter may well wish to ascertain of his client how much information he would consent to being imparted. On the other hand the social worker dealing with an offender may usually have obligations or duties either directly to the court or, for example, to the Secretary of State, and good practice involves as much consideration being given to the imparting of information to the court - quite possibly without the offender's consent. The greater danger has

tended to be in an identification of social workers with "the defence", as against
a closer awareness of what aspects of their role are independent of such considerations.

Police Powers

The Police in Scotland are a civilian force organised along Regional lines, except
that the Highlands and Islands have a unified force and Lothian and Borders Regions
constitute one force. It can be noted that outwith his own area of authority a
police officer has no more rights than, but only the same general duties as, any
other citizen. For some time police powers of apprehension and arrest for crimes
and offences have been felt to be inadequately defined, and had been governed, insofar as they could be enforced, by the so-called "judges rules", although these
never had the force of law. Now the Criminal Justice (Scotland) Act, 1980 has
attempted to codify the circumstances in which arrest and detention may occur.

Because of the particular problems which are posed, by the issue, the Act defines
the powers of the police to arrest without a warrant. There are of course many
cases, particularly the less serious ones, in which immediate arrest is not
necessary. The formula used in these instances is along the lines that "the facts
will be reported and you may be prosecuted." From this point the decision would
lie with the Procurator Fiscal: he may decide to proceed, and then arrange for the
necessary documents to be served on the person at his or her home: alternatively
he may feel that the circumstances do justify the obtaining of a warrant and the
person's arrest. In many types or instances of crime the circumstances may not be
such as to make immediate arrest without a warrant possible, but as the investigation proceeds to the point at which evidence to justify an arrest emerges, the
police may themselves be in a position to apply for a warrant for the offender's
arrest, before reporting the facts to the Fiscal. A warrant is a written authority
issued by a judge of any court authorising the apprehension and arrest of a named
individual, or the search of named premises: The basis for the granting of a
warrant is a sworn statement alleging a breach of the law, or of an order of the
court, or otherwise justifying apprehension or search.

Any decision to arrest without a warrant depends on the circumstances of each case,
but the broad test is whether the person making the arrest had reasonable grounds
for believing that without it the ends of justice might be defeated. A police
officer is entitled to arrest without a warrant:-

> i) a person committing, or attempting to commit, a serious
>   crime, including incest, or bodily harm to a child under
>   17 years,

> ii) a person in possession of goods believed to have been
>   stolen, and being unable to account for them in a way
>   consistent with innocence and if there is a possibility
>   that justice may be denied if immediate action is not
>   taken,

> iii) on information from a credible witness that a crime has
>   been, or is being, committed, and there is a similar
>   risk as above,

> iv) on seeing or being reliably informed that a breach of
>   the peace has been committed, or an outrage, or violence
>   threatening,

> v) under certain powers as granted by particular statutes,
>   for example under the Road Traffic Acts.

The powers of arrest and detention set out in the 1980 Criminal Justice (Scotland) Act are as follows:-

Section I allows that where a constable has reasonable grounds for suspecting that a person has committed or is committing an offence at any place, he may require -

(a) that person, if the constable finds him at that place or at any place where the constable is entitled to be, to give his name and address and may ask him for an explanation of the circumstances which have given rise to the constable's suspicion;

(b) any other person whom the constable finds at that place or at any place where the constable is entitled to be and who the constable believes has information relating to the offence, to give his name and address.

The Act makes certain provisions in instances where a constable does act in this way.

i) He must explain his suspicion, inform the suspected person of the general nature of the offence, and why that person is required to remain with him for the period noted hereunder. It requires a record to be kept of the place, purpose and duration of the detention.

ii) Detention during investigation is defined at S.2. It should be noted that this only relates to offences punishable by imprisonment, i.e. serious offences.

Subsection (1) of Section 2 gives the general power to detain a suspect to facilitate investigations into the offence and as to whether criminal proceedings should be instigated against that person. The detention may be at "a police station or other premises".

Subsection (2). . requires that detention shall be terminated not more than 6 hours after it begins or (if earlier) -

(a) when the person is arrested; or

(b) when there are no longer such grounds as are mentioned in the said subsection (1)

Subsection (3) prevents the repeated use of this power in regard to the same offence, but it is still possible in relation to that offence for the police to obtain a written warrant, if subsequent events call for such action.

The Act creates specific new offences of: failing to remain with the constable without reasonable excuse, or failing to give a name and address without reasonable excuse. The maximum penalty for this offence is a fine not exceeding £200 for the person actually suspected, and a fine not exceeding £50 for any other person believed to have information, who fails to provide name and address. It gives a specific power to arrest without warrant a person suspected of committing the new offences created, thus adding to the list of statutory instances in which such arrest is possible.

Important procedural matters regarding the rights of the individual are inbuilt, so that a person has a right to refuse to answer any question, other than to give his

name and address. He also has the right to have someone (including a solicitor,
as allowed for in the 1975 Act) 'reasonably named by him' informed of his detention
and the place where he is being held.

There are added powers for the police to search suspected persons for offensive
weapons and obstruction or concealment of such a weapon constitutes a separate
offence, carrying a maximum penalty of £200.

The constable is authorised to 'use reasonable force' to ensure that the suspected
person remains with him, and to verify any name and address given, provided that
such verification can be 'obtained quickly'. The Act does not stipulate what
definition is to be placed on 'quickly' and it is anticipated that guidance,
(whether from the Scottish Office or locally) may be issued to the police.

<u>Drunken Offenders</u>

The 1980 Act also introduces a new power at section 5 for dealing with offenders
who are drunk. The section says "where a constable has power to arrest a person
without a warrant for any offence and the constable has reasonable grounds for
suspecting that that person is drunk, the constable may, if he thinks fit, take
him to any place designated by the Secretary of State as a place suitable for the
care of drunken persons." Offenders cannot be detained in such places, and remain
liable to be charged and dealt with for the offence involved. It should be noted
that this section is not simply about taking people whose offence is plain drunkenness to a "designated place" - such as a detoxification centre - but contains a
much wider power. It is conceivable that places could be designated for drunken
traffic offenders, for offenders who are drunk and causing a breach of the peace,
and so on; it remains to be seen what projects will be developed, what places
designated, and what criteria used, in the wake of this enactment.

POWERS OF THE COURTS — ST 333

TYPE OF PROCEDURE	TYPE OF COURT	FORM OF CHARGE(S)	MAXIMUM PENALTIES (at common law)	PROSECUTION	TYPICAL OFFENCES
SOLEMN	HIGH	INDICTMENT	As fixed by law	Lord Advocate Solicitor General OR Advocate-Depute. Court by Crown Office.	Murder, Rape, Treason Serious crimes indicated to High Court by Crown Office.
	or by section 102			Remits from Sheriff Courts	Remits from Sheriff Courts
	SHERIFF + JURY or by SECTION 102	INDICTMENT	2 YEARS PRISON OR REMIT TO HIGH COURT	Procurator Fiscal at instance of Lord Advocate. Crown Office instruct P.F. to prosecute in Sheriff Court	Serious crimes of every kind where Crown Office contemplated Solemn procedure
COMMITTAL FOR EXAMINATION	SHERIFF (IN PRIVATE)	PETITION		P.F. takes instructions from Crown Office	Anything and everything where Solemn procedure contemplated
SUMMARY	SHERIFF NO JURY	COMPLAINT	6 MONTHS PRISON £1,000 FINE	Procurator Fiscal at own instance	Most ordinary crimes Most RTA offences Breaches of Peace, etc.
	DISTRICT NO JURY	COMPLAINT	60 DAYS PRISON £200 FINE	Procurator Fiscal at own instance	Minor thefts (e.g. shop-lifting) Domestic disputes Drunkenness Local bye-laws (e.g. begging)

Chapter 2

The Social Worker at Court: Practices and Procedures

Section 27(3) of the Social Work (Scotland) Act 1968 requires that each Local
Authority shall "make arrangements for the attendance of officers of the local
authority at court", and for "co-operation with the courts". This section outlines
the topics which require to be included in such arrangements, and describes the
procedures which should be followed by social workers who attend at courts, either
in respect of their own cases, or as a representative of their colleagues and/or
department. The detail of such arrangements will vary according to local circumstances, but the range of topics, and the essential principles which underpin professional practice, can be stated in general terms.

Social Work Functions in Court Attendance

Social workers may attend courts either in respect of their own cases or reports,
or on a representative basis, on behalf either of a particular colleague, or of
the department generally. Insofar as that attendance, on whatever basis, arises
out of, or has to do with, a case or cases with which the department is involved
by virtue of its functions under Section 27 of the Act, then that means that his
professional function *equally* involves assisting the court's purposes and functioning, *and* servicing offenders at court. These two elements of his role are
inseparable in the actual event, even though they will be discussed separately
here. It is on this understanding of his role that his status as officer of the
court is based, even if certain dilemmas may be involved in this duality. In
comparison, the attendance at court of, say a youth leader, clergyman, or voluntary
worker in respect of a case can be focused much more on assisting the individual
offender. The professional social worker on the other hand, is an officer of a
local authority which has statutory functions in relation to the court.

The social worker's function at court can be discussed under two headings: assisting the court; and assisting the offender.

Assisting the Court

Presentation of social enquiry and other reports. The Morison Committee asserted
that "ideally, the officer who prepared the social enquiry report should be available. . ." This availability becomes necessary from the legal point of view if
the defence wish to cross-examine the author, which they have every right to do.
Also any judge may take an initiative in requiring the author's presence if he
himself has any questions or observations. More importantly, the author may wish

to take an initiative himself by being available to further assist the court -
e.g. by "speaking to" the report; or by adding any new or up-to-date information.
Moreover, the author's role as officer of the court thereby becomes more readily
apparent to the offender who actually sees the social worker reporting in accordance with what should have been clearly established anyway when the report was in
preparation.

Presenting other information.   The social worker can also assist the court in the
provision of more general information about social resources.   The availability
of resources such as employment, welfare benefits, accommodation, and so on, can
be a matter of considerable relevance not only in any one particular case but for
the court's approach generally.   Equally, it can often fall to social workers to
provide information about the lack of such resources (e.g. hostel provision) for
which the department itself may be responsible.   Such information is given in
public, with press representatives present, and with the full knowledge that the
lack of such resources may mean that a custodial disposal is more likely to be
ordered.   At this crucial juncture, the reporting social worker is spokesman for
his department and needs an appropriate briefing.

Stand-down interviews.   The stand-down interview is essentially exploratory in
nature, and is most frequently requested by a court which, while contemplating the
relevance of social work involvement, is looking to the social worker for an
opinion as to the possible benefits of such a course.   Such an interview might be
requested with a view to eliciting further information if some personal difficulty
or social problem is hinted at in the hearing of the case (e.g. by Fiscal, agent,
accused himself, or by the very circumstances of the offence.)

The social worker's report on such an interview should indicate that, in the
circumstances, any factual material may be incapable of immediate verification.
The report should chiefly aim to provide an opinion as to whether fuller investigation e.g. a social enquiry report would be useful, or whether any existing
social work contact, perhaps of a voluntary nature, would suffice; this enables
the court to proceed to sentence in the normal way, on the basis of good and
readily-available information.   Whilst the result of such an interview will be
reported orally to the court, it must be distinguished from a 'verbal' report: the
latter, which either involves reading a written report aloud, or sometimes
represents a substitute for a full written report, is to be deprecated and should
not be used unless exceptional circumstances appear to justify it.

Providing a Service to the Offender at Court

This is perhaps the more important purpose to be served by actual attendance at
court, as against the submission of information to the court.   In the very nature
of the situation, the offender is 'in crisis' to a degree when he appears in court:
his pocket, if not his liberty, may be affected.   He will also be experiencing
stress and/or anxiety, which can become apparent through different forms of
behaviour.   Any court is invariably a place of tension, however subdued or controlled: the offender is by definition in conflict with society; social work
considerations can compete against other factors in sentencing; the various court
officials all have different pre-occupations.

All these aspects can be seen as, and can indeed be, constraints on the social
worker's activity, but equally provide a basic reason for his being there.   A
certain amount of professional security is, therefore, demanded of the social
worker for him to operate in a setting which is not only different from the usual
office or home-based contact with clients, but one which is essentially public,
and one where he alone represents his professional and departmental interest.

The social worker's service to clients at court can be seen as including:-

Attendance, in the following ways:

    a) Some accused (e.g. particularly women offenders) suffer
       genuine anxieties and fear about their appearance, such
       that the actual presence of a social worker is valuable.
       It might be possible for the court officials to vary the
       order of business in favour of such a person if the
       distress were sufficiently great.

    b) The actual court hearing is the first opportunity for
       an offender to see any report relating to him, but it
       might also be the first occasion on which he gleans any
       notion of the social worker's view of him. In this
       event, the presence of the report writer is for the
       purpose of discussing and interpreting the contents of
       a report prior to the accused actually going into the
       dock: this is likely both to be of value in itself and
       to secure the foundations of any possible future probation
       or after-care relationship.

    c) The social worker is present in court as a professional
       with specific tasks to perform. In this setting, people
       can suffer experiences which, while not amounting to a
       reason for statutory involvement, nevertheless, demand
       social work intervention. For example, offenders may
       come to court with quite unrealistic expectations of the
       outcome; wives may come with children, totally unprepared
       for the sort of delays all too common in courts; anxieties
       mount, and unresolved problems demand attention, which may
       amount to no more than immediate counselling or advice-
       giving, but which can extend to the creation of a voluntary
       case, or to referral elsewhere. Nothing in the performance
       of his court duties should prevent the social worker being
       alive to these aspects of the court situation, and proferring
       the assistance of the department as appropriate.

Post-sentence or post-disposal activity. The decision of the court may well create
a new situation necessitating immediate social work activity and involvement,
whether statutory or not.

The social work aspects of a sentence (e.g. probation, fine supervision) may need
further explanation, and further interviewing for the purpose; also it is important to ensure the establishment of contact with the supervising officer.

Any custodial disposal provides an immediate focus for social work involvement.
This is so, whether or not the sentence carries a period of after-care licence,
and is the more so in such an instance. The practice of automatically undertaking
a 'post-sentence interview' on any offender sentenced to custody is based on the
following essential considerations:-

    a) The consequences of a custodial disposal, both in terms
       of family functioning and of the individual's own
       reactions and future, can create a situation, akin to sudden
       death or hospitalisation, such that the tenets of crisis
       theory are applicable.

    b) "After-care begins at the point of sentence". This
       principle enunciated by 1963 Report of the Advisory

Council on the Treatment of Offenders points to the
longer-term considerations inherent in any post-sentence
interview.

Ideally, if both considerations are to receive due weight, the post-sentence interview is likely to be more productive if undertaken by the person's own social
worker. Nonetheless, many short-term aims can be accomplished in the immediate
situation, and other matters referred on to both community-based and institution-
based social workers. The problems which surface in the post-sentence interview
are directly related to the offence and derive from the court's disposal; the
immediate attitudes and reactions of the offender concerning his crime and its
sentence are germane to his response in prison and future rehabilitation. Although
a non-statutory function, the post-sentence interview is entirely in accordance
with the Local Authority's responsibilities under Section 27 of the Act, and the
social worker's role as an integral part of the correctional system, seen in the
larger terms, is to the fore.

Intake function. The situation of an offender at court who, by virtue of any
order or request of the court, is brought into contact with a social worker in
attendance thereat is essentially an intake one in terms of its casework considerations. The most frequent situation of this kind is the court's ordering of a
social enquiry report; however, the making of a probation order or the imposition
of a custodial sentence, may equally represent a point of first contact and thus
intake considerations will be paramount. Even if an offender has previously been
in contact with a social worker, a further order for involvement will produce new
considerations of intake.

The role of the social worker at court interviewing a person in respect of whom
social work involvement has been ordered, may include any or all of:-

    a) explaining the reason for social work involvement

    b) explaining the nature and methods of the intervention
       which will follow

    c) dealing with practical consequences

    d) allowing the expression of reactions and anxieties

    e) preparing the ground for the author of the report

    f) discussing confidentiality and rights of accused

It is these considerations which are basic to the presence at courts of social
workers on a representative or rota basis, and this type of interviewing will loom
large in the role of duty social workers at courts. It is important to understand
and fulfil these social work activities before the necessary administrative aspects
of court attendance can be undertaken meaningfully,

Procedural Aspects of Court Attendance

Obligatory attendance. The whole ethos of probation and after-care emphasises
the individual accountability of a supervising officer or individual report writer
for a particular case or report. Ideal professional practice is, that each supervising officer or report writer should be present in court for any hearing of the
case, in order that he may both assist the court and help the individual concerned.
However there are some situations in which his attendance is either necessary or
obligatory:-

a)   <u>Breach of Probation Proceedings</u>

Only the named supervising officer can initiate breach
proceedings: he has to attend court to depone before
the Judge, and arrange with court officials (especially
the Procurator Fiscal) for the issuing of the necessary
citation or warrant. He should also be available at any
and every hearing of the case. Once in court, it is
important that, until such time as a plea of guilty has
been either tendered or recorded, the supervising
officer should take his lead from the Fiscal. Only
after conviction or finding of guilt does the social work
role of assisting disposal commence, e.g. by provision
of a social enquiry report: prior to that, the role is
initially that of laying information as a basis for the
allegation, then acting as witness for the prosecution
if the allegation is contested.

b)   <u>Cross-examination</u>

If either the defence or the Judge wish to question a
report writer, or supervising officer in breach proceedings
attendance at court is obligatory on the part of that person.
In instances where the social worker himself takes the
initiative in attending court, he is not usually required
in Scotland to enter the witness box and give evidence on
oath: however, if the defence wish to cross-examine
either on the contents of a report, or in regard to
information for breach proceedings, evidence on oath is
necessary. Any social worker wishing to 'affirm' as
opposed to swearing on oath should seek permission of
the court to do so. Otherwise the oath is administered
by the Judge, and the questioning is most likely to
focus either on the sources of a social worker's information,
or his reasons for forming a particular opinion or view.

<u>Etiquette</u>.   The social worker in respect of the performance of his professional
duties should observe court etiquette. Three matters deserve mention:-

a)   <u>Dress</u>

All other court officials have a particular dress
appropriate to their function. Social workers should
ensure that their general demeanour is calculated to
reflect the professional nature of their task, and the
fact that they are representing the department in this
particular setting.

b)   <u>Approach</u>

It is normal practice to bow to the court (i.e. a slight
inclination of the head) if going forward of the bar for
any purpose, and especially if approaching specifically
to address the bench. If the social worker's seat is
in front of the bar, he should also bow at any entrance
and/or recession of the Judge. The bow acknowledges the
court as representative of the Crown. High Court Judges
are addressed as 'Your Lordship' or 'My Lord'; Lay Justices

as 'Your Honour'.

c) Access to Cells

The Police have responsibility for the security of
persons held in custody, and whilst social workers often
have official cause to interview such persons, they need
to be aware both of this general responsibility of the
police, and also of the particular arrangements which
apply for access. It is recommended that any social
worker attending at a court for any reason has with
them a means of indentification.

Social Work Liaison with the Courts

Section 27(3) of the Social Work (Scotland) Act indicates that the arrangements
for the co-operation of local authorities with the courts "may include the appointment of one or more Sheriffs having jurisdiction in their areas to the Social Work
Committee and to any Subcommittee thereof". Such appointments are usually determined either in the Authority's probation scheme approved by the Secretary of State
under Subsection 3 or by the Social Work Committee.

There are other possibilities, at a more day to day or practical level, for contact
between judges and social workers, which can be grouped under two headings:-

Discussion of individual cases. A system known as that of Case Committee played
an important part in the organisation of the former probation service. This was a
Sub Committee, comprising Magistrates and/or Judges who sat on the larger probation
committee, and it met with the officers from time to time; whilst local practice
varied, a common feature was often that any potential breach, or potential early
discharge, of a probation order was discussed at this Committee prior to action in
the court. Some Sheriffs, and to a lesser extent Lay Justices, are still content
to see either report writers or supervising officers to discuss individual cases
if either side wishes it. Whilst in general this practice is desirable in respect
of a social worker's own case(s), another practice attracted the following observations in the Report of the Committee on 'The Sheriff Court' chaired by Lord Grant
(1967): . . . the practice, which is not unknown, of the probation officer seeing
the Sheriff in private when the accused and the prosecutor are not present,
especially before the hearing of a case. It would be regarded as highly improper
for the Sheriff to see the prosecutor, the accused person, or the representative
of the accused person, in private, and we are strongly of the view that he should
not see the probation officer". The same considerations apply, mutatis mutandis,
to the social worker.

General discussion. Some areas have found value in an adaptation of the Case
Committee idea whereby Sheriffs and/or Magistrates have been prepared to meet with
groups of social workers, at different levels, for more general discussion. Such
meetings have discussed more general aspects concerning the use of probation and
reports, as well as other aspects of the Social Work Department's work.

Administrative Co-operation With Courts

At the administrative level, Social Work Departments need to have arrangements
which include the following provisions and which allow for certain eventualities.

Probation Orders. The law requires that a copy of the probation order shall be
given to the probationer by the Clerk of Court. The arrangements which are made
to cover these requirements need to include:-

a) Agreement that, if service is actually made by the
    social worker, he is acting on behalf of the court, and
    will fulfil this responsibility.

b) Arrangements for the immediate availability of copies of
    the order in instances where the order includes either
    in-patient treatment or hostel residence, as a copy is
    required by the appropriate institution before the
    probationer can be admitted.

c) Parallel agreements and arrangements in regard to orders
    discharging or amending probation orders.

Breach of probation.

a) In the institution of proceedings for breach of require-
    ment, the supervising officer needs to make arrangements
    to depone before a judge, and needs to know from the
    court officials how this can be arranged.

b) Supervising officers need to liaise with Clerks of Court
    for the necessary issuing of process after deponing, or
    in the event of an offender being brought back to court
    for a breach by further offences; and the procedures
    for this need to be known.

c) There needs to be an arrangement whereby a breach by
    further offence can be dealt with instantaneously if
    the court is both competent and wishes to do so: this
    chiefly involves the Clerk of Court locating the papers
    relating to the original offence in respect of which the
    order was made. Adoption of such a procedure avoids the
    necessity for separate or later proceedings if a custodial
    disposal is ordered in relation to the new offence.

d) There need to be arrangements for the availability of
    supervising officers at any hearing of a breach of
    probation case, whether the function involved is one
    of giving evidence, or of assisting the court's disposal.
    This problem is particularly acute when a probationer is
    arrested on warrant, especially at weekends, and it may
    be that courts will be asked to accept that a short remand
    may be necessary: in this case, the view of the super-
    vising officer as to any need for custody might be helpful.

Social enquiry reports. The submission of reports to courts is a matter requiring
careful arrangement. The essential principle is that the report is the court's
property, and is only distributed by the court at the relevant point in the proceedings.

a) In any case where the report is ordered pre-trial all
    copies should be lodged with the Clerk of Court, who will
    only make them available after conviction or finding of
    guilt. There needs to be an arrangement for the destruction
    of the report if the accused is acquitted, or the case not
    proven.

b) In the more normal instance of reports prepared after

finding of guilt or conviction, reports should be
submitted to all relevant parties in good time for
their contents to be read and digested, ideally the day
prior to the hearing. Nonetheless, all the reports
should go to the court in the first instance, and it
is up to the Fiscals, agents and anyone else who is
entitled to a copy, to make arrangements with the court
to obtain their copy.

c) The duty social worker should ensure that all accused,
especially those who are unrepresented, have seen a
copy of a report relating to them, and he should have
sufficient copies for this purpose.

d) Duty social workers should also arrange for an extra
copy of any report to be submitted to the court in the
event of any custodial disposal being ordered, for despatch
to the relevant institution.

e) There should be a general agreement between courts and
social work departments about the period of time allowed
for reports, especially when the accused is detained in
custody. The administrative arrangements of social
work departments should reflect a great sense of urgency
in getting full information about an accused in respect
of whom a social enquiry is ordered to the local social
work office as soon as possible.

f) This point is particularly to be emphasised when an
outside department is involved. It may also be necessary
to reach agreement about joint compilation of a report
if an offender is held in custody outwith his home area.

g) There needs to be an agreed arrangement to cover the
event of a report not being prepared in the time allowed,
in the event of maladministration.

h) There should be an agreed arrangement as to what grades
of staff are authorised to sign reports without needing
a counter-signature.

i) It is helpful if methods of liaison are developed with
psychiatric hospitals in the event of both social enquiry
and medical reports being ordered simultaneously.

Court business and availability. The ideals of court attendance are in reality
restricted by the amount of court business which does not directly concern social
workers, and especially in the larger areas, by the sheer number and diversity of
courts sitting which may deal with a case in which social work is either already
involved or may become so. The Morison Committee urged that a degree of consideration should be afforded to social workers, comparable, for example, to that given
to lawyers, but where agreed liaison procedures exist, the more likely is it that
a productive relationship will develop. Social workers in turn should be aware of
the pressures imposed on court officials by the sheer amount of business. All
concerned need a sense of balance which arises from mutual acceptance of the other's
function. Nonetheless, there should be arrangements to cover:-

a) Court Lists

The social worker cannot operate efficiently without
information about the charges against those appearing.
This information is at first glance obtained from court
lists, supplemented by the prosecutor's account of the
actual circumstances. The list may well also show the
distribution of court business, especially as between
solemn and summary courts.

b) Previous Convictions

There should be arrangements with the police authorities
for the obtaining of previous convictions, as the list
supplied by the Fiscal is inadequate for social enquiry
purposes. The police may need to be satisfied that the
persons about whom such information is requested will
be the subject of reports. This information, once
gleaned, needs to be passed on immediately to the report
writer.

c) Court Coverage

There needs to be an agreement with the court and its
officials concerning which courts will be covered by
social workers attending on a duty basis. By implication,
this agreement should extend to include two other events:
the first is the absence of a duty social worker dealing
with one case when another arises; and secondly, the
method of transmitting adequate information from another
court in which he is not normally expected to be present.
Moreover, the cases in which reports are involved may be
distributed among more than one court, and acceptable
arrangements for obtaining disposals, etc. need to be
made.

d) Availability

Experience suggests that the availability of one or more
full-time liaison officers to supervise and monitor all
aspects of both the professional and administrative topics
in court attendance which have been outlined can be helpful
to both courts and social work departments, and to the
relationship between the two.

Specimen referral form for use in court social work. This form is designed to
give expression to the points made in the text above in reference to the effect
that referrals taken at court involves both the obtaining of full and detailed
information, and also the use of social casework skills in relating to the offender
who has been referred by the court for action by the Social Work Department. The
form is divided in two main ways: firstly, the front side is for detailed information, and the reverse side for recording social work activity; secondly, the upper
portion of each side is for recording the point of referral, and the lower part for
recording disposal and its consequences: occasionally these two moments may occur
at one and the same instance - for example, the immediate imposition of a prison
sentence without a previous report, but where a post sentence interview is undertaken.

* = Ring where applicable

NOTICE OF:- * Order for S.E.R. * Fine Supervision Order * Other Disposal	COURT MAKING ORDER:- * High * Sheriff (Summary) * Sheriff * District (Solemn)
DATE OF ORDER: DATE OF CONTINUED HEARING:	Indicate whether: *Post Conviction or: *Pre-trial

SURNAME alias	FIRST NAME(S)	age: d.o.b.: Marital Status:

ADDRESS - Indicate status of address & permancy.	*Cited to appear *Ordained *Bail(amount) *Custody (location)	*Advice of Panel *Medical Report *Community Service Report

OCCUPATION:	AGENT/SOLICITOR

OFFENCE(S)

    Circumstances:

PREVIOUS CONVICTIONS AND/OR INVOLVEMENT WITH SOCIAL WORK DEPARTMENT
   (indicate source + comprehensiveness of information)

ANY FURTHER CONTINUATIONS AND DEFERMENTS

FINAL DISPOSAL

  . . . . Court on . . . .(date)

 *Judge: *Sheriff: *Magistrate   (name)

 Any remarks by sentencer.

                                Fine payments . . . .

                                Driving
                                Disqualifications . . . .

This form should be returned along with completed reports (6 copies)
to   (address)   NOT LATER THAN   (date)

RECORD OF SOCIAL WORK ACTIVITY AT COURT:-

AT POINT OF ORIGINAL ORDER OR REFERRAL

      Indicate whether accused interviewed: YES/NO
      Report on (e.g.)   availability; hours of work;
                      any other family or friends present at Court;
                      re-action of accused to hearing and/or reports;
                      any problems discussed/action taken;
                      any matters of extreme confidentiality.

AT POINT OF SENTENCE OR DISPOSAL

      Indicate whether accused interviewed or not:-   YES/NO

1.   Remarks or Instructions of Sentencer:-

2.   Re-action of accused

3.   Problems raised

4.   Action taken: advice or instructions given

5.   Any further referral

Our View:

In essence this area of operations presents Scottish Social Work Departments with challenges to display a range of skills in the most public of settings, in view of a potentially critical audience, both professional and lay; to demonstrate ability across a spectrum of stress situations, in dealing with hostile, angry, bewildered people; to actively demonstrate that 'co-operation with the courts' has a day to day practical use which makes the social work contribution indispensable to the administration of justice.

In the nature of things these challenges can only be met by individual social workers, performing their duties with professional competence, effeciency and dignity.

Chapter 3

Social Enquiry Reports

The term 'social enquiry report' does not appear in Scottish law. The law in-
corporates both some general powers and some specific obligations concerning
reports.

An earlier term in common use was 'probation report'. This term reflected a
situation in which a report was only asked for if the court had, for whatever
reason, already reached a stage at which the use of probation was being contemplated
as a disposal. Such a report was not obligatory, but the court was looking for an
opinion as to the offender's suitability for probation. It has been written that
'at that time, the probation officer certainly felt himself to be on the side of
the offender. He was then an employee of a voluntary charitable body with a strong
religious ethos, who saw his purpose as keeping people out of prison, and to effect
this, persuasion and special pleading were not out of place.' (Jarvis, 1969, p98).

The Legal Basis for Reports

The 1949 Criminal Justice Act established some important general principles and
specific obligations concerning reports, and subsequent acts have extended the
range of situations in which a report has to be considered.

General Power to Order Reports

Section 26 of the 1949 Act established a general power to order reports. This
power is now to be located in the Criminal Procedure (Scotland) Act, 1975, at
section 179 (for cases on solemn procedure), and section 380 (for cases on summary
procedure). These sections, in describing the court's power to adjourn cases,
declare that this includes power:-

> 'to adjourn the case for the purpose of enabling inquiries
> to be made or of determining the most suitable method of
> dealing with the case.'

The following points should be noted:

    i)   such adjournment must follow a plea or finding of
        guilt, but precedes disposal.

    ii) no such adjournment shall exceed a period of three
        weeks at any one time.

    iii) the definition suggests two purposes for such an
        adjournment:-

        a) the simple making of inquiries

        b) assisting the court's disposal of the case

    iv) the function of assisting disposal does not specifically
        refer to probation as the contemplated course.

The position now established, therefore,is one in which the 'report is intended as
an essay in objectivity. The purpose is to provide the impartial, professional
appraisal of the offender and his situation which is vital to effective sentencing
as now understood.' (Jarvis, ibid.)

In the 1949 Act, schedule 3 made it clear that the undertaking of such inquiries
was a task for the then probation service. Section 4 of schedule 3 defined the
duties of probation officers as including one 'to inquire, in accordance with any
directions of the court, into the circumstances or home surroundings of any person
with a view to assisting the court in determining the most suitable method of
dealing with his case.'

In 1969, this duty passed to the newly created Social Work Departments of Local
Authorities. Section 27 of the Social Work (Scotland) Act refers to 'making available to any court such social background reports and other reports relating to
persons appearing before the court which the court may require for the disposal of
the case'.

Obligatory Reports

The law requires that reports shall be considered before a custodial sentence can
be passed on certain offenders, or in certain situations. A persistent refrain in
the sections which define these is that the report's use is to help the court determine that 'no other method of dealing with him is appropriate'. The business of
considering alternatives is therefore implicit in the report writer's task.

Young offenders: aged 16 to 21 years. Ever since the 1949 Criminal Justice
(Scotland) Act, courts have been obliged to consider a report before sentencing any
young offender to any period in custody. The obligation is now to be located in
the Criminal Justice (Scotland) Act, 1980, at section 45 which states:

    'the court shall not impose detention on a person unless it
    is of the opinion that no other method of dealing with him
    is appropriate (and further) to enable the court to form an
    opinion it shall obtain . . . such information as it can
    about the offender's circimstances. . . and take into account
    any information before it concerning the offenders character
    and physical and mental condition.'

Imprisonment. In 1960 the First Offenders Act introduced an obligation on courts
to consider a report before sentencing any first offender to imprisonment, whatever
his age. The rule was incorporated in the Criminal Procedure (Scotland) Act, 1975,
at section 417, but only ever extended to cases on summary procedure.

The Criminal Justice (Scotland) Act, 1980, has now extended the obligation to consider a report before a sentence of imprisonment. Section 42 of that Act requires

    'a court shall not pass a sentence of imprisonment on a
    person of or over 21 years of age who has not been previously

sentenced to imprisonment or detention. . . unless the
court considers that no other method of dealing with him
is appropriate; and for the purpose of determining whether
any other method of dealing with such a person is appropriate
the court shall obtain (from an officer of the local authority
or otherwise) such information as it can about the offender's
circumstances'.

What was colloquially known as the 'first offender rule' has now become a 'first
time rule', and the 1980 Act includes courts of solemn procedure. It can be noted,
however, that the 1980 Act introduces a subtle change of wording for persons in
this situation; where the 1975 Act says (in relation to young offenders) 'the court
shall obtain information', the 1980 Act says that it shall 'obtain such information
as it can'.

Children. Offenders age under 16, or age up to 18, but already under the supervision of a Children's Hearing.

The law requires that courts consider reports in those cases where children are
prosecuted, rather than being referred to the Reporter. There are specific considerations which apply to their consideration of reports in these circumstances,
and we deal with the whole issue subsequently.

Rights of Offender

There is one all-embracing obligation concerning every report prepared to assist
the court, and that is that a copy of it shall be given to the offender, or his
solicitor. This obligation was enacted by Section 10 of the Criminal Justice
(Scotland) Act 1949, and is now to be located at Sections 192 and 393 of the
Criminal Procedure (Scotland) Act 1975 in regard to solemn and summary cases
respectively. These Sections also allow that if a child is appearing before the
court and is not legally represented, the report shall be given to his parent or
guardian, if present. The law states that this duty of giving the report to the
offender is one for the Clerk of Court, but in practice it is often undertaken by
either the social worker writing the report, or the social worker on duty at the
court. Although reports are regarded as the property of the court that ordered
them, the law is silent as to the rights of the offender to retain his copy: the
word 'given' suggests he has such a right. Moreover, we follow the view of the
S.W.S.G. document 'The Social Worker Reports' (April, 1974) that, as a report can
include statements about an offence, a breach of a rule of criminal law occurs if
the prosecution does not also receive a copy. Accordingly, the administrative
arrangements for the submission of reports should include this practice.

The Content of Reports

This topic has been considered by a number of influential bodies. The discussion
in the Report of the Interdepartmental Committee on the Business of the Higher
Criminal Courts (the Streatfeild Report, 1961) represents perhaps the most substantial contribution. Although this document was only concerned with England and
Wales, the Interdepartmental Committee on the Probation Service (the Morison Report,
1962), which did include and extend to Scotland, largely endorsed the recommendations made by the Streatfeild Committee. Furthermore, in Scotland the S.W.S.G.
document 'The Social Worker Reports' (April, 1974) gave further guidelines on the
presentation and compilation of written reports. It was the Morison Committee who
urged the adoption of the term 'social enquiry report' as the most appropriate
name to describe its function. That is the basis for the current usage of this
now more familiar phrase.

There seems to be general agreement that a social enquiry report should include:-

> 'essential details of the offender's home surroundings and
> family background; his attitude to his family, and their
> response to him; his school and work record, and spare-time
> activities; his attitude to his employment; his attitude
> to his present offence; his attitude and response to previous
> forms of treatment following any previous convictions; de-
> tailed histories about relevant physical and mental con-
> ditions; an assessment of personality and character'.
> (Morison, quoting Streatfeild).

Neither the law nor these authorities lay down any standard format for a report.
The general principle is that the format should reflect and be derived from the
essential points in any particular case. It is on this sort of subject that mutual
understanding between sentencers and report writers is essential. There should be,
within Social Work Departments, a format of sufficient flexibility to enable report
writers to operate freely within this general principle.

Opinions as to Disposal in a Report

The propriety of expressing an opinion as to disposal in a social enquiry report
received detailed consideration in both the Streatfeild and Morison Reports. They
both agreed that it was the report writer's duty to express a helpful opinion if
he were able and competent to do so. The Streatfeild Report advanced the suggestion that such an opinion might legitimately go beyond the question of probation, if
the expertise of the probation service and research findings justified it. The
Morison Committee expressed some reservations that the state of knowledge at that
point in time (1962) did not justify such an extension.

In Scotland the matter was discussed at a Conference in May, 1964, which was chaired
by the Lord Justice Clerk, Lord Wheatley. In his summing-up, Lord Wheatley came to
the following conclusions:-

> The judge would decide what opinions he wanted in a report.
> The unsolicited offering of views by a report writer
> represented a departure from his terms of reference.

> The question of the sources of the material included in a
> report was crucial if an opinion of any kind was to be
> offered.

> Two aspects of a report could be differentiated: the social
> enquiry report, and a suitability for probation report. The
> latter comprised all the information for a social enquiry
> report (as defined above), together with an opinion about
> the chances of probation diverting the offender from crime.

Clearly the author of a social enquiry report in Scotland should both be aware of
this range of views and also be familiar with the source material. The most recent
pronouncement is the S.W.S.G. document of April 1974, 'The Social Worker Reports'.
We offer the following guidelines as being applicable:-

> There is no obligation to offer *any* opinion. A good social
> enquiry report as such assists the sentencing process.

> Report writers could usefully acknowledge in their reports
> that the sentencing decision is one for the court. The
> use of the word 'recommend' (or 'recommendation') in a
> report tends to suggest the reverse.

> The most appropriate opinion, if any is to be offered, is

one relating to the offender's suitability for probation.
In particular, the court's concern is with the degree of
probability that probation will divert the offender from
further crime.

Considerable thought and caution should be exercised before
offering any other opinion. The crucial question is whether
or not the report writer's expertise and competence justifies
such a departure.

At all times, the offering of an opinion is related to the
social and rehabilitative possibilities of any suggested
disposal. These factors do not represent the totality of
sentencing considerations which the court must bear in mind.

Technical Problems

There exist a number of technical problems related to the compilation and presentation of reports.

Previous Convictions and the Rehabilitation of Offenders' Act. Reference to past
criminality is an integral and necessary part of any social enquiry report. It is,
therefore, necessary to deal with the question of the social worker's authority for
both giving and obtaining information about this subject in the course of the preparation of a report.

Normally, information about an accused's previous convictions is made available to
a court by the prosecution; either after an admission of guilt by the accused; or
after conviction or finding of guilt; but prior to disposal. Occasionally such
information is adduced earlier during trial proceedings in certain exceptional
situations. In earlier times, the existence of previous convictions was regarded
 especially if of like nature as·an 'aggravation' of the charge with which the
court was dealing. However, the legal relationship of previous convictions to
present sentence is now stated in the Criminal Procedure (Scotland) Act 1975,
(Sections 159 and 356), thus:-

> A previous conviction may not be libelled as an aggravation
> of an offence.

> Where a person is convicted of an offence, the court may
> have regard to any previous conviction in respect of that
> person in deciding on the disposal of the case.

> Nothing in this section shall affect the sentence which a
> court may pass on a second or subsequent conviction.

The number and type of previous convictions, coupled with their associated disposals,
represent crucial factors in sentencing, but the matter is one for the policy and
the interpretation of the courts.

The practices of prosecutors in the quotation of previous convictions therefore
become very important, as usually this is the only source of such information
available to courts prior to sentence. Although the letter of the Rehabilitation
of Offenders' Act does not apply to this practice, prosecutors have been encouraged
to operate the spirit of the Act's provisions in quoting previous convictions. The
effect of this practice can often be:-

> i) Appearances before a Children's Hearing are not shown,
>   unless the accused is <u>currently</u> subject to a Supervision
>   Requirement under Section 44(1) of the Social Work
>   (Scotland) Act 1968, because in this instance the Court
>   is obliged to obtain the Advice of the Hearing and

therefore needs to know of the existing supervision.

ii)   A person who appears as a 'first offender' may not
have an unblemished record.

iii) Often only like convictions are listed (particularly,
for example, in relation to drunkenness, traffic offences).

In any event, prosecutors may only quote offences considered by them to be relevant.
It is also worthy of note that only convictions prior to the date of the offence's
commission, which may have occurred some months before the trial, can be quoted.

The function of a report writer in obtaining and, in turn, relaying to the court
information about a person's past criminality has a different focus. He is seeking to assist the court's disposal of the case and, in pursuit of this aim, it
becomes part of his professional function to analyse and interpret, as far as he is
able, the offender's behaviour: in particular, he is looking for any indications
that social work supervision could significantly 'divert the offender from further
crime'. (Streatfeild).

From these general considerations derive the essential principles governing actual
practice. The detail has been dealt with in two Circulars - SHHD 26/75 and SW11/76.

The report writer needs to have access to full information about the extent and
nature of an offender's past criminality. In many areas, the general practice is
that the local Police arrange to supply the Social Work Department with a full list
of all appearances made by an accused before both Courts and Hearings. As noted
above, information about an accused made available by a court will only be that
quoted by the prosecutor, and may well, therefore, not be an adequate list for this
purpose. The Rehabilitation of Offenders' Act does govern the disclosure of information about previous convictions by any agency possessing it to any other person.
In this context, the Circulars make it clear that 'in the view of the Secretary of
State, the disclosure of convictions by the Police to social workers for the purpose
of social enquiry reports should not be regarded as contrary to the Rehabilitation
of Offenders' Act'. The practice is seen as falling under the heading of being a
disclosure to 'persons who have a lawful use for information about convictions'.
The first point to emphasise here is that the disclosure is authorised only by
reference to the preparation of a report - i.e. a specific function under Section
27 of the Social Work (Scotland) Act - and not for general information or idle
interest. A second important point is that lists supplied by the Police contain
information over and above actual sentences. Because of this, the list needs editing before any of its contents can appear in or are attached to a social enquiry
report. The following should not appear in any social enquiry report:-

No Action (by Reporter) - but Referral Discharged by
hearing is acceptable

No proceedings

Desert Pro Loco Desert Simpliciter

Not Guilty

Not Proven

Continuations or Deferments.

The report writer, then has a lawful use for the information. The following considerations apply to his use of that information in the actual content of a report,
according to the circulars:-

There is no statutory requirement on the social worker to
provide a full list of convictions (i.e. as an end in itself).

He may do so if he wishes, but particularly if he thinks
it either relevant or necessary to the purposes of the
report.

He should try to obtain and supply a full list if the court
specifically asks him to do so. Such an expectation may
be an accepted part of the relationship between Court and
Social Workers in any area.

He need not supply a full list if he considers it unnecessary.

In practice, the following guidelines help towards better practice, though it is
important for report writers to know the practices and expectations which obtain
in the Courts in their area.

The obtaining and use of information about previous convictions in a social enquiry report is an authorised function
under the Rehabilitation of Offenders' Act.

The more information gained in its preparation, and the fuller
his reference to significant factors in criminality, the
more useful his report.

More important than giving a list of appearances and disposals
is the analysis of the offender's pattern of criminal behaviour.

In practical terms, therefore, any information given by a report writer is likely
to exceed that supplied by the prosecutor. It will, therefore, represent extra
information in the court's disposal of the case and the court will need to put its
contents to the accused in the ordinary way, so that he can accept that the details
apply to him. For example, appearances before a Children's Hearing are more likely
to be relevant to the report writer's purpose than to the prosecutor's. A report
writer will be constrained to refer to any probation or after-care supervision,
even if the relevant appearance is not listed by the prosecutor. It is more
important to emphasise the report writer's role of 'giving information about'
previous convictions within the context of the report's over-all function, rather
than to see him simply as the compiler of an alternative and often larger schedule
of previous convictions. There can be no doubt that to perform his function
adequately, the report writer must initially possess full information about an
offender's crimes, but possession alone does not guarantee the expertise and
objectivity necessary to a proper use of it. The function of the report is to
provide an analysis, and lists should be used constructively to this end.

Pre-Trial Reports

As indicated above, the law only allows for the ordering of reports after a plea
or finding of guilt but prior to disposal by means of an adjournment of court proceedings for the purpose. As a matter of administrative convenience, however,
reports may be requested in advance of a trial. There are very important implications for report writing and preparation in these 'pre-trial' situations, over and
above the more normal 'post conviction' considerations already discussed.

It is the practice of the High Court to issue a written request for a 'social
background report' when a person under the age of 21 has been fully committed and
served with an indictment in a case to be heard by that Court. This practice
derives from the seriousness of the matters tried by the High Court, coupled with
the obligation placed on all courts to obtain and consider reports before any
person of such an age can receive a custodial sentence.

A similar practice obtains in some areas in regard to persons in the same age group committed for trial on solemn procedure and for identical reasons.

Social workers may bring an accused's circumstances to the court's attention either because he is already subject to statutory supervision, or because he is otherwise in contact with the Department. The method chosen is the advance preparation of a report. The situation occurs more frequently, though not exclusively, in cases cited to appear on summary procedure.

In all these pre-trial situations, great care must be taken in regard to:-

Consent. The accused and/or his solicitor must consent to the preparation and submission of the report. This will necessitate the social worker explaining in detail:-

> - the basis of the request for the report
>
> - the subject matter to be covered and methods of inquiry
>
> - the role of the report in the administration of justice.

The accused has the right to refuse preparation at this stage. Furthermore, the attempted stipulation of conditions by an accused should be construed by the social worker as constituting a refusal - hence the importance of a detailed initial explanation.

Plea. The establishing of the accused's intended plea is of paramount importance. An intended plea of 'not guilty', while not of itself preventing the preparation of a report, does preclude the social worker from making any reference to the alleged offence(s). A logical extension of this is that the expression of any opinion concerning disposal is thereby also precluded.

Two other possibilities must also be mentioned:-

> i)   The accused intimates a plea of guilty to alternative or lesser charge(s). Report writers should avoid this potential hazard by stating, 'I understand that . . . pleads not guilty to the charge(s) as libelled,' and proceed as above.
>
> ii) The accused, whilst intimating plea(s) of not guilty, makes an open admission of the charge(s). In this rare situation, report writers are obliged, in any report prepared at this stage, to state the full truth, and to inform the accused that they are duty bound to do so.

Submission of report. Once prepared, the report should be lodged with the Clerk of Court. Any requests for 'advance copies' from any source (e.g. offender or his agent, or any other interested person) should be resisted. The report is the court's property and will be made available by the court to all those with proper authority to have a copy at the appropriate point in the court proceedings.

The chief objection to the preparation of reports pre-trial is that, whatever the intended plea, the full circumstances of the offence(s) have not been disclosed by the prosecution, and accordingly, any discussion of an accused's attitude towards his crime(s), which is a proper and necessary part of a report, is more than usually premature and hazardous.

Non-cooperation of the accused. Whilst accused persons may not be in a position to prevent the court ordering a report in their case, they can create difficulties for the report writer by various degrees of non-cooperation. The following considerations can be stated at the outset:-

> The ordering of a report is not a 'referral', in the sense of a request to the Social Work Department to perform a certain task. It is, in fact, an order of the court, and the report writer has both authority and obligation to obtain the information necessary to the court's purpose in sentencing. The report writer is acting in his capacity as 'officer of the court'. This is the approach, therefore, that the social worker brings to the task of report writing.

> Section 27 of the Social Work (Scotland) Act imposed a responsibility on the Local Authority to 'make available . . . reports . . . which the court may require'. The courts, in their turn, work under an obligation to 'obtain information about the person's circumstances from an officer of the Local Authority' (e.g. Section 208 of the 1975 Act). In most courts' interpretation, the views and wishes of the accused are of little account, and report writers will want to emphasise this position to an accused who may be seeking to impose restrictions on the enquiry. An accused who de facto (e.g. by silence) refuses cooperation runs the risk of being in contempt of court.

A court has a number of options open to it when ordering a report: it may remand the offender in custody for the purpose - with this often being interpreted as an indication of the seriousness of the situation, or it may release him on bail, and under the terms of the Bail Act, 1980, may insert a specific requirement that he makes himself available to the writer of the report.

The matter of availability is the first main area in which any degree of non-cooperation may manifest itself. There is a specific remedy in the case of an offender who is made the subject of a bail order with a special requirement that he make himself available under the 1980 Bail Act: in this event the social worker's report as to his non-availability may form the basis of a subsequent prosecution, and thus his documentation of and evidence for the non-cooperation needs to be suitably full. Even with those offenders who may be ordained to appear, any report as to their non-cooperation should be adequately itemised.

The provisions of the Bail Act have significantly changed the situation in which reports may be prepared and the fact that a breach of the requirement respecting the preparation of the report is of itself an offence creates for the reporting social worker a completely new authority position with which he should be conversant and capable of responding appropriately in the event of problems arising or the bailed person failing in his commitment to 'make himself available'.

Even if an offender makes himself available, or is forcibly made available by virtue of the fact that he has been held in custody, he may be uncooperative by manner, evasion, or restriction on information, to the point that no adequate report for the court's purposes can be submitted. In particular the social worker will need to judge whether, or in what degree, the offender's wishes in regard to confidentiality can be met without undue sacrifice to the value of the report. We offer the following guidelines to assist towards good practice:-

> The court has opportunity when ordering a report to explain its scope and purpose. The accused and/or his agent can make known any reactions or objections.

Either in lieu of, but preferably in addition to, this the
social worker on duty in the court should, in an interview
with the accused, explain this matter more fully. Any
immediate problems should be noted, and the issues referred
to the person who will actually compile the report.

The report writer, should, at the commencement of his
enquiry, explain either orally or in an introductory
letter the purpose and scope of the report.

It is implicit that the first contact should be with the
accused personally, prior to any question of meeting his
family, speaking to employers, etc. A corollary of this
is that any enquiry should be begun as soon as possible
after notice is received.

On meeting with a refusal to cooperate, or with a specific
objection which nullifies the value of a report, the report
writer should satisfy himself that the accused fully under-
stands the position and the potential consequences of refusing
cooperation.

If the accused is represented, the report writer should
immediately confer with the accused's solicitor with a view
to resolving the difficulty.

If the issue remains unresolved, the judge who ordered the
report should be advised without delay.

A report should be submitted to the court, outlining the
steps followed, and the conclusion of the inquiry.

The court is then in a position to do one of three things:-

i)   Proceed to sentence on the basis of the available
     information.

ii) Continue the case for a further period, having ruled
     on the difficulties which have arisen.

iii) Remand the accused in custody, and order a further
     period for the report's preparation.

The prime objective of the written document, the social enquiry report, is to
assist the court in disposing of the case, frequently to the point of determining
that 'no other method is appropriate' other than custody, and in all this the
'client' is in a very real sense the court. It is also true that the individual
offender who is the subject of the report is a 'client' in the more familiar sense
of the word in social work circles. The social worker has to provide a service to
both, but there are no circumstances in which a social work service to the accused
person may interfere or impede the delivery of service to the courts, as laid down
by the statutes.

The Right of Refusal: Implications for Social Workers Preparing Reports
for Childrens' Hearings

It may be said that prior to a decision to proceed with the case to a hearing, the
child and his parent(s) have a right of refusal to cooperate in the preparation of
any report. Their position is analogous to the accused person who has not yet
appeared before a Court, and until the child and his parent(s) have been formally
notified that the matter is being referred to the hearing and the grounds of
referral stated, they have a perfect right to remain silent.

When so notified, the decision as to whether they will accept the grounds; a decision which may be made independently or in consultation with a solicitor, is for them. Following on that, if they decide to accept the grounds then no valid reason exists for delaying the preparation of a report.

It is, however, a highly unsatisfactory arrangement when the social worker in pursuance of information for a report is the bearer of the initial information that the child is to be referred to a hearing. The child and parent(s) are entitled to notification and a period of reflection and deliberation before being requested to comply with the investigations of the social worker in preparation of a report.

It is, therefore, an issue of considerable value for the social worker and for the family if the social worker's earliest contact, be that by letter or visit, proceeds at the correct pace in relation to the knowledge and determined position of child and parent(s). Accordingly, any initial contact must clear this ground. Firstly, to take the pre-decision investigative report. It may be that sufficient information exists within the Social Work Department, or that Department acting in concert with e.g. the child's school to provide sufficient, but not all available information, which would enable the reporter to arrive at a decision. In illustration, the fact that on three occasions in the past year Mrs. Smith had sought aid and advice about Jimmy's conduct coupled with an alarming truancy rate over the past three months would probably constitute sufficient information for the reporter in referring to the hearing a child alleged to have stolen £5.00. On the other hand, the fact that 10 years ago a sister now married and living away from home, had an illegitimate child can hardly be seen as germain to the reporter's task at this point.

There is no prohibition in the statute, to the passing of relevant information between the Social Work Department and the reporter in this way, for this purpose, but the usual considerations of confidentiality must be preserved, and it is within that, that decision would be taken about an approach to the people concerned. Any such approach must be clear that the intention of the investigation is strictly limited to aiding the reporter in his investigative task.

Secondly, there is the preparation of a report for the hearing. The initial contact should start from the point of clarifying with the child and the parent(s) that they have been duly notified by the reporter as to the nature of the grounds on which the child is being referred, the date, time and place of the hearing.

From that the social worker should ascertain if they intend to accept the grounds as stated. It is not part of the social work task to persuade people in either direction and if a genuine doubt is expressed, the best guidance is that the advice of a solicitor should be sought.

The pressures to produce a report, must in these circumstances, be resisted. If such be the case then the appropriate communication to the reporter, for transmission to the panel members is simply that the child and parent(s) have been contacted and have indicated that the grounds, as stated, will be denied, and that in the circumstances no further enquiries have been undertaken. It would be quite wrong to, e.g. reproduce a previous report, or compile a report from departmental records in these circumstances. Whatever inconvenience is occasioned to the social worker, the reporter or to panel members is very secondary to the primary responsibility to acknowledge and safeguard the fundamental rights of the citizen.

If the child and parent(s) do go to the hearing and deny the grounds and the decision is to refer the matter to the Sheriff for proof, it should be clearly understood that the Sheriff would not seek, nor indeed would have any use for a social work report during these proceedings.

If written communication is the chosen means of initial contact, then
in the investigative stage a suitable letter might adopt the following form:

> Dear Mr. and Mrs. Smith,
>
> I have been advised by the reporter to the children's
> hearing that your son, James, has been reported to him by
> the police for an alleged offence of theft. The reporter
> has requested my help in reaching a decision as to whether
> James should be referred to the children's hearing in
> respect of the above matter.
>
> I would like to call to discuss this and propose visiting
> at 7 p.m. on 14th inst. If this is inconvenient, or if
> you wish to seek the advice of a solicitor before my visit,
> I would be obliged if you would let me know at your earliest
> convenience.
>
> > Signed.

At the stage of compiling a report for the hearing:

> Dear Mr. and Mrs. Smith,
>
> I have been notified that your son, James, is to appear
> before the children's hearing on 14th inst. and that you
> have received notice of this, together with a statement of
> the grounds of referral, which I understand relate to an
> alleged offence of theft.
>
> Subject to James and you agreeing the grounds of referral
> as stated, the hearing will require to consider a report
> compiled by this department on his social background and
> personal circumstances and for this purpose I propose to
> call on 10th inst. at about 7 p.m. It would be helpful if
> I could see James in addition to discussing this matter
> with you.
>
> If for any reason this is inconvenient or if you intend to
> deny the grounds of referral, as stated, I would be grateful
> if you would let me know as soon as possible.
>
> > Signed.

Obtaining and Using Information

While there is no statutory obligation on the police to supply information to
Social Work Departments in respect of the preparation of social enquiry reports
there is an expectation that local arrangements arrived at between Chief Constables
and Directors of Social Work will meet the needs of reporting social workers without placing undue strain on the police service. Difficulties which may arise in
given localities should therefore be subject to resolution at appropriate levels
in the respective organisations.

The 1976 Circular (SW11/76) 'Social Enquiry Reports' noted 'Although sections 68
and 356 of the Criminal Procedure (Scotland) Act 1975 provide a formal method for
the libelling of previous convictions, there seems to be authority for the view
that a local authority officer charged with the duty of preparing a social enquiry
report may include in such a report previous convictions which were not libelled
by the prosecutor. If, therefore, a social worker considers that details of an
accused's previous criminality, either in whole or in part, were necessary for the
purposes of an adequate report to the Court then such convictions may be referred
to in his report, notwithstanding that this exceeds the list libelled by the

prosecutor.' This underlines the view that the social worker should use the information received in the social analysis of the offender's situation, and not simply provide for the court a formal list of previous offences. The provisions of the C.P.(S)A.75 provide for the libelling of a full list of previous convictions by the Fiscal, but does not remove his discretional power to be selective in the compilation of the list. We regard the primary social work task as being that of social analysis and comment. The use of provided information, including the list of previous convictions is but a particular aspect of the task, albeit one which requires considerable skill in the interpretation of events and potential patterns of criminal conduct as revealed by such a list.

In respect of reports on child offenders the 'list of previous convictions' does not apply, and care should be exercised in the presentation of patterns of conduct so that the court dealing with the child is in no doubt or difficulty respecting this but at the same time a list of appearances before hearings, or known instances where discretion has been exercised by either reporter or police is not presented in such a way that it becomes a 'list of previous convictions' in all but name. The desirability of comprehensive reports on children is now well recognised and as an aid to the identification of appropriate information sources SWSG issued a circular SW16/74 'Children subject to court proceedings' following a House of Commons statement by the then Secretary of State, in which inter alia, the following points were made:

A) <u>Information to be supplied to Social Work Department</u>. If the social worker is to provide a satisfactory service to the court, it is clearly desirable that he be fully aware of the way in which the Police and the prosecuting authorities proceed in relation to decisions on prosecution and detention in custody. This knowledge is necessary if he is to play his full part in the court process. His main contribution, of course, will be the provision of social background reports and, for purposes of these reports, it is important that the Social Work Department be given, in each case, details of the nature of the charges on which the prosecution is based. It is understood that, where proceedings are being taken against children, Procurators Fiscal will send to the Social Work Department a copy of the charge. In most cases this should provide for the social worker sufficient information about the offence. At times, however, he will require further details of the charge and it is hoped that, in such cases, Procurators Fiscal will be prepared to provide additional details in response to specific requests by social workers.

B) <u>Assessment of information received by Social Work Department</u>. It is important that the Social Work Department should be able to identify cases that require special attention and, for this purpose, it is recommended that an experienced officer in the Department should scrutinise the information received from the Procurator Fiscal.'

This, as with the police requires clear lines of communication between social work and the Fiscal, and in the circumstances covered by the circular provides a broad indication of the inter-related nature of the services being provided when children face criminal charges and courts have to make decisions which will reflect the seriousness of the situation and the needs of the child offender.

<u>Examples of Letters and Communications Relevant to the Preparation of Reports</u>

The essence of social enquiry reporting is an ability to communicate information and relevant opinion. Such ability is also required in the preparation stages of a report, and we give examples of letters and forms which may be of use in enhancing the explanations, requests, purpose of the writer to those whom he may need to contact; and also by their ready access here to save the writer time.

Contact with the offender. Given the frequency with which contact for a report
is made by letter, it is appropriate that the writer's purpose and authority
should be comprehensively conveyed. As the basis of that authority within the
general purpose of a report may differ according to matters such as:- the age of
the offender; the stage at which the report is ordered; the basis of the remand;
and so on, a number of alternative models are necessary.

General introductory letter

                                                      Area Office ....

                                                      Date   ....

Dear Mr. Smith,

        I have been informed that you appeared before the Hamilton Sheriff
Court on the 5th of January, 1980, and pled guilty to an offence of theft of a
motor car. I understand that the court continued your case until the 26th of
January and ordered a social enquiry report.

        This report, which it is my duty to prepare, is ordered by the court to
assist it make a decision in the case. The court considers that information about
your background, family, personal circumstances, and about any previous offences,
is relevant to its decision, and calls for the report in order to obtain such
information. The information will be confidential to the court, but you will see
a copy of the report before the court makes its decision, and you will be able to
comment on, or take objection to, anything that is said in it.

        In order to take this matter further, I would like you to call and see
me at the above address at 2.00 p.m. on the 13th of January. You may wish to
consult a solicitor, but if anything to do either with the report itself, or with
regard to this appointment, causes you anxiety or difficulty, please contact me
as soon as possible.

                                Yours sincerely,

                                Social Worker.

Variations

a) Pre-trial report (see   above).

                                                      Area Office ....

                                                      Date   ....

Dear Mr. Jones,

        I have been informed that you are due to appear before the High Court
at Ayr on the 4th of February charged with culpable homicide. Because you are
under 21 years of age, the court will require a social enquiry report in the event
of your being convicted and in considering that custodial sentence is necessary,
and it makes a practice of asking the Social Work Department to prepare this
report before you come to trial. At this stage the report can only be prepared
with your consent, but if you are convicted that consent would not be necessary.
If you agree to the report's preparation now, it will only be used if you are
convicted, and nothing in it can be mentioned in court until that stage; if you
are not convicted it will be destroyed.

        The report will cover your background, family, personal circumstances,
and any previous offences, and would be used by the court to help it make a
decision in the case. The report is confidential to the court, but you would see
a copy and have the opportunity to comment on, or take objection to, anything said

in it before the court makes its decision.

In order to take this matter further, I would like you to call and see me at the above address at (time) on the (date). You may wish to consult a solicitor, but if anything to do either with the report itself, or with regard to this appointment, causes you anxiety or difficulty, please contact me as soon as possible.

Yours sincerely,

Social Worker.

b) **Availability as a specific requirement of bail**. The general introductory letter would be amended to read:-

In order to take this matter further, I would like you to call and see me at the above address on (date) at (time). I should point out to you that the court has made it a specific condition of your bail that you make yourself available for the preparation of this report; and that if you fail to do so you make yourself liable to be charged with the specific offence of failing to do so, which, if proved against you, would render you liable to an additional penalty over and above that which you may receive for the present offence. (Then as before . . .)

Note: a registered letter or the use of recorded delivery is to be recommended in this instance.

c) **Child offender**. The main variation to consider here is whether the letter should be to the parents. If the 'child' is under 16 years of age, such a course could be recommended, but there is more flexibility when the 'child' is one by virtue of his being a 17 year old but under the supervision of a Children's Hearing.

Area Office ....

Dear Mr. and Mrs. Brown,   Date ....

Either (post-conviction)

You will know that your son, James, appeared before the Inverness Sheriff Court last Tuesday, the 26th February, and pled guilty to an offence of shoplifting, after being arrested the previous night and being charged along with a number of older boys. The court has continued the matter until Tuesday the 17th of March, and ordered a social enquiry report, which it is my duty to prepare.

The court considers that information about James' background, family, personal circumstances, and about any previous trouble or difficulty, is essential to its decision, and calls for the report in order to obtain this information. The information will remain confidential to the court, but you will have the right to see it in court, and to comment on, or take objection to, anything said in it before the court makes its decision.

In order to take this matter further, I propose to call on you at your home on . . . . (as before)

Or (pre-trial)

Area Office ....

Dear Mr. and Mrs. Brown,   Date ....

I have been notified that your son James has been cited to appear at the Inverness Sheriff Court on the 24th of March to face a charge of shoplifting. The law requires the Social Work Department to prepare a report about James' background family, personal circumstances, and about any previous trouble or difficulty, and to obtain a report from his school, for use by the court before it makes a decision about what to do with him.

At this stage the report can only be prepared if you, as his parents, agree, but if he is convicted, a report could be ordered by the court without that consent. The report is confidential to the court . . . (as before).

Contact with Other Agencies or Outside Departments

The Police.   As indicated, the Police are under no obligation to provide information to report writers about an offender's previous convictions, and any communication to the Police can usefully indicate its nature as a request, not a demand, for information. In the light of circulars SWSG 11/76 and SHHD 7/76, as discussed in the text, many areas have a clear policy about this matter, and report writers should familiarise themselves with its content. In any event the request for information should contain sufficiently full detail to enable the identification of the correct offender, and should satisfy the Police authorities that it is related specifically to social enquiry or allied purposes. It should also be noted that the information supplied by the Police may be in a form which it is not appropriate simply to attach to a report, and may thus need editing in line with the guidance given above.

The Chief Constable   Area Office ....
Police HQ   Date ....
                For the attention of the Officer in charge of records

Dear Sir,
                          Social Enquiry Report

I am required to submit a social enquiry report on:-

                John Albert Smith   (d.o.b. 12.10.50.)
                No Fixed Abode   (currently remanded in custody)

who is to appear at Perth Sheriff Court on the 20th of this month on 3 charges of Theft By Housbreaking.

I should be obliged if you would inform me at your earliest convenience of any previous convictions recorded against him, so that I can prepare my report.

                              Yours faithfully,

                              Social Worker

Outside Departments.   In those cases where an offender lives outwith the immediate area of the court or the social work division or district which services it, speed of administration and the fullest possible detail are both essential. It is particularly helpful if the written request and its associated detail can go directly to the office from which the person who is actually to prepare the report works, and a telephone call to ascertain this can prevent days of delay; the use of first class post is also to be recommended. Nonetheless it is also important to ascertain and respect allocation procedures in different areas.

In those instances where the offender lives in England or Wales, a further enquiry is necessary, especially in the cases of younger offenders, to establish whether the local probation office or local social services department is the most appropriate for the task. Moreover it is important to provide the

English or Welsh authorities information about the disposals and powers available to the Scottish Court dealing with the case.

A further complication arises if the offender is held in custody at a prison which is far removed from his home area. The practicalities demand urgent negotiation with the home-based social worker to establish a clear arrangement for the offender to be interviewed in custody.

In all cases copy correspondence, clearly indicating the addressee, and the date and method of despatch, is to be recommended, in the event of postal delay and other problem eventualities.

Example;

Dear   Area Officer ....
                                                       Date ....

       Re. Michael Williams (age 25)
       Address:4 Grey Street,Whitetown.

The above-named appeared today at Edinburgh District Court from custody, and pled guilty to an offence of breach of the peace. The case was continued to (date) for the purpose of obtaining a social enquiry report. Williams was released on bail with a specific condition that he make himself available for the report's preparation. I attach all the detail I have about him;-
     (itemise) copy of the complaint
            convictions libelled by the Fiscal
            referral form and interview record
            name of duty solicitor

I would be grateful if you would arrange for the report to be prepared and (number of) copies sent to (address) on or before (date).

                Yours sincerely,

                Social Worker

In this example an English authority would need comment on:-

     the disposals and powers available to the district court
     the significance of the specific bail condition
     the limitations of the fiscal's list of convictions
     the arrangements operated by the department for the submission
     of reports to the court.

As these matters are noted in the text we do not propose to elaborate further upon them. Also the content of the above example would need to be varied in the event of the report being requested pre-trial, with adequate information about the practices used in regard to that by the requesting area. It can be noted here that many English Crown Courts ask for pre-trial reports as a matter of course on categories of offender for whom reports are not obligatory under Scottish law: the potential report writer may be prepared to observe English practice in this instance (example - an offender over 21 who is not going to prison for the first time); or he may reply to the effect that he would be prepared to do a report post conviction, as this would be in accordance with Scottish law.

Outside Departments will also require to be informed by letter of the outcome of the case.

Example: Letter Notifying Disposal

Dear
                                                      Area Office ....
                                                      Date ....
             Re. Michael Williams (age 20)
             Address:4 Grey Street, Whitetown.

         Thank you for your report on the above named. When he appeared today at
the Edinburgh District Court he was sentenced to 60 days detention in a Young
Offenders Institution. I return spare copies of your report, together with our
Court Social Work form which shows the post-sentence activity undertaken after
the hearing.

                              Yours sincerely,

Communication to Courts when Reports are NOT Available

There are three main types of circumstances in which reports may not be available:-

        i)   Maladministration - by either the court or the social worker

       ii)   Non-availability of the accused

      iii)   Non-co-operation of the accused

Maladministration.   It can happen that reports are not prepared as a result of
maladministration: it could be that the Social Work Department was not informed by
the court officials of the request for one; or that the Social Work Department
concerned either loses or delays the referral so that preparation is impossible in
the time originally allowed. In either event it is important that any communication
to the court exonerates the accused, and the communication should be seen by him as
if it were a report.

Non-availability of the accused. Any non-availability on the part of an accused
which results in a report not being ready by the due date could be open to a
number of interpretations. At one end of the scale it may be that a combination
of time and circumstance for which he is not to blame produces a situation in
which the report cannot be completed in time. At the other there may be downright
evasion on his part which could result in him incurring further penalty.

The social worker's communication to the court needs to be sufficiently detailed
to help the court determine which end of the scale any particular instance represents. Under the first heading:-

Example:
        The Clerk of Court   Area Office ....
        (address)   Date ....

Dear Sir,
             Re. Henry McIntosh (d.o.b. 20.4.40)
             Address:12 Burns Road, Seatown.

         The above named appeared at (name and location of court) on (date),
when the case was continued for a social enquiry report until (date): the accused
was ordained to appear under the provisions of the Bail Act 1980.

         I have to inform the court that since his appearance in court,
Mr. McIntosh has started a new job which involves him working away from home for
long hours, and that I have been able to verify this. As a result, however, two

appointments which I arranged proved abortive, and the report will not be ready in time for the due date. I would in no way attribute this to any lack of co-operation by Mr. McIntosh, and if the court still requires a report, I have ascertained that it could be accomplished within a further two weeks after the due date.

Yours faithfully,

Social Worker.

Under the second heading (evasion), it becomes important to provide very full detail and documentation:-

The Clerk of Court   Area Office ....
(address)   Date ....

Copy to the Procurator Fiscal

"   "   " solicitor for the accused

Dear Sir,

Andrew MacEwan (age 24)
Address:14 Scott Road, Penthills.

The above named appeared at (name and location of court) on (date), and was convicted after trial of (offences). The case was continued for a social enquiry report and the accused given bail, with the condition that he make himself available for the report's preparation. This was explained to him in court, and he was seen immediately afterwards by (name - court duty social worker) and expressed his understanding of the position.

I have to inform the court that no report will be available on the due date, because Mr. MacEwan has not made himself available. I have written to him three times (and attach copies of those letters), and visited his address twice: on each occasion it was confirmed that he was resident there, and that both my letters and the fact that I had visited had been passed on to him. I would regard Mr. MacEwan as being in breach of the terms of his bail.

Yours faithfully,

Non-Co-operation. It is quite possible for an accused person, whilst making himself available for the preparation of a report, to fail to co-operate with that preparation to an extent that it is null and void: we deal with this situation in the text above.

Example:
The Clerk of Court   Area Office ....
(address)   Date ....

Dear Sir,

Re. William MacIver (age17)
Address:S. A. Hostel, Green Road,

The above named appeared at (name and location of court) on (date), on charges of (.........), and his case was continued until (date) for the purpose of obtaining a social enquiry report.

I visited Mr. MacIver at his home on (date) and explained the purpose and use of the report, and he indicated that he understood. However, I have to

report to the court that I am unable to submit a proper report to the court, which
I attribute to Mr. MacIver's non-co-operation.

He refused to disclose to me the whereabouts of his parents or other
family members, or to give any information about his home life beyond the stark
fact that they originated in Glasgow. He also refused to discuss his previous
offences with me, in spite of the list (copy attached) which shows a number of
appearances, including time spent in detention as a result of unpaid fines. Because he refuses to disclose his home address I am unable to locate any social work
records which may exist.

I would be in a position to describe his present accommodation, and to
ascertain whether or not he is in the employment he claims, but I consider that a
totally inadequate report for the court's purpose, and that the inadequacy is due
to Mr. MacIver's non-co-operation.

Yours faithfully,

Social Worker.

Chapter 4

Child Offenders: Court and Hearing

Under the provisions of Part III of the Social Work (Scotland) Act 1968, a system of Children's Hearings replaced the former Juvenile Courts: the new system came into effect in April 1971. The Children's Hearings have a wide jurisdiction both over matters which in an adult would constitute a criminal offence, and over children who are deemed to be in need of care or protection. A full account of the Hearings System is available in the S.W.S.G. booklet, 'Children's Hearings', revised and re-issued in 1976. We deal here with the specific issue of an important minority of children who find themselves before the criminal courts.

Before the introduction of the new system, juvenile offenders (i.e. those under 16 years of age) were dealt with by the same type of courts as adult offenders. However, juveniles were dealt with in private and in buildings, or parts of them, separate from those in which cases against adults were heard: there was protection from publicity, and the attendance of parents was essential. Identical powers were available for dealing with juveniles as were available for adults, e.g. probation, fine, etc., but removal from home was generally in terms of a specific Approved School Order, although detention in a Remand Home for a period not exceeding 28 days was also a possible disposal. The over-riding duty placed on the courts was to act in the best interests and for the welfare of the juvenile.

PROSECUTION OF CHILDREN BEFORE COURTS

Section 31 of the Social Work (Scotland) Act provides that no child shall be prosecuted for any offence except on the instructions or at the instance of the Lord Advocate: nor can the District Courts deal with children so prosecuted. A child is also defined in the Social Work Act (Section 30) as :-

1) a child who has not attained the age of 16 years.

2) a child over the age of 16 years who has not attained the age of 18 years and in respect of whom a supervision requirement of a Children's Hearing is in force

3) a child whose case has been referred to a Children's Hearing under Part V of the Social Work Act i.e. because he is the

> subject of a supervision or care order made by a
> juvenile court in England and Wales.

The Lord Advocate has issued instructions as to which categories of offence are
to be considered for prosecution in the courts. In respect of these, any police
report will also go to the Procurator Fiscal as well as to the Reporter, and these
two will liaise either generally, or on a specific case basis, or both, as to
whether the child should be prosecuted, or be referred to a Hearing: if, on the
face of the evidence, the Fiscal considers that prosecution by the solemn
procedure is necessary, that view will take precedence over referral to a Hearing,
and Crown Office will be consulted by him in the normal way.

This leaves Procurators Fiscal considerable scope for interpretation, thus
influencing the numbers of cases which are referred to the Hearings. The following considerations govern the prosecution of children:-

1) No child under the age of 8 can be prosecuted for an offence.

2) No child under the age of 13 can be prosecuted for an offence
   except on the specific instructions of the Lord Advocate.

3) All very grave crimes (murder, culpable homicide, rape etc.)
   which would normally be tried by the High Court will be
   brought to the attention of the Fiscal.

4) Children who are involved with adults (i.e. persons aged
   over 16) can be prosecuted before the courts, if it is
   considered prejudicial to separate the accused.

5) Any offence which involves the possession of an offensive
   weapon can be prosecuted in the courts, as the Hearing
   does not have power to order the forfeiture of any such
   weapon.

6) Driving offences which carry disqualification can be
   brought before the courts if the prosecution consider
   there are reasons for disqualifying someone who, although
   under the legal age to drive, may nonetheless be considered
   suitable for such disqualification, which might then delay
   the age at which he could legally drive : the Hearing has no
   power to order disqualification from driving.

In general, the prosecuting authorities note the intention of Part III of the
Social Work (Scotland) Act, and only prosecute children before the criminal courts
if a special reason under these headings exists.

BRINGING CHILDREN TO COURT

Once the decision to prosecute a child in the courts has been taken, he can be
cited to appear on a particular date, but is equally liable to be arrested,
detained in Police custody, and brought before the court on the next day. This
will automatically happen if the charge is a serious one which merits the
consideration of solemn procedure.

If a child is to appear before a court, Sections 40 and 308 of the Criminal
Procedure (Scotland) Act 1975, require the Chief Constable to notify the local
authority of the charge and the date and time of the court appearance: the local
authority is, in turn, obliged to submit a report "which shall contain such

information as to the home surroundings of the child as appear to them will assist
the court in the disposal of the case, and the report shall contain information,
which the appropriate education authority shall have a duty to supply, as to the
school record, health and character of the child". In practical terms this means
a social enquiry report, together with a school report, which is obtained by
adapting the usual procedures applicable in relation to appearances at a
Children's Hearing. Great care should be taken to ascertain:-

1) by what method of procedure (solemn or summary)
   prosecution is being made.

2) whether the child has been cited to appear, or has
   been arrested and thus already appeared.

3) whether the report is prepared pre-trial or after
   conviction.

If a child is to be remanded for any purpose by the Court (e.g. reports) or is
committed for trial, special considerations apply to the place of his detention:
these are set out at Section 329 of the 1975 Act:-

i) If the child is under 16 "the Court shall commit him
   to the local authority in whose area the court is
   situated, and the authority shall have the duty of
   placing him in a suitable place of safety chosen by
   the authority instead of committing him to prison".

ii) If he is over 16, yet still a child, by virtue of being
    subject to a supervision requirement from Children's
    Hearing, he can nonetheless be remanded in the normal
    way.

iii) If he is over 14, but not yet 16, he can be committed
     to custody instead of to the local authority, if the
     court grants an 'unruly certificate'; on the grounds
     that he is too unruly or depraved to be detained in a
     place of safety organised by the local authority.

A place of safety is defined in the Social Work (Scotland) Act as "any residential
or other establishment provided by a Local Authority, a Police Station, or any
hospital, surgery or other suitable place, the occupier of which is willing
temporarily to receive a child". The Criminal Procedure Act requires that the
Local Authority or Remand Centre, as appropriate, be named in the warrant authorising the detention. The evidence which constitutes the ground of unruliness or
depravity is not defined, but Section 329 of the Act empowers the court to issue
an unruly certificate simply "where it appears ..... that he is unruly or
depraved", without first necessarily considering a place of safety. Information
from the Social Work Department e.g. in regard to persistent absconding, or to
any previous violence within a residential institution, would be essential to any
prosecutor who wished to allege unrulinesss or move for the detention of a child
in custody: the child (or his agent) would then have opportunity to rebut such
evidence or allegation. The simple non-availability of a suitable place of
safety on the part of the local authority is not a good or sufficient legal
ground for the granting of an unruly certificate. The Children Act 1975,
Section 70, amends the provisions of the Criminal Procedure (Scotland) Act 1975
in the following respect: '..... the court shall not so certify a child unless
such conditions as the Secretary of State may, by order made, or by statutory
instrument prescribe, are satisfied in relation to the child'. No such statutory

instrument has as yet been prescribed by the Secretary of State, but the position
is one to be watched with care, and good practice would dictate that the spirit
of the Act be observed.

Disposal of Cases Involving Children

Sections 172 and 371 provide that "every court in dealing with a child who is
brought before it as an offender shall have regard to the welfare of the child
and shall in a proper case, take steps for removing him from undesirable surroundings". As noted above the court will have before it reports on which
to base this decision.

Children who are not subject to supervision who are found guilty or plead guilty
to an offence:the court has a choice of action:

A)   It may, instead of making an order, remit the case to the reporter to
     arrange for the disposal of the case by the Children's Hearing
     (S.S.173(1)(a) and 372(1)(a)).

     When the court does it, it relinquishes all jurisdiction in respect
     of the child who then becomes subject to the measures available to
     the Hearing (S.S.173(4) and 372(4)).

Or

B)   It may, on a finding of guilt or a guilty plea request the reporter
     to arrange a Hearing for the purpose of obtaining their advice as to
     the treatment of the child (S.S.173(1)(b) and

     On obtaining this advice, the court can either deal with the case or
     remit it to the Hearing for disposal (S.S.173(3) and 372(3)).

The Hearing advice follows the format of consideration given in terms of the
Hearing with the full inputs of social work, school and other appropriate reports.
The parameters within which the Hearing works in this respect are broader than
those normally observed in the Hearing and due regard is to be paid to the wider
powers of the courts.

It is important to realise that children appearing before the courts are liable
to ordinary court penalties, such as fine, probation, disqualification, etc.
which would not be the case before the Children's Hearing. Additionally, there
are provisions for orders for Residential Training and other custodial measures
appropriate to the most serious offences, which are subsequently outlined
Children under 16 cannot be sentenced as adults might be.

The references in the above are qualified by the provision at S.S.173(5) and
372(5) that these arrangements do not apply in a case in respect of which the
sentence is fixed by law. In these cases the powers of detention of the child
are stipulated at S.S.206 and 413 respectively and of course where the fixed
penalty is monetary then this is applied in the usual way, with the court exercising in appropriate cases its power to impose fine supervision. But it may be
that the Secretary of State will decide that a prison service institution is
suited for the detention of a child subject to one of these other orders under
Section 206(1) and (2) and Section 413, especially as he grows to adulthood.

The law allows for, and in some cases ensures, that courts relate to Children's
Hearings in the disposal of any case involving a child. The provisions are set
out in the Criminal Procedure (Scotland) Act at Sections 173 (cases on solemn

procedure) and 372 (summary procedure):-

i)   If the child is *not* already under supervision from the
     Children's Hearing, the court may simply remit the case
     to the Hearing for disposal. That means that it may view
     the types of supervision available to the Hearing as
     adequate to the case, and consider that there is no special
     reason (e.g. disqualification, forfeiture) for a court
     penalty to be imposed. An important corollary of such a
     remit for disposal is that the court's powers of remand
     or detention lapse at that moment, as the case now simply
     stands as "referred to a Children's Hearing", like any
     other.

ii) If the child is already under supervision from the Children's
     Hearing, the court *must* obtain the advice of the Panel as to
     disposal. This involves a remand for the purpose and involves
     the convening of a Children's Hearing to consider the case
     and all the reports in the interim. Hearing members, therefore,
     need to be familiar not only with the resources directly avail-
     able to their own tribunal but with the philosophy and content
     of the various sentencing options open to the court: this
     equally applies to the social worker who is writing reports
     for the Hearing in such a case. Once the advice of the
     Hearing has been obtained, the court may either remit to the
     Hearing for actual disposal, or proceed to sentence in
     whatever form it sees fit.

Attendance of Children at Court

Children may have to attend courts in capacities other than as offenders. The law
governs the attendance of children at courts:-

i)   No child under the age of 14 years shall be permitted
     to be present in any court during the trial of any
     other person except when his presence is required as
     a witness or "otherwise for the purposes of justice"
     (e.g. to be identified in the process of evidence being
     given).

ii) Where a child appears in any proceedings relating to an
     offence against, or conduct contrary to, decency or
     morality, the court may direct that all persons not
     officers of the court, counsel or solicitors, and
     persons directly involved in the case, be cleared from
     the court, during the taking of that child's evidence.
     Courts are particularly sensitive to the trauma faced
     by a child having to give evidence in court of any kind,
     especially if the child concerned was the victim of or
     witness to a sexual or violent offence. Bona fide repre-
     sentatives of newspapers and newsagencies need not leave
     the court but are subject to the over-riding consider--
     ation that nothing published shall in any way lead or lend
     itself to an identification of the child.

     Schedule I of the 1975 Act gives a list of offences which
     allow a court to proceed in the absence of the child/victim
     if that presence is not essential to a just hearing of the

case.   These offences include:-

a)   any offence under the Criminal Law Amendment
     Act, 1885, which relates to certain sexual
     offences, brothel keeping etc.

b)   any offence in respect of a child under the
     age of 17 which constitutes the crime of
     incest

c)   any offence under Sections 12, 13, 14, 15,
     22 or 33 of the Children and Young Persons (Scotland)Act
     1937 (e.g.child neglect, etc.) now Sch.1.C.P.(S)A 75.

d)   any other offence involving bodily injury to a
     child under the age of 17.

Moreover, if an adult is convicted or found guilty of any
of the offences listed in this schedule, this shall
represent authority for the court to refer the child who
was the victim to the Reporter, and such an offence
against the child shall constitute a ground of referral.

iii)   Children occasionally have to attend court who, although not
       being prosecuted in the courts for an offence, are nonetheless
       appearing before the Children's Hearing on account of unlawful
       behaviour, or as being in need of care and protection.   There
       are two such situations:-

a)   The child or his parent(s) denies the ground of
     referral and the Hearing refers the matter to
     the court for a finding as to whether the facts
     alleged establish a ground.   The normal rules of
     evidence apply, and the case is heard in private:
     No press are present.   If the ground of referral is
     established, the Sheriff cannot dispose of the case,
     and the matter is returned to the Hearing for disposal:
     if the ground is not established, that is the end of
     that particular matter.

b)   The child or his parent(s) or both wish to appeal
     against the decision of the Hearing: the appeal is
     against the Hearing's disposal, not against the
     establishment of the grounds of referral.   The appeal
     must be lodged within 3 weeks of the Hearing's
     decision: the Reporter makes available to the Court
     all the reports used in reaching the disposal, together
     with the 'stated case' of the Hearing members as to
     their reasons for reaching such a decision.

The Sheriff may call for further reports to help him reach
a decision: he has 3 options for disposing of the appeal:-

1.   Reject the appeal, and confirm the original
     decision.

2.   Grant the appeal, and discharge the case.

OR. 3. Grant the appeal, and remit the case
back to the Hearing with his reasons for
so doing, and instructing the Hearing to
reconsider.

A further appeal within 7 days is permitted in respect of the
second disposal decision.   Finally, any decision by a Sheriff
relating to a child i.e. either a sentencing decision or a
decision on appeal can be appealed to the Court of Session.
The ground of such an appeal is an alleged irregularity at
law (e.g. sentence of detention centre training) or of
conduct (e.g. public present in court): this appeal can be
made by either the child or his parent(s), or by the Reporter.
The Court of Session does not dispose of the case but sends
it back to the Sheriff with its findings and instructions.

Parents

If a child is prosecuted before the courts, Sections 39 and 307 of the Criminal
Procedure (Scotland) Act require his parent or guardian to attend. The attendance
is necessary "if he can be found and resides within a reasonable distance", and
must be for all the stages of the proceedings, unless the court is satisfied that
it would be unreasonable to require the attendance. Parents must also be warned
by the Police after any arrest of their child that they are so liable to attend.
Moreover, if the father is not the parent or guardian having actual possession
and control of the child, his presence may nonetheless be required. The only
exception allowed to the attendance of parents is in the situation where, prior
to the institution of proceedings, the child has been removed from their custody
or charge by an order of the court. In any case, where the Local Authority is in
loco parentis (e.g. under Section 16 of the Social Work (Scotland) Act) in
relation to a child, the presence of the supervising social worker will be
necessary under this heading.

Sections 37 and 304 allow courts to order parents or guardians to give security
for their child's good behaviour. This can be done if the parent, having been
required to attend court, has failed to do so, but "no such order shall be made
without giving the parent or guardian the opportunity of being heard". Non-
payment is enforceable against the parent or guardian (e.g. by civil diligence or
by imprisonment) as if the parent or guardian had himself been convicted of the
offence with which the child was charged.

Attendance of Social Workers

S.W.S.G. Circular 16/1974 discusses the arrangements for co-operation between
courts and Social Work Departments in any case where a child is prosecuted before
a court. It amplifies in greater detail the obligations on court officials,
especially the Fiscal, to notify the Social Work Department of the prosecution of
any child. However, it also emphasises the importance of the social worker's
attendance : "careful consideration should be given in each case as to whether
the circumstances justify the presence of a social worker both during the journey
to the court and throughout the court proceedings. Whether or not special
arrangements are made for young children e.g. the use of a Policewoman, the
earlier identification of potentially difficult cases should make it easier to
have a social worker present in court to provide any necessary assistance in the
management of the child or to provide assistance to the parents. Such arrangements should be made as a matter of routine when children under the age of 13 are
being prosecuted before the courts". In any case, where a child is before the
court and is already the subject of a supervision requirement from the Children's

Hearing, the presence of the supervising officer is justified on similar principles, and in particular, the subject of escort arrangements needs careful
attention in any case where a residential supervision requirement is in force.

CHILD OFFENDERS AND THE CHILDREN'S HEARINGS

The Children's Hearing system which replaced the Scottish juvenile courts system
came into operation in 1971 and from that time constitutes the principal tribunal
to which children 'in trouble' may be referred. Children are 'referred' to a
hearing, they are not prosecuted unless, as noted, the decision has been taken to
bring them before a court on specified criminal charges.

The statutory grounds on which a child may be referred are:

> that he is beyond the control of his parents.

or

> that he is falling into bad associations or is exposed to moral danger.

or

> lack of parental care is likely to cause him unnecessary suffering or
> seriously to impair his health or development.

or

> any of the offences mentioned in Schedule 1 of the C.P.(S)Act 1975 has
> been committed in respect of him or in respect of a child who is a
> member of the same household.
>
> (Schedule 1 offences are those of a sexual nature, including incest
> and any offence involving bodily harm to 'a child under the age of 17
> years'. This latter qualification is important because of the distinc-
> tion made elsewhere about persons aged 16 and over being 'adult' in the
> context of being subject to prosecution in the criminal courts.)

or

> the child being a female is a member of the same household as a female
> in respect of whom an offence which constitutes the crime of incest
> has been committed, by a member of that household.

or

> he has failed to attend school regularly without reasonable excuse.

or

> he has committed an offence.

or

> he is a child whose case has been referred to a children's hearing
> in pursuance of part V of this Act.
>
> (Part V of the '68 Act relates to children who are in process of
> transfer between England, Wales or N. Ireland and Scotland or vice
> versa, and also children who abscond from places of safety or
> residential establishments and those who harbour them.) (S.32 S.W.
> (S)A.1968 as amended by Schedule 3 S.54 Children Act 1975)

The Reporter: There can be no possible doubt that the key person in the juvenile
justice system is the reporter. The office did not exist prior to the passing of
the 1968 Act. It is a tribute to the foresight of the Kilbrandon Committee that
the term which was coined in their report (1964) should survive the long debate
and appear both in title and substantially in the spirit in which that Committee
thought it should do.

The origins of the office of reporter are to be found in Scottish legal

procedures, deriving from the long and honourable traditional links which exist
between Scots law and the European family of laws. Such office is unknown in
English procedures and the, at times strident, calls in England for ' a Scottish
system' fail largely to take account of the fundamental differences in approach
to the prosecution of crime which has, historically, characterised the two
countries.

The concept of the office of reporter stemmed from the public prosecution system
in Scotland, and the demonstrated fact for over a century, that an effective,
economical system can function on the basis of clear responsibility placed in an
office in which there is public confidence. By these criteria the office is
defined as being free from administrative or political interference, secure in
that the incumbent is free to exercise his discretion without fear or favour,
and legally competent to carry forward the intentions of the statutes in the
spirit in which the legislators intended.

The reporter has several functions. One is to act as the filter for children
referred to the system. The second is to be the administrative arm of the Panel
and Hearing system. The third is to act as the community watchdog in respect of
the observance of the statutory rules governing the Hearings. The fourth is to
act as the legal representative of the Hearings, when it is necessary for representation to be made in the courts. In none of these, save in the first, does
the reporter make active disposal decisions regarding children.

The office of reporter was established at S.36 of the S.W.(S) Act, amended by the
Local Government (Scotland) Act 1973 to meet the requirements of the created
regional authorities and by the Children's Act 1975 at S.82 to regularise the
practice of reporters appearing before the Sheriff in their official capacity.

Sequentially the duties which the reporter discharges have been listed; in effect
they are discharged simultaneously as the volume of work comes to him.

When a child offender is referred by the police he has in fact been processed
through the elaborate decision making associated with the police role and function
under the Act, so that what reaches the reporter has been 'sifted'. His task is
now, on the basis of the police complaint and such reports as they may supply, to
make a decision as to whether the child should be brought before a Hearing.
There are certain complications in this. The referral from the police is a formal
documented one; it is, in the strict sense 'official'. Like the Fiscal the
reporter has to decide on a question of process. He is concerned with disposition
but not with disposal, he has no power to make orders of any sort. He has to be
satisfied on a number of grounds, so far as the child offender is concerned.
These are: that the offence is well founded in law, not whether he did it, but
simply that if called upon to do so he could say that in law there is a prima
facie case to answer, and secondly that, on the evidence available, the child is
in need of compulsory measures of care. He may be satisfied on the first count
but not on the second, and on that basis may decide to take no further action. He
may decide that informal action will suffice and often sees the child and
parent stressing the danger of involvement in illegal acts, and maybe, arranging
for private restitution to be made to the injured party. He may on occasion refer
the case to the Social Work Department for informal advice and aid. These things
he is empowered to do under S.39(1)(2).

By these strategies the reporter acts as a diversion agent and many child offenders are thus taken out of the system. If, on the basis of the evidence he decides
to take the matter to a Hearing, then he has the responsibility of convening the
Hearing, allocating to the Social Work Department a request for social background
information, disseminating this and other reports to the members and notifying

the child and parent of time, date and place of the Hearing.

In the Hearing the reporter has no decision making function or responsibility, he may advise either the members or the child and his parents about legal or procedural points at issue and is responsible for stating the grounds on which the child has been referred. If the child denies the grounds, it becomes the respons- ibility of the reporter to make application to the Sheriff for a finding as to whether the grounds are established, and as shown, in the event of appeal, from either side, it is the reporter who represents the panel at the Sheriff Court and who becomes the responsible person for the presentation of the case for the panel.

A secondary source of referral in respect of child offenders which administrat- ively places them in the same category as other 'in need' cases is provided by S.37, as amended by S.83 C.A.'75.

This provides that:

'Where a local authority receive information suggesting that a child may be in need of compulsory measures of care' (irrespective of the nature of the grounds) 'they shall - a) cause inquiries to be made into the case unless they are satisfied that such inquiries are unnecessary or b) if it appears to them that the child is in need of compulsory measures of care, give to the reporter such information as they have been able to discover'.

This, however, runs into the difficulty of social work being seen as being involved in a range of activity which properly is the province of the police, and this reference ought therefore to be regarded as one where the commission of an offence is incidental to broader aspects of the information alleging a 'need for compulsory measures' and where the social work department does come in contact with offence commission, is it always advisable to consult the police as there are times when the implications extend beyond the individual child.

While the focus of the present work is on offenders and in this context, on child offenders, no consideration is possible outside the framework of the principles and practices of the Scottish juvenile justice system. The Act (S.32(1)) states that:

> "A child may be in need of compulsory measures of care within the
> meaning of this part of the Act if any (of the foregoing) conditions
> is satisfied with respect to him".

Following the Kilbrandon Report (Comm. 2306) 1964, and the 1966 White Paper 'Social Work and the Community', the Act proceeds from the premise that if any of the above conditions is satisfied, then that may be a point for social inter- vention, in any one of a number of forms, blanketed in the above by the term 'compulsory measures of care' and defined at S.32(3) as 'includes protection, control, guidance and treatment'. Punishment has no place in this scheme, but the commission of an act which in an adult could lead to considerations of criminal prosecution, constitute the 'ground of referral'.

There are three situations where the Hearing cannot deal with offences; one as mentioned relates to offences prescribed by the Lord advocate, which by virtue of their serious nature, or question of disqualification from driving or the confiscation of offence weapons. Another noted is where the child is jointly charged with an adult and the prosecution requires, in the interests of the administration of justice, that both appear 'jointly charged'. The third is where the child 'denies the ground of referral'. For the panel to proceed with the Hearing it is necessary for the child and his parent to 'accept the grounds stated by the reporter for the referral' (S.42(2)(a)). Where the grounds of referral are that the child has committed an offence, the grounds must be stated by the reporter in the referral, and communicated to the child and his parents in writing prior to the Hearing not less than 7 clear days before the date of the Hearing (Children's Hearing (Scotland) Rules 1971, Rule 14) and where the grounds are of an offence, that offence must be stated in the form 4A provided by the rules: "that he has committed the offence specified........".

In support of the stated condition the reporter must employ the same standards of specification as would the prosecution in a criminal case, so that the specification might read:

> "that on 12th November, 1979 between the hours of 6 p.m. and 10 p.m. at 6 Highgate, Seatown, he did steal £5.00 in money, the property of John Smith of the said 6 Highgate, Seatown.'

As this is an offence contrary to Common Law no statutory reference is necessary in the specification.

Thus the child faces a specific allegation, namely that he did steal a sum of money, from a named individual at a certain time, in a certain place. He may admit that such is so, 'agreed the grounds' as stated, in which case the Hearing may proceed. He may dispute the fact but not the act, and say 'but it was not £5, it was £3'. The Hearing is empowered and S.42(b) to proceed where 'the child and his parent accept these grounds in part, and the Hearing considered it proper so to do'.

He may, and is entitled to, 'deny the grounds'; in short he may be saying either 'prove it', (and it may be worth making the point that denial in these circumstances may equate a 'not guilty plea' in court. In either case the person concerned does not have to prove anything; that rests with those who mount the proceedings) or 'I did not do it'. The Hearing in these circumstances can do one of two things. It can either 'discharge the referral' (S.42(2)(C)) - abandon the matter, or direct the reporter to 'make application to the Sheriff for a finding as to whether such grounds for the referral, as are not accepted by the child or his parents are established'. In terms, this means that the reporter has been given the task of presenting to the Sheriff Court the facts, and of calling of supportive evidence, in respect of the 'grounds of referral' in this case, an offence, as stated. If the sheriff, who will hear the application in chambers, within 28 days of the application being lodged, decides that the grounds have not been established then the application is dismissed and the referral discharged (S.42(4) and (5)). This means that the matter is closed and, in the stated form, cannot be re-opened. If, however, the sheriff finds the grounds established then the matter goes back to the Hearing for consideration and for disposal.

There are two matters pertaining to these issues taken to the court for proof. The first is that there is no right of legal aid or, in the strict sense, legal representation at the hearing. (The explanatory leaflet 'To tell you about the children's hearings', issued by SWSG, and sent by the reporter to each referred child, says that if the person who comes along with the child and parents 'to help' 'happens to be a lawyer, his legal fees will not be covered by legal aid'.) If, however, the matter is taken for proof to the sheriff, then there is full right of legal representation and consideration in the usual way, of legal aid, if needed. Secondly, the Act provides (S.42(6)) that in hearing such cases the sheriff shall 'apply to the evidence the standard of proof required in criminal cases'. The standard of proof required in criminal cases is that the issue be decided 'beyond reasonable doubt' on the basis of what Walker (1969) described as 'The rules of evidence determines what must be proved, and by what means, and incidental argument may arise as to the admissibility or pertinency of some of the evidence'.

Once the child is back before the hearing, he stands in the same relationship as the child who agrees the ground of referral. The majority of cases proceed at the hearings without going to proof, but there are no circumstances whereby the child and/or his parents may be denied the exercise of their right to have the issue decided before the Sheriff.

The principle on which the hearings operate is that of arriving at a decision on the basis of a round table discussion. This entails a free flowing discussion based on the concept of seeking to establish what is in the child's best interests and of deciding on the appropriate measures calculated to secure these. This places the child offender on exactly the same footing as any other child facing the hearing or any of the 'welfare related' grounds, and the questions of guilt and punishment are not within the reference frame.

The responsibility for presenting the grounds of referral lies with the reporter; beyond that his task is to advise the hearing on appropriate matters and to record the reasons for the decision, which must, at the end of the hearing, be made out and signed by the chairman (Rule 9 (2)).

The responsibility for the conduct of the hearing rests with the chairman, and in accordance with the above this will entail the exercise and display of the necessary qualities of chairmanship which will enable the members to question, comment and exchange views with the child and the parents, and will also enable the child and parents, in their own words and in their own way to comment on the issue constituting the ground of referral and on the general situation at home and in the environment which affects or contributes to the child's present needs.

The only persons who may be present at a children's hearing, in addition to the three panel members (one of whom must be a woman), and the child and his parent(s), are a representative of the Social Work Department who may be the writer of the report submitted concerning the child, any person being the chairman or member of the Children's Panel Advisory Committee, other panel members or possible panel members, in training, any approved student or researcher, or/and 'any other person whose presence at the sitting may in the opinion of the chairman be justified by special circumstances' (Rule 12). The discretionary power of the sitting chairman extends to all of the above and comes directly under the terms of S.35(2) which requires that ' the chairman shall take all reasonable steps to ensure that the number of persons present at a children's hearing shall be kept to a minimum '. The press have right of access but must not identify the child, either directly or by reference to circumstance. In practice it is most uncommon for the press to evince any interest in the hearings, and this reflects the broad sympathetic view which the Scottish Press have taken in respect of this form of juvenile justice.

The provision, above, about the ability of the chairman to admit 'any person whose presence may be justified by special circumstances' means, in effect that school teachers, youth club leaders, staff of homes etc., can be admitted and given the opportunity to contribute to the discussion.

The child and parent(s) are obliged to attend under threat of penalty (£50 fine on summary conviction S.41 (3)) unless the hearing considers it would be unreasonable to require his attendance or that his attendance would be unnecessary to the consideration of the case (S.41(2)). It is a fairly common phenomenon for children to appear with mother, but without father, and the provisions of S.41(2) make it possible for this to be tolerated, although hearings are known to insist on the attendance of an individual parent.

Reports and the decision making process: the hearings procedure is that (Rule 6)
the reporter shall give to the members of the hearing, notice of the time and
place of the hearing, 'whenever practicable at least seven days before the date
of the hearing' and shall give to them 'not later than three clear days before the
date of the hearing:

A)   A copy of a report of a local authority on the child and his
       social background.

B)   A copy of the statement of the grounds for the referral.

C)   A copy of any judicial remit or reference or any reference
       by a local authority.

D)   Where the child is subject to a supervision requirement, a copy
       of that requirement.

S.S. 38 and 39 lay responsibility on the reporter for initial investigation of the
case, and decision to proceed to the hearing. That decision is his, and his alone
and in relation to the above S.39(3) is quite clear that 'where it appears to the
reporter that the child is in need of compulsory measures of care, he shall
arrange a children's hearing and further, (S.39(4)) *where he has arranged* a
hearing, he shall request from the local authority a report on the child and his
social background.'

There is at least scope for debate as to the place and timing of a social work
report in this complex decision making process (see e.g. Brown et.al. 'Community
and Legality' A.P.P. 1979). There are two distinct phases in the process:

Phase one: The reporter is called upon to 'make such initial investigation as he
may think necessary' (S.38 (1)). The following sub-section places on the police
a responsibility at this point to make available to the reporter 'such reports as
required'. There has grown up in some areas a practice of supplying to the reporter
at this stage a social work department report. It should be clearly understood
by workers preparing such reports that what they are doing, and doing quite
properly, is acting as the investigative arm of the reporter in his decision-
making as to whether or not to take the matter forward to a hearing. It is in the
nature of the exercise, unwise to go beyond that; and such reports should be
confined to supplying the reporter with such information as will enable him to
decide if the child is to be taken before a hearing, as being in need ' of
compulsory measures of care'.

Phase two: Having taken his decision to proceed (and in passing, he is entitled
not so to do,)the reporter is then required 'to request from the local authority
a report on the child and his social background', as noted, and at that point 'it
shall be the duty of the local authority to supply the report which shall
contain information from any such person, *as the reporter*, or the local authority
may think fit'.

The right of the reporter to indicate to the reporting social worker the potential
sources of information is not one generally recognised or applied, but has a
potential for positive co-operation between the two, as in the course of his
initial investigations and on receipt of police information, the reporter may
well be able to indicate positive lines of investigation by the social worker;
or taking another example, the provision of specific specialist reports concerning the child can be facilitated in this way, without embarrassment, as this

provides a clear legal remit for such approaches to be made.

In addition to the social work report, the hearing will have a report from the child's school, and if the matter has been continued for custodial reports, a comprehensive statement from the establishment to which he was sent for observation.

These documents will be in the hands of the members at least three days in advance of the hearing, so that they will come to the hearing prepared by and possibly influenced by the information in advance of any discussion, by any 'summary and recommendations' about disposal put forward, especially by the social worker. While some social workers have adopted practices which vary from person to person of showing the report, reading the report, or explaining the contents to the parents and child, before the hearing, certain problems do exist.

The members have advance information. What is provided for in the rules (19(4)) is that the chairman 'shall inform the child and his parent of the substance (emphasis added) of any reports .... if it appears to him that this is material to the advice that will be given and that its disclosure would not be detrimental to the interests of the child'. Thus there is a distinct possibility of variable practice, both in respect of hearings and in respect of social workers writing for the same hearing. So far as the social worker is concerned he is free to follow his own practice, but the potential dichotomy of the child and parents being told more by the social worker than by the chairman, or conversely, less by the social worker than by the chairman does lend itself to the possibility of the recipients having feelings that somebody in the hearing was 'keeping something back.' Accordingly it is probably better for the social worker to observe the letter of the law and leave the communication to the chairman. In the course of the hearing the worker will have opportunity to bring any matter of importance from his professional standpoint out for discussion.

The issue of 'recommendations' is a long standing problem which in the hearing has been justified by the rationale that the panel members are 'volunteers and amateurs.' This is both insufficient and discourteous to a body of people who have undergone training in preparation for their task.

The practice which appears to be one compatible with natural justice is for the avoidance of specific, and by definition, exclusive 'recommendations' by the reporting social worker. The function of the report writer is to advise on the child and his social background, and to offer professional opinion and views, if requested, on the range of possible disposal open and available to the hearing. In accordance with this view it is suggested that a 'multiple-choice' presentation with valid, well argued, speculation of what each might mean for the particular child, is calculated to serve the interest of the hearing in seeking a disposal facility in keeping with the needs of the child.

While the decision is arrived at by a process of discussion, the attendant social worker, if invited by the chairman, may be able to contribute, in elaboration of aspects of the written report or in elucidation of matters touched upon in discussion about which a professional input or assessment may be of value. However, the responsibility for arriving at a decision and of making that decision known to the child and parents rests with the panel members at the hearing. This is the fundamental distinction between the consideration of the case and the making of a decision which separates the advice and discussion from the legally enforceable disposal of the referral. In relation to the hearing's responsibility in this, it may continue the hearing for further investigation and may in that context require the child 'to attend or reside at any clinic, hospital or establishment during a period, not exceeding 21 days' (S.43(4)). This provision is backed by the power to issue a warrant for his detention if such a course is necessary.

Power of the hearings to detain: The civil nature of the hearings has the effect that child offenders are dealt with by civil and not criminal process. It remains that within that process there are statutory powers of detention. These are defined and are structured to meet given situations where the needs of the child and the administration of justice demand that he be detained.

Where a child is brought before a hearing and it is unable to dispose of the case, if the hearing 'has reason to believe' that during any adjournment the child would fail to attend any subsequent hearing, or attend any ordered examination or investigation or fail to comply with any requirement under S.43(4), for him to be subjected to such investigation, then if they are 'satisfied that detention of the child is necessary in his own interest', they may issue a warrant requiring him to be detained in a place of safety for a period not exceeding 21 days. Such a warrant may be renewed by the hearing 'on cause shown' for a further 21 days on application by the reporter.

If further remand is necessary beyond this period of 42 days then an application by the reporter to the sheriff, a further 21 days may 'on cause shown' be granted, and this may be further extended by 21 days on application by the reporter to the sheriff. There are no circumstances whereby a child may be detained for a period in excess of this cumulative total of 84 days without his case being disposed of.

The authority for this is now to be found at S.84 C.A.75, which amends S.40(7) and (8) of the S.W.A. by the substitution of new sub-sections and by the addition of new sub-sections '8A and 8B'. The intention of the statute in giving the hearings a power of detention is firmly based in need to create a facility whereby, in the interests of the child he may be legally detained in pursuance of the need of the hearing to dispose of his case competently. Thus if the hearing wished to secure a specific residential placement and there was good cause to believe that if the case was continued in the normal way the child, for whatever reason, his own problematic behaviour, or of the absence of a supportive home base, would not attend then such power could be exercised. By the same token if medical, psychiatric, psychological or social investigation was a consideration and the hearing had reason to doubt if the child would co-operate if at liberty then power of detention for this purpose could be ordered. The limiting factor inbuilt in the legislation is to safeguard the child from any processes of remands pending an 'ideal' placement becoming available. The power of the sheriff to extend the 21 days plus 21 days available to the hearing is subject to the reporter satisfying the sheriff that such further remand is necessary in the child's own interest. Administrative convenience or problems about obtaining information or reports will not suffice, the detention must be justified throughout by the laid down criteria: firstly, that there is cause to believe that if detention be not ordered the child may not attend or be made available, and secondly, that such detention is necessary in the child's own interest.

These provisions which are specific to cases before the hearings and which are subject to the authority of the hearing are to be differentiated from the power rested on 'a constable or any person authorised by a court or by any justice of the peace' to take to a place of safety, a child who has been offended or who is in such danger. This power under S.37 of the S.W.A. is now subject to the amendments under S.83 C.A.75: following sub-section (1), sub-section '1A', in substitution of sub-section 2 the new 'sub-section 2' and by the addition of new sub-sections 5A and 5B after sub-section 5.

Disposal Possibilities Open to the Hearings

The considerations which relate to the 'control, protection, guidance or treatment' and are subsumed under the term 'compulsory measures of care' are
extremely wide, although the system since its inception has been haunted by a
spectre of 'too few resources'. It is within the ambit of what exists in mobilising
the resources of the community that the resolution to this problem is to be found.
Experience indicates that the mere provision of more residential, custodial facilities will not of itself solve the problem and there is a school of thought which
has it that demand for residential facilities expands to meet available resources.

The hearings are empowered (S.44(1)(a) and (b)) to take one of two courses,
assuming that they decide neither to discharge the referral or take no action on
it.

They can make a supervision order which requires the child to 'submit to supervision in accordance with such conditions as they may impose.'

N.B. the language of the section: submit, conditions, impose. The order can, and
should be tailored to the specific and defined needs of the child. The fact that
he is an offender may say something about the condition. It may indicate that the
control/guidance element is more necessary than the protection/treatment one;
again it may not. Supervision of itself, if it relates to some kind of outdated
'report every week, all's well', routine is for the majority of little value save
perhaps to instil a sense that offending, if caught, carries a penalty, and the
name of that penalty is boredom.

If the preparatory work in the report stage has been done, if the discussion at
the hearing has been meaningful then the hearing ought to have a clear view of
what the probable conditions are. These ought to be positive, calculated to
enhance social skills, improve educational performance and effectively control
deviant behaviour. The range of possibilities is as wide as the span of human
activity in a modern civilisation. Many, if not most of the measures require
neither money nor buildings; they require imagination, energy, commitment and the
ability to recognise community resources. The experience of community service in
the adult courts, both in Scotland and in England and Wales is sufficiently
encouraging to lead to the conclusion that for many what is lacking is the opportunity and the help to capitalise on latent personal resources. For many it may
be that the best way to give them help is actively to engage them in giving help
to those less fortunate than themselves, and children are particularly sensitive
to this kind of appeal. Some of the child offenders (and others) who come to the
hearing are heavily underachieving educationally and socially. The supervision
requirement ought to identify these areas and make possible through the social
work and educational services the necessary inputs of interest, concern and
professional skill to affect positive change over time.

The requirement at S.44(1)(a) may stipulate residence and such requirement may
extend to England or Wales where arrangements have been made, so that if home and
accommodation problems are in evidence, an 'open' order could 'require the said
John Smith to reside at 12 White Street, Blacktown, with his sister Mrs. D. Brown
at that address'. It is in essence an extremely flexible instrument, and to
take a further example, in illustration, if what is now popularly referred to as
'Intermediate Treatment' is seen in a broad, non-institutional way, then the
instrument for its implementation is to hand.

Secondly where such appears to meet the needs of the child the hearing (S.44(1)(b))
may require him to reside in a named establishment. This may be a 'List D'
school, ('List D' arose when S.W.S.G. took over responsibility from Home and

Health Department and the former Home and Health Department 'Approved schools' were listed; as it happened lists existed for other establishments A to C, so List D) it may be any other residential establishment suitable for and willing to accept the child under order. There is also the provision at S.44(4) for the hearing to notify the Education Authority where it encounters a child suffering from disability and the powers of the Education Authority under S.63 Education (Scotland) Act 1962, which relates to the authority's duty to ascertain children suffering from disability, need to be exercised. The responsibility of the Local Authority to exercise the supervisory function in respect of children subject to orders is well recognised. What requires to be reiterated is that under S.44(5) for the purposes of the Act such child is deemed to be in the care of the Local Authority so that the general oversight afforded to children formerly in care of either the Local Authority or a voluntary body is seen to be a similar function and more importantly the rights and duties of the Local Authority under S.16 as it now reads by virtue of S.74 of the Children's Act 1975 apply. This has wide implications for the child under supervision who for any reason requires more aid and succour than might otherwise be forthcoming from normal hearing intervention.

Duration of supervision: Supervision requirements made at Hearings are of a different order from Sentences imposed or orders made on child offenders in the courts. The latter, except in serious cases where the child is detained during Her Majesty's pleasure, are all of stated duration, determined by the nature of the sentence or order and the jurisdiction of the court making it. The Hearing, on the other hand, empowered as it is to take wide sweeping powers for the welfare of the child may make orders for what, in an adult, would be extremely lengthy periods.

S.47(2) says that 'a supervision requirement shall cease to have effect when he attains the age of 18 years', and this could mean being under the supervision of one form of social work or another for a truly lengthy period. Because of the potential for this S.47(1) makes a specific stipulation that 'no child shall continue to be subject to a supervision requirement for any time longer than is necessary in his interest' and goes on to state that the Local Authority should take active steps to advise the reporter with a view to the case being reviewed, so that the Hearing may have the opportunity either to continue, vary or discharge the order. This calls for close attention to be paid to orders held, as the statute intends that where possible, positive action be taken to activate the hearing review, rather than simply await the stipulated periodic review of the case.

The function of the supervisor, and if the child is in residence, then the residential representative and the liaising social worker, is to advise the Hearing of progress, change or deterioration in the child's circumstances or conditions. If issues have been raised at the Hearing or in previous reviews, then the social work representative has a clear duty to give an account of how these issues have been met and the responses obtained to any intervention made for or with the child. The in-built flexibility of the system is demanding of a dynamic rather than a static approach to the problems posed by children who have been defined as being 'in need of compulsory measures of care'.

Review: The general principles which are outlined in respect of probation orders, relative to the rights of the individual or the supervisor to request change or discharge have been taken further in the Social Work Act as it applies to the hearings. A formal review system was established at S.48 with certain rights established at S.44(5) for the supervising Local Authority.

S.48 lays down that any supervision requirement (residential or otherwise) shall be reviewed where the Local Authority so recommends. That means in effect that

the supervisor can require a review,and must then justify that in open session, as
the child and parent must be present. Such review could stem from a desire to
terminate the order on the grounds of good progress, a desire to have further
conditions inserted as experience indicates are necessary, the deletion of conditions or the varying of the order in more substantial ways by the substitution,
either of an 'open' requirement for a residential one or a residential requirement for an 'open'one. Where the request emanates from the supervisor then he
must produce the evidence in support of the proposal. Secondly, the requirement
may stem from the authority in a more formal sense, inasmuch as the authority
may, e.g. wish to request the deletion of a residential requirement as the child
has come into the care of the Local Authority by virtue of other circumstances
and the authority has assumed parental rights. The request may come from the
child or parent, and there may be scope for the view that, like probationers, many
are inadequately advised of their rights to petition for the variation of order or
for their termination ahead of time. The stipulated periods for review are given
at S.48(3) and (4).

A)   Where an order remains in force for a period of one year without review
      that order will automatically cease to have effect.

B)   At any time after the expiry of 3 months from:

      i) the date of making the order
   or
     ii) the date of a review which varies the requirement of the order
   or
    iii) for the child or his parent: at any time after the expiry of
         6 months from the date of a review which did not vary the
         requirements of the order.

The processes referred to of referral to the hearing and the review system may
be regarded in terms of a deliberate allocation of the child within an operational matrix which is sufficiently wide as to lend itself to the exercise of
highly skilled judgments about what may be 'in the child's best interests' and
this dimension does require the exercise of highly developed assessment skills in
the advisers, and equally well developed critical abilities in those receiving the
advice and making the disposal decisions.

OPERATIONAL MATRIX IN THE WELFARE/JUSTICE SYSTEM

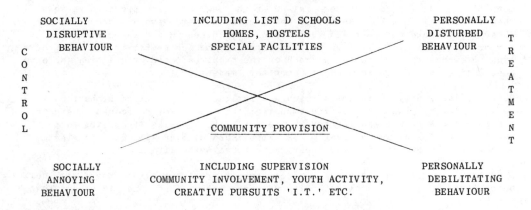

RESIDENTIAL PROVISION

Appeals from Children's Hearing Decisions

The right of appeal from a hearings order may be based on either irregularities in the procedure or disagreement with the disposal ordered. There is no case whereby a child can, as he may do in court, appeal against a finding of the grounds of referral. If he does not agree the grounds the hearing does not proceed.

To take the possibility of an appeal on irregularities in procedure:

S.41(1) and (2) of the S.W. Act state that (1) 'the parent of a child shall have the right to attend at all stages of a children's hearing who are considering the case of his child', and (2) states that when the child's case is being considered by a children's hearing 'his parent shall attend at all stages of the hearing unless the children's hearing are satisfied that it would be unreasonable to require his attendance or that his attendance would be unnecessary to the consideration of the case'.

The interpretation is that e.g. a discussion between the members and the social worker is a 'stage of the hearing'and the adjournment of the members (for coffee) during which they continue to deliberate about the case, is 'a stage of the hearing' and as such are clear breaches of the statute and would constitute irregularities about which an appeal could be mounted.

Or if, say, the chairman invited his neighbours in to witness his virtuoso performance then that too would be an irregularity in breach of the rules, and would constitute grounds for appeal.

The 'round table discussion' is just that. The decision may well 'be arrived at',but as has been made clear the responsibility for that decision rests with the hearing, and if the child or/and parent decide, within a period of three weeks from the date of the decision that they wish to appeal it, they may do so (S.49). In the first instance appeal is to the Sheriff who will hear it in chambers.

In such cases the reporter is required to furnish the court with all documents and reports relating to the case, and with the chairman's written reasons for the decision. The Sheriff may examine the reporter, and the Children Act Schedule 3 S.57 amends the S.W. Act to read 'The reporter, whether or not he is conducting the proceedings before the Sheriff, may be examined by the Sheriff', so that even if the reporter engages an advocate to conduct the case he may still be examined. If the Sheriff finds for the appellant and allows the appeal he may (S.49(5)(b):

Either, 'discharge the child from any further hearing or other proceedings in relation to the grounds for the referral of the case'. In short the child is freed from any future proceedings whether by hearing or court in the offence stated or he may 'remit the case with the reasons for his decision to the hearing for re-consideration of their decision'. In other words, if e.g. the appeal had been against a residential requirement to take up residence in a named establish- ment 100 miles from home and for a variety of reasons the Sheriff had allowed that appeal then he would give to the hearing his reasons and invite them to reconsider the matter. The child would still be subject to the decision of the hearing but the earlier requirement would be abandoned in favour of whatever new facts and disposal possibilities come to light.

In the nature of court business, appeals take time and S.49(8) permits where an appeal is lodged for the child or his parent to make application to the hearing for the requirement to be suspended, pending the appeal; and it is left to the discretion of the hearing either to grant or refuse that application.

In respect of the aforementioned appeal against the hearing no further appeal is possible, the Sheriff's decision is binding, the hearing will proceed on the basis of his remit back to them (S.50).

However, in the case of any alleged irregularities in the matter before the Sheriff, appeal lies to the Court of Session. 'The object of an action is to enforce a legal right against a defender who resists it or to protect a legal right which the defender is infringing' (Scottish Office 1975); in this instance the latter definition applies, the object of the appeal is to protect a legal right. Appeals at this stage may be lodged (S.50(1)) at the instance of the child or his parent or both, or by the reporter acting on behalf of the children's hearing and no further appeal shall be competent. The procedures here are that the Sheriff is required to 'state a case', ie. to explain to the court of session the case and his reasons for reaching his decision. If the court finds against the appellant then the Sheriff's decision stands, if however it finds for the appellant then its judgment is handed down to the Sheriff for disposal 'in accordance with such direction as the court may give'.

Added final safeguards are inbuilt inasmuch as under S.51 where a Sheriff remits a case to a hearing for reconsideration the child or his parent may within 7 days of the hearing decision appeal to the Sheriff as they might have done in the original instance. It is thought that this provision is very much a last stage defence and that things would be very much at variance with the norms of the system for it to be activated.

The Act (S.52) provides for the Secretary of State to terminate a supervision requirement (whether residential or 'open') if he considers in all the circumstances and the interests of the child such a course is justified. This is a 'democratic appeal' procedure which could be activated through an M.P. if the case appeared to be exceptional enough to warrant such action.

The broad considerations respecting residential training under these arrangements was set out in a SWSG Circular SW13/71.

The circular, which was in anticipation of the workings of the then S.58A C. & Y. (S) Act 1973, now S.413 C.P.(S)A. '75, made a number of points, the main ones being summarised as:

A)   Since the ultimate responsibility for children committed under
      section 58A (now S.413) will rest with the Secretary of State, and
      they will not be statutorily in local authorities' care, any costs
      incurred by local authorities on accommodating them or on arranging
      for their assessment will be reimbursed by the Social Work Services
      Group.

B)   The local authority concerned will be free to decide where to hold
      the child in the light of their knowledge of the child and the
      circumstances of the case. If they were unable to provide
      accommodation from their own resources - for exanple, where the
      detention of the child in conditions of security was thought
      necessary - they would be expected to make arrangements with
      another authority having suitable accommodation.

      In exceptional cases a local authority may reach the conclusion that
      no accommodation which it can provide from its own resources or by
      arrangement with another authority would be suitable for holding the
      child; in such an event reference should be made at the earliest
      possible stage to the Social Work Services Group. Where the local

authority felt it necessary to recommend that a child should be held in a prison service establishment a fully supported case would need to be made at the earliest possible opportunity; it is only in exceptional circumstances, however, that the Secretary of State would agree to placement in a penal institution in the case of any child under the age of 16.

C)   In formulating their recommendation to the Secretary of State on the placement of the child the local authority would be expected to consider the whole range of accommodation available in the social work field, as would be done in the case of a child found by a children's hearing to be in need of compulsory supervision on a residential basis: in special cases it may be necessary to consider also specialised accommodation in educational and other fields.   In a case where a local authority wished to specify an establishment not under its own management (i.e. one operated by a voluntary body, a hospital board or other local authority) the necessary enquiries and consultations regarding placement might need some time to complete and the initial approach should where possible be made at an early stage in the local authority's consideration of the case: where, however, the local authority is likely to recommend placement in an approved school these enquiries should be in all cases directed to the Social Work Services Group rather than to the school managers. In the latter case it would be open to the local authority in making its recommendation to specify a school which it considered particularly appropriate for the child; but whether or not this was done it would be for the Social Work Services Group to secure the vacancy by direct arrangement with the managers concerned.

It is recognised that the final decision on the placement of the child may contain some element of compromise in matching the needs of the child to the facilities, and vacancies, available. Where the placement which would have been preferred in any instance is found not to be practicable because of lack of a vacancy or for any other reason, this should be explained and a recommendation for an alternative placement made.

D)   Assessment and recommendation for placement. In assessing a child committed under section 58A the local authority are asked to apply the same criteria as to the nature and extent of any examination to be carried out as they would in the case of a child who may require residential supervision and who is referred for assessment by a children's hearing. Following assessment full case papers should be submitted to the Social Work Services Group together with the local authority's recommendation as to placement. In all cases the papers submitted should include a copy of the social background report prepared for the court and a medical report on the child. It would be for the local authority to decide whether any additional information or examination of the child was necessary beyond this in order to reach a view on the appropriate placement for the child. Where psychological examination is considered necessary and the local authority are unable to arrange this, a request for the services of one of the psychologists attached to the approved schools should be made (in good time to avoid delays) through the Social Work Services Group. Referral of a child to a psychiatrist or consultant paediatrician should be arranged as necessary and his report included in the case papers.

E)   Under section 58A(3) (now 413) a child sentenced under the section
        may at any time be released conditionally or unconditionally.
        The managers of the establishment will therefore be asked to review
        each case at fixed intervals in conjunction with the local authority
        and submit a report to the Social Work Services Group. They will
        also be asked to report to the Social Work Services Group immediately
        they think that a child should be considered for release, or if they
        think that transfer to another establishment is necessary. Where
        placement on release away from the home area is proposed the
        managers will be asked to include in their report the views of the
        local authority in whose area it is proposed that the child should
        be placed as well as the views of the home local authority. A
        recommendation for the release of a child should include an indication
        of the arrangments which could be made for the accommodation of the
        child and his schooling or employment as appropriate.

        Where a child is released the local authority would be responsible
        for his supervision in terms of section 27(b)(ii) of the 1968 Act.
        The authority supervising a child who had been released would be
        responsible for advising the Social Work Services Group, after
        consulting the establishment from which the child was released, if
        they considered at any point that the Secretary of State should ex-
        ercise his power to recall the child.

        These cardinal points require to be to the forefront of planning
        placements. The essential feature is that the courts' responsibility
        to have regard for the welfare of the child is both underlined and
        safeguarded. The assessment and planning responsibility is firmly
        vested in social work and as the circular makes clear the intention
        is that appropriate placements geared to the perceived needs of the
        child are the first consideration. The involvement of the Government
        department responsible at a direct level has tended to create the
        mistaken view that such cases are, or have to be simply put into
        some sort of administrative pipeline for disposal, as distinct from
        positive allocation. It cannot be emphasised too strongly that this
        provision relates to cases where the Sheriff (summary) court has
        made a decision that a sentence of residential training is the
        appropriate one, and that this consideration is but one of a number
        to be considered by the court in its sentencing function.

The 1980 Consultative Document

At the time of going to press a Consultative Memorandum on Part III of the Social
Work (Scotland) Act was issued by the Secretary of State inviting "consideration
and comment".

The purpose of including reference to the Memorandum is that if, as appears
likely, some or all of the proposals secure support and find their way into legislative action, areas of operations in the Children's Hearings system dealt with in
the text, would be subject to revision. It is to be expected that the Scottish
Juvenile Justice system should reflect changes in the public perception of dealing
with children and indeed a cardinal feature of the legal system as such is that it
reflects public attitudes and is responsive to community need over time. This is
the second consultative document issued since the inauguration of the Hearings.
The first being that of 1975 which the present one duly acknowledges while formulating a number of more substantive changes than hitherto.

It is a recognised hazard of venturing into this field that change over-takes writers. In the present instance it can but be drawn to attention the form in which intending change is likely to be presented.

In setting out in a brief note, the philosophy of the Hearings system, the Memorandum draws attention both to criticism that the Hearings do not have sufficient measures of discipline and punishment available and to the view which may be held by children and their parents that compulsory measures of care particularly those entailing removal from home may in fact be seen as punishment. From this the Memorandum directs itself to questions as to whether the powers of the Hearings are adequate to deal "purposefully with the persistent and generally older offender who apparently thinks that he can flout the law". It is a significant feature of the Memorandum that it employs for the first time since the introduction of Part III of the Act the concept of punishment in relation to the Children's Hearing System.

It returns to the suggestion contained in the Kilbrandon Report that the imposition of caution would call for a constructive effort on the part of the parents and seeks views on a proposal to confer power on the Hearings to refer parents to the Court with a recommendation for the imposition of caution and on the penalties which might be imposed in the event of caution not being found.

The Committee on Reparation by the Offender to the Victim in Scotland considered that there was scope for the inclusion of reparation in the Children's Hearings System. The Memorandum accepts the argument put forward by that Committee that the Hearings should be encouraged to make use of reparation in the absence of a supervision requirement and continue cases specifically in order to see whether children had fulfilled agreements to make reparation.

There is some practice within Scotland of informal arrangements being arrived at with children and parents for some token of atonement but this proposal is quite specific that the Hearings should, in selected cases, focus quite specifically on this particular aspect. Linked with this is the quite specific proposal which would require legislative change, that the Hearings should have the power to defer disposal for periods up to six months with a review at the end of the specified period. Such "deferred disposal" would, as with the case of deferred sentence in the Courts, not be a disposal in its own right but would merely be a prelude to a decision being made. This is a quite radical departure from determining whether or not the child is in need of compulsory measures of care. Clearly, if the child is not in need of compulsory measures of care this concept introduces a quite new dimension into the work of the Hearings.

Equally, the Secretary of State's decision to reintroduce the question of fines into the Hearing System places question marks against the concept of what the Hearings have been concerned about "in the spirit of Kilbrandon".

The consideration that the growing development of what has been termed Intermediate Treatment schemes is a juvenile equivalent of Community Service has had the effect of inclining the Secretary of State away from any notion of extending the powers of the Hearings towards the formal introduction of Community Service Orders.

There is a proposal in the Memorandum that in future offenders over the age of 16 years should go direct to Court but this in no way would change the Courts' power to refer the child back to the Hearing either for advice or to remit him for disposal. This clearly would have implications for a core of "child" offenders who technically are adults but because of supervision requirements remain under the age is of the Hearings System.

We have dealt at some length with the technicalities of residential training under

section 413 of the Criminal Procedure (Scotland) Act 1975. This Memorandum proposes certain changes which would transfer the Secretary of State's responsibility
to the Children's Hearing and if carried forward this would have a quite substantial bearing on the way that such cases would be handled. There are a number of
complex issues involved in this proposal and it would be unwise to venture further
comment pending positive legislative proposals.

A number of minor proposals are contained which relate to the removal of the existing requirement that the High Court should remit to the Children's Hearing for
advice in cases of children already under supervision found guilty of grave
offences and extending the provision for treating a child in the same household as
a female child against whom an offence has been committed so that the founding of
a conviction in solemn procedure would be the equivalent to the establishment of
the grounds for referral in one as it now is in the other.

The Memorandum proposes an extension of the power of detention for a child await-
ing a Court Hearing of the ground for referral from 7 to 14 days; and to provide
for detention for three days between the finding of the ground established by the
Court and convening the Children's Hearing to consider the case. It is further
proposed to extend to the Hearings the power to order forfeiture of weapons and if
carried forward this would mean that a number of cases now taken to Court simply
at the level of the need for forfeiture could conceivably reach the Children's
Hearings instead.

In an effort to "stiffen up" the work of the Hearings there is a proposal that
where children under supervision commit further offences the Hearings should take
note and have the opportunity of seeing the child and discussing with him and his
parents the need to avoid such behaviour.

The Memorandum poses a quite new concept in relation to the Hearings. Its general
tone would, so far as offenders are concerned, make the disposal possibilities
much more in line with juvenile justice models as distinct from the welfare orient-
ated model which has characterised the Hearings to date. The essential feature of
the Hearings procedure is of course preserved but as these proposals either in
whole or in part take legislative form it will be necessary both for panel members
and practitioners to re-evaluate the focus which they bring to bear in respect of
some offenders and some categories of offender appearing within the Hearings System.
To this extent the present text would need to be read in the light of change and
of changing circumstance. Practice, as ever, must needs conform to the legislative
structure it would seek to serve. To do this, a clear understanding of what the
legislation intends is necessary for individual practitioners, both in terms of
the discharge of their own particular functions, and in terms of their dealings
with people with whom they come in contact because of a Hearing commitment.

PART TWO: NON CUSTODIAL MEASURES

Chapter 5

Absolute Discharge; Admonition; Deferred Sentence;
Fines and their Enforcement; Caution; Compensation

The non-custodial measures available to courts are essential components in the
armoury of the administration of justice in Scotland.

These, following the 1980 C.J.(S)Act are:-

1) Absolute Discharge (it should be noted that Conditional Discharge is not a
competent Scottish Disposal;   2) Admonition;   3) Deferred Sentence;   4) Fine;
5) Caution;   6) Compensation.

1   Absolute Discharge

The effect of an absolute discharge is that the accused leaves the court
without any penalty being imposed. The law states that the court may make
such an order, provided that the penalty is not otherwise fixed by law, 'if
it is of the opinion, having regard to the circumstances, including the
nature of the offence and the character of the offender, that it is inexped-
ient to inflict punishment and that a probation order is not appropriate.'

The order of absolute discharge is available to courts hearing cases on both
solemn and summary procedure.

In cases of solemn procedure, Section 182 of the Criminal Procedure (Scotland)
Act 1975 makes it clear that such an order is made "instead of" a sentence.
Section 191 further adds that the original conviction does not count for any
purpose 'other than the purposes of the proceedings in which the order is
made, and of laying it before a court as a previous conviction in subsequent
proceedings for another offence.' It is, however, possible to appeal against
the conviction itself (subsection 3 of Section 191).

In cases on summary procedure, an order of absolute discharge is made
'without proceeding to conviction' (Section 383 of the Criminal Procedure
(Scotland) Act 1975). The offender can still appeal against the finding
that he committed the offence as if that finding were a conviction (Section
392(4)). Similarly, an order of absolute discharge made in cases on summary
procedure can be referred to in subsequent criminal proceedings, but in all
other aspects a conviction is not regarded against the offender.

2. Admonition

In this instance, the accused leaves the court without any penalty being imposed, but the admonition represents a warning and *does count* as a conviction, whichever method of procedure is being used. The relevant Sections (181 and 382 of the Criminal Procedure (Scotland) Act 1975) simply state that a court 'may, if it appears to meet the justice of the case, dismiss with an admonition any person found guilty by the court of any offence.'

3. Deferred Sentence

This measure was enacted by Section 47 of the Criminal Justice (Scotland) Act 1963, although it seems to have operated in the practices of courts before that time. The power to defer sentence is now to be located at Sections 219 (solemn procedure) and 432 (summary procedure) of the Criminal Procedure (Scotland) Act 1975, and is expressed in very general and wide-ranging terms: 'it shall be competent for a court to defer sentence for a period and on such conditions as the court may determine.' It should be borne in mind that a deferred sentence is not a substantive sentence: at the later date a substantive sentence will be imposed - offenders do not 'get' deferred sentences.

The deferred sentence can have a variety of uses, but in common practice is used in such instances as:-

- to test behaviour over a specified period of time.

- to see how the offender responds to a recently-made period of supervision.

Less frequently, it can be used as a stated alternative to a period of imprisonment. It has also been used on occasion to enable an offender to perform a specific task or service, but it is not a suitable vehicle for the ordering of 'community service'. It is a useful instrument when issues are in doubt, or the intentions of the offender need to be tested.

The more frequently used periods of deferment are 3, 6 and 12 months. There is no objection in law either to longer or to repeated deferments, but in practice, courts do arrive at a point at which a sentence is imposed. The prosecutor will, at the date of the deferred hearing, inform the court of any convictions against the accused which have been recorded in the intervening period: any outstanding charges at that time can also be brought to the court's attention.

Courts can and do order either supplementary or even full social enquiry reports for the date of a deferred hearing. However, any supervision undertaken during such a period can only be voluntary, unless some other statutory order is extant.

The Criminal Justice (Scotland) Act 1980 at Section 53 has now made clear that it is possible to make a probation order after a period of deferred sentence: previously this was only possible in cases on solemn procedure. A further objective for a period of deferred sentence can now be to test the offender's preparedness to consent to probation, perhaps by further interviews, or by requiring a specific activity on his part (e.g. finding a job) during a short period of deferment. The submission of further reports on the outcome of such a period of deferment is quite appropriate, even if not formally ordered by the court.

The same Act at Section 54 also makes it possible to return an accused to court, either by a warrant for his arrest, or by citation, if he commits a

further offence during a period of deferment. Previously this was not so,
and the original offence could only be dealt with on the duly deferred date,
even if other convictions intervened. Now, if returned to court as a result
of a further offence committed during the period of deferment, the offender
can be sentenced for the original offence in any manner it would have been
competent for it to deal with him on the originally scheduled date of deferment. Moreover, if it is the same court which originally deferred sentence
before which the offender appears for the fresh offence during the period
of deferment, it can deal with both matters simultaneously.

4   Fines and their Enforcement

The fine is the most commonly used of all disposals, especially in courts of
summary procedure. Not only do the arrangements for payment of fines
dominate much court procedure at the time of their imposition, but the
problems of enforcing their payment represent a major pre-occupation for
court officials. The policies and methods of fine enforcement have been
discussed in Scotland in the reports of both the Scottish Council on Crime
and the Thomson Committee on Criminal Procedure. Whilst these reports came
to somewhat different conclusions, both agreed that some tightening up of
the procedures was necessary, especially in view of the ability of some
more persistent defaulters to manipulate the present arrangements.

Two approaches to the fine have been identified. One, which has been
described as the 'old view' sees the fine as representing to the accused an
opportunity to avoid a prison sentence: in crude terms he can 'buy himself
off'. A 'newer' view, in contrast, sees the fine as a punishment in its own
right, but with imprisonment as a necessary sanction for non-payment. It is
under this heading that offenders can end up in prison in consequence of
offences which of themselves do not carry imprisonment as a potential
penalty (e.g. especially drunkenness). One report (Wootton Committee on
Non- and Semi-Custodial Penalties) has argued that prison should never be
the outcome of a non-custodial disposal, and penal reform groups are quick
to point to the high proportion of people in prison who are there as a
result of fine default. Under the present arrangements, however, few
practical alternatives exist, and the question of fine enforcement very
quickly runs into the procedures and methods of imprisonment in default of
payment. Social workers will find it helpful to inform themselves of the
policies, procedures and interpretations used by courts in their area in
regard to the minutiae of fine collection, especially in regard to areas of
discretion or de facto practices operated by the appropriate clerical staff.

Until the enactment of the Criminal Justice (Scotland) Act, 1980, different
sets of considerations governed the enforcement of fines according to
whether the case was on solemn or summary procedure. Now the Act has
extended to cases on solemn procedure all the arrangements which previously
applied only to cases on summary procedure, with the effect that the
considerations *are the same irrespective of the type of procedure*. The
following sections deal with the methods and mechanics of fines, their
imposition and enforcement.

Imposing the fine

Courts of solemn procedure have no limit to the amount of fines which they
may impose. The Sheriff Summary Court is normally restricted to a maximum
of £1,000, and the District Court to a maximum of £200, except in the case

of those statutory offences in which the Statute specifies a different
amount, which will be shown in the notice of penalty which accompanies the
complaint.

i) The law insists at section 395(1) of the 1975 Act that the
means of the offender shall be taken into account in actually
fixing the amount of the fine. This can be seen as an example
of individualised justice, and might represent one reason for
an apparent discrepancy in penalties when other circumstances
seem equal. At this stage, the means of the offender can only
usually be ascertained by a series of direct questions to him
in court *without* the possibility of any independent verification, or necessary reference to previous or out-standing
payments.

ii) However, any money found on the offender at the time of his
apprehension can be applied by the court towards payment,
unless:-

a) the court is satisfied it belongs to someone else

b) the court is satisfied the loss of such money would
be more injurious to his family than his imprisonment or detention. (Section 395(2)). The accused may
apply, either orally or in writing, even if he has
been committed to prison, that any money so found
should not be applied towards the fine, and the
court may make various enquiries on receipt of such
an application. (Section 395(4)).

iii) Section 396 ensures that the court must allow at least 7 days
to pay a fine, or the first instalment thereof, unless:-

a) the offender appears to have sufficient means to
enable him to pay forthwith. This can be interpreted as going beyond point ii) above, because the
accused could arrange for money to be brought from
home, or work, or a savings account.

b) the offender does not ask for time to pay. The
Court can none-the-less still allow time to pay,
and has the power to order the use of civil
diligence to recoup the money, rather than permit
the offender to 'do time' of his own accord in lieu,
at public expense.

c) he has no fixed abode. The definition of what
constitutes a fixed abode represents a problem
for the interpretation of the court, as it is not
defined in the statute. This problem is notoriously
one in which social workers often feel themselves at
variance with the judges or officials of various
courts. Legal niceties and social realities are
often poles apart as regards the status of the
lodging house, night shelters, etc. However, unless
Social Work Departments can provide satisfactory
alternative residential care, or even speedy
independent verification of such matters, it is

hardly appropriate for them to protest overmuch.

    d)   the court is satisfied for any other special reason
          that no time should be allowed. In this event,
          however, it must state and minute its reason. A
          practical example is the offender who is already
          serving a prison sentence in respect of some
          other matter.

iv) The court must *not* when allowing time to pay, fix the
    alternative sentence in the event of future default (Section
    396(4)) unless:-

    a)   the offender is present before it,

and b)   the gravity of the offence   ) make it expedient to impose
) such an alternative without
or c)   the character of the offender   ) any further enquiry, i.e. a
) Means Enquiry Court, and
or d)   some other special reason   ) again the reason must be given

    v) normally the court orders payment of a fine either within a
        stipulated period, or by instalments, which are almost
        invariably expressed in terms of a weekly amount. It can
        specify a starting date for payment by instalments which
        is longer than a week (e.g. if a first wage packet is not
        due for a fortnight). In the case of a person who is
        already paying a fine, it needs to specify whether payment
        of the new fine should commence on completion of the
        existing one, or whether the amount stated is in addition
        to it. The whole question of any outstanding fine payments
        is one which can always usefully be raised in any social
        enquiry report about a new offence.

    vi) special considerations apply to young offenders as far as
        ordering an alternative sentence of imprisonment in default
        of payment is concerned. These are included in detail in the
        sections which follow on fine supervision and Means Enquiry
        Courts.

It can be seen that the essential intention of these provisions is that the
burden of payment should first of all be put on the offender without the
immediate imposition of sanctions. The spirit behind the exceptions is
reasonably clear from their specific content, and from the requirement that
reasons be given, which would be relevant in the event of an appeal.

Fine Supervision

Fine supervision was made possible by the 1963 Criminal Justice (Scotland)
Act. It was originally only available in cases on summary procedure, and
the legislation was subsequently located at Section 400 of the Criminal
Procedure (Scotland) Act 1975. Now Section 47 of the Criminal Justice
(Scotland) Act has extended this provision to cases on solemn procedure
also. Originally it was one of the duties of the probation service, but
under Section 27 of the Social Work (Scotland) Act 1968, the duty of
supervising such cases passed to Local Authority Social Work Departments.
There is no stipulation in the law as to the grade of the person appointed
to supervise such cases, and indeed in some areas the work has been under-

taken by Social Work Assistants recruited specifically for the purpose.
Whilst, in regard to probation, the statute clearly emphasises the word
'officer' of the Local Authority, in regard to fine supervision, it
speaks simply of the 'person appointed'.

Fine supervision can be ordered in relation to offenders of any age.
Indeed, one of its aims has been described as providing a means of
entry for the social worker into the processes of family interaction
(by way of discussing budgeting) by imposing it on selected adult
offenders. The law *requires* at Section 400(4) that young offenders,
i.e. offenders aged 16 but under 21, be made subject to such supervision before any period of imprisonment can be ordered in default,
unless the court is satisfied that it is impracticable to place them
under such supervision. No definition of 'impracticable' is given in
the 1975 Act: in common-sense terms it can be seen as including
the young offender 'of no fixed abode', but the absence of any supervision by the Social Work Department could not justifiably be construed
as rendering the making of such an order 'impracticable'. Section
400(5) requires that the reason for any decision as to impractibility
must be minuted by the court. The intention and spirit of these
provisions is clearly preventive, if not in explicit social work terms,
then clearly in terms of precluding unnecessary imprisonment.

The duties of the person appointed to supervise are defined in Section
400(3) as twofold:-

   i)   to communicate with the offender with a view to
       assisting and advising him in regard to payment of
       the fine.

  ii)   to report to the court without delay as to the
       conduct and means of the offender if payment is
       not made.

The law also requires, at Section 400(7) that the Clerk of Court give
to the offender a notice of the order placing him under supervision,
but as with probation, the practice is often that copies of this
notice are given to the person appointed, who in turn gives them
to the offender.

Where an offender under supervision defaults, and is cited to the
Means Enquiry Court, the court will require a formal report from the
person appointed to supervise and will issue a notice to that effect
by virtue of Section 400(6). Although the report may be given either
orally or in writing as far as the law is concerned, all the general
considerations, both of principle and of casework considered in
respect of social enquiry work apply in this case e.g. right of
accused to know contents; importance of social worker's presence;
expression of opinions as to disposal. Although not a full social
enquiry report, a Means Enquiry Report should contain information
about:-

   i)   basic (elementary) details of the home set-up of the
       offender,

  ii)   details of his present employment together with
       comment on the frequency of any job changes, duration
       of any unemployment, efforts to find work, etc. with

particular reference to the period under review.

iii) full details of personal finances and commitments,

iv) response to social work intervention in any form,

v) opinion as to whether supervision will be effective in assisting enforcement of the fine.

A fine supervision order stays in force until:

i) the order is transferred to another court area:
however, in this instance the new court may - and
often does - order the continuation of supervision,
if all other things remain the same,

or ii) some other court order is made in respect of the fine,
especially imprisonment in default,

or iii) the fine is paid in full.

The fine supervision order is something of a hybrid. It is not a
probation order and is not primarily concerned with grand goals of
rehabilitation: the offender's consent is not necessary, nor can he
be compelled to receive visits from or make visits to the person
appointed to supervise. On the other hand, its aims are essentially
preventive, both in terms of social work and penal policy: that it
is not in any sense a debt-collecting function is clearly reflected
by the law's designation of it as a social work and not a court
official's function. Numerically, it exceeds probation in importance in Scotland.

Means Enquiry Courts

Once time has been allowed for payment, no order for imprisonment
in default can be made without a further court hearing, (Section
398 of the 1975 Act). This hearing is known as the Means Enquiry
Court.

It is possible under Section 397 for an offender to make application
to the court, either orally or in writing, for a variation in the
arrangements for paying his fine and receive a written notice from
the court in response. This does not require the convening of a court,
but is dealt with by court officials, in consultation with the
appropriate judge if necessary. The court must allow further time,
unless it is satisfied that the failure of the offender to pay has
been wilful or that he has no reasonable prospect of being able to
pay if further time is allowed. The practices of the officials may
also include the issuing of a warning letter if payments slip behind
before the formal decision to order a hearing at the Means Enquiry
Court is taken. It should also be possible at this stage for a
supervising social worker to receive a copy of such a letter sent to
any person under fine supervision.

Once it is decided to order an investigation into the means of an
offender who defaults, the procedure is to issue a citation requiring the offender to appear at a court hearing for an enquiry into
his means. Should the offender not respond to that citation, a

warrant can be issued for his apprehension. Thus the offender
who, owing a fine, moves his address and defaults on payment is
liable to arrest. The Police treat these warrants with some
discretion, and often arrange for the offender to present
himself at a subsequent hearing. However, it is quite proper to
detain a defaulter in custody, and thus Means Enquiry cases on
warrant can form part of normal daily court proceedings. Social
workers whose clients owe fines can do a general service to prompt
an initiative on the offender's part by advising him as to these
potential consequences and experiences if he defaults.

The investigation which the Means Enquiry Court conducts is again
a series of direct questions to the accused about his means, without
any real means of independent verification. The possible outcomes of
the investigation are:-

  i)   vary the period of time originally allowed for payment

  ii)   vary the arrangements (either in terms of amount or
        frequency) for paying instalments

  iii) order fine supervision, together with any such variation

  iv)   continue any existing supervision, together with any such
        variation

  v)   order a period of imprisonment in default of payment being
        made, or being made on time, in future

  vi)   order imprisonment in default forthwith

  vii) take no action.

Imprisonment, either forthwith or in the event of future default,
cannot be ordered in relation to young offenders unless:-

       a)   they have previously been under fine supervision

or   b)   the court is satisfied it is impracticable to place
            the offender under such supervision.

However, the ordering of imprisonment, either forthwith, or in the
event of future default, terminates the existing fine supervision.

Other Provisions in Regard to Fines

  i)   Subject to all the requirements and procedures of the
        preceding sections, the periods in default of payment of
        fines are now defined at Section 50 of the Criminal
        Justice (Scotland) Act 1980 as:-

Amount of Fine				Maximum period of imprisonment
Not exceeding £25				7 days
Exceeding	£25 but not exceeding		£50	14 days
"	£50 " " "		£200	30 days
"	£200 " " "		£500	60 days
"	£500 " " "		£1,000	90 days
"	£1,000 " " "		£2,500	6 months
"	£2,500 " " "		£5,000	9 months
"	£5,000			12 months

ii)   If a fine has been paid in part before the alternative prison
sentence comes into effect, the period of that imprisonment
will be proportionately reduced. Equally, an offender
imprisoned in default of payment can secure his release if
the balance of the fine is paid e.g. by a relative or friend
to the Governor of the prison.

iii) If a child i.e. person under 16 is fined, and defaults on
payment, the court may 'if it considers that none of the other
methods by which the case may legally be dealt with is suitable,
order that the child be detained for such period, not exceeding
one month, as may be specified in the order, in a place chosen
by the Local Authority in whose area the court is situated'.
Such place would be a residential facility normally available
to the Local Authority: it would not, by definition, be an
establishment under the control of the Prisons Division of the
Scottish Home and Health Department.

iv)   A young offender who is sentenced to detention in respect of
a further offence may apply through the Governor to the
Secretary of State to have any outstanding fines remitted.
The Secretary of State may, if it appears that such a course
will assist the offender's rehabilitation, remit the fine in
whole or in part.

Whilst it is normal practice for penal establishments to give
any help needed in such cases, it is not their responsibility
to identify unpaid fines. If a social worker considers that
the offender's rehabilitation can be aided by so doing, he
should advise the institution of any outstanding fines.

5   Caution (pronounced 'Kay-Shun')

Courts may require offenders to lodge a specified sum of money as a
security for their future good behaviour. The money is referred to as
caution, and an order for caution will stipulate:-

i)   the amount of money to be found. In Sheriff summary courts this cannot exceed £1,000, and in District Courts, £200,

ii)   a period of time within which it must be lodged with the
      Clerk of Court,

iii) a period of time, not exceeding one year, during which
      the offender must be of good behaviour.

The offender may recover his money from the Clerk of Court, with interest
calculated at the current rate of deposit, at the end of this period, if
he has been of good behaviour. Any further offence of which he may be
convicted during this period makes him liable to forfeit the money, and
the initiative in making a motion to this effect usually rests with the
prosecutor.

The Law allows that non-payment of caution in the period allowed shall
be treated as a non-payment of a fine Section 289(1) of the 1975 Act.
The procedures for enforcement, and the alternative periods of imprisonment, are operated and calculated as discussed above in relation to fines.
This means that a Means Enquiry Court has to be held. However, it is not
possible to order the payment of caution by instalments. The provisions
for fine supervision make no reference to supervising the finding of
caution, but courts have been known to request social work assistance in
regard to the finding of caution precisely because it cannot be paid by
instalments: such assistance would, however, have to be on a voluntary
basis.

Caution may be required, at the discretion of the court, for any offence
for which imprisonment is not being imposed, and without regard to age or
any other consideration. Caution may also be ordered as a requirement of
probation.

6.   Compensation

The 1980 Criminal Justice (Scotland) Act has introduced a new measure
known as the 'compensation order' (section 58). Prior to its enactment
no such specific power had been available, and the deferring of sentence
had represented the main device by which offenders were afforded an opportunity to make repayment to the individual victim who had suffered loss or
injury. Given that any crime or offence may have two 'victims' i.e. both
society in general and an individual who suffers directly as a result of
its commission, the new measure affords courts an increased opportunity
for ensuring that in appropriate cases and circumstances individual
victims may be compensated through punishment imposed on the offender.

Important general aspects of the new order are:-

i)   it may be imposed in addition to other penalties, as well
      as instead of them.

ii)   if a choice has to be made between a fine and compensation,
      compensation should be preferred.

iii) imprisonment is available as a sanction in default of payment.

iv)   all the procedures applicable to fine enforcement apply to such
      orders.

The compensation order is available to courts of both solemn and summary procedure. Section 59 (1) requires that a court when determining whether to make an order, and in determining its amount, should take the offender's means into account. There is no limit to the amount which may be awarded in cases on solemn procedure (Section 59(2)). In cases on summary procedure, subsection 3 of section 59 restricts the maximum amounts to:-

    sheriff and stipendiary magistrates courts - £1,000

    district courts   -   £200

although it should be noted that these maximum amounts apply to each offence, and not necessarily to the cumulative total.

Compensation orders may be ordered as a penalty in their own right, and section 63(1) declares that 'for the purposes of any appeal or review, a compensation order is a sentence'. More importantly, perhaps, compensation orders can be made in *addition* to other penalties, thus giving effect to the 'two victims' notion; it is possible, for example, to order an offender to perform unpaid work for the community under a community service order, and to require him to make compensation to the individual who suffered injury or loss as a result of his offence. There are two exceptions to the possibility of ordering compensation in addition to other disposals: - section 58(1) (a) prevents the combination of compensation with an order for absolute discharge; and with probation. In the latter situation, as will be seen, it is possible to make the payment of compensation a requirement of probation but that requirement is not made in terms of the 1980 Criminal Justice (Scotland) Act, and the enforcement procedures of the 1980 Act do not apply to compensation as a requirement of probation.

The enforcement of compensation orders made under the 1980 Act is a matter for the court, and payments are made to the court (section 60). Sections 61 and 62 arrange that if a fine and compensation are both considered appropriate but the offender's means do not run to both, a compensation order is to be preferred: even in cases where both fine and compensation are ordered jointly, such payments as the offender makes go first to the compensation and only thereafter to the fine. Section 65 extends all the fine enforcement procedures discussed above, to the enforcement of compensation orders, thus directly extending the range of social work department duties in this respect.

An interesting liability on offenders for compensation is created by subsection 2 of section 58. This allows that in cases involving dishonest appropriation of property i.e. theft, reset, fraud, etc., or in cases of taking and driving motor vehicles (under section 175 of the Road Traffic Act, 1972,), if the property, or car, is recovered but has been damaged while out of the owner's possession, 'that damage (however and by whomsoever it was in fact caused) shall be treated ...... as having been caused by the acts which constituted the offence'. Subsection 3 of section 57 provides that no compensation order shall be made in respect of:-

    a)   loss suffered in consequence of the death of any person

or b)   injury, loss, or damage due to an accident arising out of the presence of a motor vehicle on a road, except under the heading of subsection 2 above which we have just considered.

The introduction of compensation orders does not prevent the individual

victim taking action in the civil courts, even if a compensation order has
been made by a criminal court in the case. Section 67 deals with the
relationship of amounts awarded by the civil courts to the compensation
ordered by criminal courts. Subsection 2 of section 67 requires that the
damages in the civil proceedings be assessed without regard to the
compensation order i.e. by the ordinary criteria of the civil courts. The
assessment of the civil court may exceed the amount of compensation
ordered by the criminal one, but the civil court's actual order for
damages may not exceed the amount, if any, by which its assessment exceeds
what has been paid under the compensation order. Subsection 3 deals with
the situation where all or part of the compensation order remains unpaid,
and damages are awarded in civil proceedings; unless the person against
whom the compensation order was made has ceased to be liable for the
amount which he has not paid (e.g. he has been sent to prison in default;
or has successfully had the original amount reviewed and accordingly
reduced) the following restrictions apply to the civil court's award for
damages:

   a)   if the assessed amount of damages do not exceed what is unpaid
        under the compensation order, the order for damages shall not be
        enforced.

   b)   if the assessment for damages exceeds what remains unpaid, the
        actual order for damages shall only be for the difference.

Section 64 allows that, if a civil court assesses the loss or damage at
an amount less than that ordered by way of compensation in the criminal
court, or if the property whose loss is reflected in the order for
compensation is recovered, the offender may apply to the latter for a
review of the amount of compensation it ordered.

Some examples may be needed to help clarify these situations:-

1. a)   Smith is ordered by a criminal court to pay £100
        compensation to a victim. He pays it in full. The
        victim takes the case to a civil court, which
        subsequently assesses the damages at £150: it can
        only actually order £50 (the difference) to be paid.

   b)   Smith pays nothing of the £100 compensation and
        serves a period of imprisonment in default: the
        civil court can then order the full £150 to be paid.

2. a)   Jones is ordered to pay £500 compensation, and pays
        £250 of it, but suffers no penalty for his default
        before the civil court's judgement occurs. The civil
        court assesses the damages at £250, and therefore
        cannot enforce any payment: if it had assessed them
        at £400, it could only have ordered payment of the
        £150 difference.

   b)   Should the civil court only assess the damages at
        £250 in the above instance, Jones could apply under
        section 63 to the criminal court for a review of
        the original compensation order - with a view to it
        reducing the amount to the £250 which was the civil
        court's assessment, and which was the amount he had
        already paid.

Apart from the specific extra task for social work departments of
supervising offenders who default on compensation orders, the introduction
of the order has important implications for the writing of social enquiry
reports.   In their function of assisting the court to dispose of a case,
report writers need to extend their thinking on the subject of offering
opinions as to disposal to encompass the suitability and the possibility
of that disposal incorporating some compensation to the victim.   Not only
will they need to be familiar with the legislative detail of section 58
to 67 of the 1980 Act as discussed here, but also two important considerations arise

    a)   whether in principle the concept of reparation to which the
           compensation order is designed to give effect can suitably
           be combined with the objectives of other disposals which may
           be under consideration; and in particular whether the
           compensation should be the independent or additional disposal
           outlined.

    b)   the sheer practicalties of the offender's willingness
           and/or motivation to fulfil such a responsibility and
           make payments, as against the possible need to revert
           to imprisonment in default when otherwise prison might
           not be under consideration for the original offence:
           especially does this suggest a very detailed presentation
           of his financial situation as well as a thoughtful analysis
           of his feelings towards the victim as evidenced by his
           attitude to the offence.

PART THREE: SOCIAL WORK MEASURES

Chapter 6

Probation

Definition

The law says that probation is 'an order requiring the offender to be under supervision for a period to be specified in the order of not less than one and not more
than three years'. This definition was established by the Criminal Justice
(Scotland) Act 1949. Prior to 1949, probation was available as a disposal, but,
the legal method of enforcing it was somewhat different. Since 1949, the probation
order has been an entity in its own right and powers to deal with breaches of an
order were set out in the Act. The definition of probation is now to be located at
Sections 183 and 384 of the Criminal Procedure (Scotland) Act 1975, in regard to
cases on solemn and summary procedure respectively.

A purely legal approach provides but the bare bones of an understanding of probation.
Probation cannot properly be understood apart from its basic purpose of rehabilitation, from which its other statutory requirements derive. The essence of probation is that a legal order depends on it having a social work content to be
meaningful.

The question of probation's social work content is in turn equally bound up with
the methods of its adminsitration. It was integral to the 1949 Act that it also
contained (in Schedule 3) organisational provisions for the probation service.
This close inter-relationship of legal intention and social work meaning received
its classic expression in the Morison Committee's definition of probation: "we
understand by probation, the submission of an offender whilst at liberty to a
specified period of supervision by a social caseworker who is an officer of the
court: during this period the offender remains liable, if not of good conduct, to
be otherwise dealt with by the court."

In Scotland, the organisational framework of probation was changed by the Social
Work (Scotland) Act 1968. It was not the intention of that Act to affect adversely
the meaning or practice of probation: Section 27 transferred the duty of supervising persons on probation to the newly created Social Work Departments of Local
Authorities. While the emphasis on supervision remains, this in no way limits the
type of help or social work method which the individual supervisor may use: while
he remains responsible to the court for implementing the order, he may use a
variety of resources and persons in working towards the offender's rehabilitation.

Although the social worker is not a direct employee of the court, the contractual

relationship with the court is still a direct one for the purposes of probation.
Indeed, the notion of a 'contract' provides a useful shorthand description of
probation. There is a contract between court and offender represented by the
terms of the order: there is a contract between the court and the supervising
officer for the implementation of supervision: and the term 'contract' is
latterly much in vogue to describe the relationship and activity between social
worker and client.

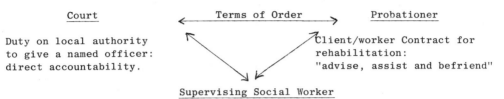

Court   Terms of Order   Probationer

Duty on local authority   Client/worker Contract for
to give a named officer: rehabilitation:
direct accountability.   "advise, assist and befriend"

Supervising Social Worker

Preliminaries

The law ensures that various matters are borne in mind before a probation order
can properly be made. The main effect of these considerations is that probation
emerges as an extremely versatile measure, with little restriction from the purely
legal point of view, on its possible usage and potential content. The stipulations
contained in the law also seek to ensure that the making of a probation order shall
have an impact.

Availability

i) A probation order can be made in respect of any offender who has attained
    the age of criminal responsibility. In Scotland that means aged 8 and over
    (Section 170 of the Criminal Procedure (Scotland)Act 1975). Children can
    sometimes be brought before the criminal courts, and probation is a possible
    disposal.

ii) A probation order can be made in respect of any offence for which the penalty
     is not fixed by law. Fixed penalties are very few, and are unlikely to come
     to the attention of social workers. Murder carries a fixed penalty, but
     culpable homicide does not: at the other extreme, contravention of parking
     bye-laws may carry a fixed penalty.

iii) The law makes no mention of previous convictions as representing, of them-
      selves, a necessary bar to the use of probation.

It can be seen at a glance then that probation is available to offenders of both
sexes, all ages, varied records, and for almost all crimes and offences.

Decision

The Morison Committee concluded "that there was an 'a priori' case for the use of
probation when four conditions exist:-

a) the circumstances of the offence and the offender's record must not
    be such as to demand, in the interests of society, that some more
    severe method be adopted in dealing with the offender.

b) the risk, if any, to society through setting the offender at liberty
    must be outweighed by the moral, social and economic arguments for
    not depriving him of it.

c)   the offender must need continuing attention, since otherwise, if the
     second condition is satisfied, a fine or discharge will suffice.

d)   the offender must be capable of responding to this attention whilst
     at liberty.

It is axiomatic that, whilst it is in some instances legally competent to do
without one, a social enquiry report should be considered before any probation
order is made.

In all other respects, the guidance afforded by the statute refers simply to
expediency. The governing sections which allow for the making of probation orders
both state that "the court, if it is of the opinion having regard to the circumstances, including the nature of the offence and the character of the offender,
that it is expedient to do so, may ...... make a probation order".

Making the Order

i)   The court must explain to the offender the effect of probation.

ii)   The explanation must be in 'ordinary language'.

iii)   The explanation must include reference to any additional
       conditions or requirements which it is proposed to include.

iv)   The explanation must specifically refer to the offender's
       liability to be sentenced for the original offence if he:-
       either commits another offence whilst on probation
       or fails to keep any of the requirements of the order.

v)   The offender must express his willingness to comply with
       all these requirements - that is to say, with the standard
       requirements applicable to all probation orders (see below)
       as well as any extra requirements that may be included in
       the order.

These stipulations, although all contained within the one subsection (6) of
Section 183 and 384 have been here set out thus fully to underline the importance
of a moment in court proceedings which can often be under-emphasised. The offender
enters into an undertaking with the court; the importance of his understanding of
that undertaking is crucial. Furthermore, any person, other than the supervising
social worker, who will also be affected by the contents of a probation order
(e.g. hostel warden, doctor, community service placement organiser) must also be
consulted, as unless they agree to the inclusion of a requirement which affects
them it is impracticable to include such a requirement.

Legal Effects of Probation

Probation is an order, not a sentence. Certain consequences follow of which it is
important to be aware.

Punitive aspects

The effect of probation is that successful completion of the order means that the
offender receives no punishment for the original offence. Probation is often
described as the 'sword of Damocles'; it employs the technique of the stick as
well as the carrot. The court retains its right, if the offender either commits
another offence or is brought back to court for not observing one or more of the
requirements, at any time during the probation period, to deal with him for the

original offence as if the probation order had never been made.

Probation must be distinguished from:-

  i)   the deferred sentence - which has looser conditions and still involves
                              the imposition of a sentence at a later date.

  ii) the suspended sentence - which involves the initial fixing and impos-
                              ition of a prison sentence which takes effect
                              automatically if a further offence occurs
                              during the period of suspension.

Whilst successful completion of the order obviates the imposition of any punishment for the original offence, it is an inescapable facet of probation that it
involves some degree of deprivation of the probationer's liberty, and it may well
be that he experiences its requirements as restrictive and irksome.

Solemn and Summary Procedure

In Scotland there is an important difference between probation orders made under
the two different types of procedure. This distinction does not apply in England
and Wales.

  i)   In cases on solemn procedure the accused stands convicted of the
       offence but the order is made "instead of sentencing him". (Criminal
       Procedure (Scotland)Act 1975, Section 183(1)). However, this conviction
       "shall be deemed not to be a conviction for any purpose other than the
       purposes of the proceedings in which the order is made, and of laying
       it before a court as a previous conviction in subsequent proceedings
       for another offence". (Section 191(1)).

  ii) In cases on summary procedure, the order is made "without proceeding
       to conviction" (Section 384).

Until the enactment of the 1980 Criminal Justice (Scotland) Act, one consequence
of this distinction was that in cases on summary procedure probation could not be
ordered together with a disqualification from driving, thus restricting its
availability for those offences where disqualification was mandatory: nor,
technically, was it possible to order probation in cases on summary procedure
after a period of deferred sentence, as the latter involved the recording of a
conviction.   Sections 53 and 55 of the 1980 Act have remedied this situation by
allowing for the combination of probation with a disqualification from driving in
the appropriate instances, and by making probation available after a period of
deferred sentence. The original distinction now remains as one of mainly legal
rather than practical significance.

Considerations as to the legal standing of a probation order also arise in cases
where an accused is to be sentenced on more than one charge. It is clearly
inappropriate to order both probation and a custodial sentence (however short in
relation to the proposed period of probation) simultaneously. Whilst there is no
necessary impossibility in ordering probation on one charge and, say, a fine on
another, the overall rehabilitative intention of probation must be borne in mind,
and indeed this intention is reflected both in the legal status of the order, and
in the rehabilitative considerations which apply to probation, as compared, for
example, with sentences such as a fine .

It is clearly inappropriate to order probation and a period of custody simultaneously. However, instances are known of offenders shortly to be released from

custodial sentences appearing before the courts on new charges and being put on probation - especially if it is known that they are not to be subject to statutory after-care.

At all times the aim of probation in terms of the offender's ultimate rehabilit-ation in the community should be borne in mind in any case involving more than one charge. The total circumstances of the case would have to be borne in mind before any consideration of mixing probation on one charge with other disposals.

The Probation Order

The statute determines that a probation order "shall be as nearly as may be in the form prescribed by Act of Adjournal". (Criminal Procedure (Scotland) Act 1975, Sections 183(2) and 384(2) as appropriate. A specimen probation order is given at the end of this section. The 1975 Act also directly ensures that the following arrangements shall be included.

    i)   the name of the local authority area in which the offender resides or is to reside.

    ii)   provision for the offender to be under the supervision of an officer of the local authority for that area.

    iii)   provision, if the offender resides or is to reside in a local authority area where the court making the order does not have jurisdiction for the order to name the appropriate court for that area of residence; and to require the relevant local authority to arrange for supervision.

These requirements underline the direct accountability of the supervising social worker. In turn, subsection 3 of both these governing Sections (183 and 384) obliges the offender to be under the supervision of an officer of the local authority: *he* might justly claim that a lack of supervision could amount to a breach of the law.

Serving the order

The 1975 Act requires (subsection 7 of Sections 183 and 384) that copies of the order shall be given by the Clerk of Court to the supervising officer; to the probationer; and to any person in charge of an institution in which the probation-er is to reside as a condition of probation (e.g. hospital, hostel). In practice, the administrative arrangements are often such that all these copies are given to the supervising officer for distribution.

The importance of the supervising officer serving, and explaining, the order is paramount. It could be held legally that the probation order is not completely made until this is done. More importantly, casework possibilities are inherent in the situation, and this serves to illustrate the marriage of legal and social work elements in the probation contract. The order should be served at the earliest appropriate moment, and the procedures of the local authority will need to reflect a suitable sense of urgency.

The supervising officer should ensure that the probationer signs one of the copies to be retained by the supervising officer to the effect that he, the probationer, has received his copy: the supervising officer should also sign to the effect that service of the order has been made, and the date of the event.

The importance of speedy administration is even greater when the probationer is to

reside in a different area. It is incumbent on the duty social worker in the
court making the order to ascertain immediately the nearest social work office;
and to notify that office in writing of the making of a probation order on a
person resident in that area as soon as possible, enclosing all available information. (See also Ref. below).The duty social worker should also attend to the
probationer's needs in terms of fares and subsistence, where appropriate, and to
other practical arrangements: he should, moreover, give the necessary instructions - not 'advice' - as regards contacting the relevant office, as he is at this
point acting in his capacity as officer of the court on behalf of the future
supervising officer. This will facilitate both early contact with the probationer
and appropriate allocation of case prior to the bare details of a request for the
name of a supervising officer arriving from the appropriate court.

Appeal

Probation is an order and not a sentence: it is, therefore,still possible to appeal
against the original conviction or finding of guilt if the plea was one of 'not
guilty'.

If the High Court, sitting as an Appeal Court, makes a probation order in place
of a sentence previously imposed by another court, the period of probation may
be calculated as effective from that earlier date, although in practical terms its
effective length will be somewhat shorter.

Requirements of probation orders

Probation is an order requiring an offender 'to be under supervision'. The
provisions of the law not only define the essential outlines of the probation
contract, but also relate directly to the content of the supervision. It is
crucial to the successful enactment and operation of these requirements of supervision that sentences are aware of and have confidence in social work methods and
administrative practices; and in turn, that supervising officers appreciate the
aims and pre-occupations of the court when ordering probation. Without such a
common frame of reference probation loses both significance and substance.

Standard requirements

All probation orders made in Scotland, following the Act of Adjournal, contain
three general requirements:-

i)   to be of good behaviour

ii)   to conform to the directions of the supervising officer

iii)   to inform the supervising officer at once if he/she changes
        his/her residence or place of employment.

It is instructive to compare these with those common in England and Wales,
viz:-

i)   to be of good behaviour and keep the peace.

ii)   to notify the probation officer at once of any change in
        residence or employment.

iii)   to keep in touch with the probation officer in accordance
        with such instructions as may from time to time be given,
        and in particular, if the probation officer requires, to
        receive visits at home.

It is important to note that powers are available to bring offenders back to court who, though they have neither been convicted of a fresh offence, nor have broken one of the specific requirements to be discussed below, are none-the-less, not co-operating with the spirit and intention of probation, and are thereby in breach of the contract they made with the court.

The problem of defining and interpreting what constitutes 'good behaviour' highlights the importance of a common frame of reference and of discussion between sentencers and supervising officers, and of clear guidelines being given by supervising officers to probationers.

General power to include extra requirements

The statute contains a general power to include, during the whole or part of the probation period, extra requirements (sections 183(4) and 384(4) of the 1975 Act). Such requirements must meet two commonsense criteria:- they must be reasonable and legally enforceable; and they must be capable of being supervised.

Again, the close relationship of meaningful sentencing to effective, and developing social work practice lies at the heart of the matter. The law itself gives a guiding principle concerning such extra requirements:-

> "as the court, having regard to the circumstances of the case,
> considers necessary for securing the good conduct of the offender
> or for preventing a repetition by him of the offence, or the
> commission of other offences".

Extra requirements relating either to residence, or to medical treatment, or to unpaid work, are the subject of different and specific subsections, and are considered separately below. Those in common use which can be regarded as both feasible and meaningful are listed below. It is open to a report writer to suggest the inclusion of extra requirements in giving an opinion as to suitability for probation: implicit in such an offering is an acceptance of the responsibility to supervise and implement any such requirements which are inserted.

Employment

A probation order can gain added strength from a specific requirement concerning employment, almost as a matter of course. The requirement can be regarded as a method of bolstering the probationer's incentive to stay in a job, and provides the supervising officer with a useful tool in attempting to enlarge his client's social horizons e.g. by use of the training and rehabilitative facilities of the Department of Employment. Equally, it prevents the probationer using excuses for living on statutory benefits and not taking employment available to him.

In common practice, three refusals to take jobs offered either by the Job Centre or after interviews arranged by the supervising officer would be regarded as a sufficient basis for breach proceedings being instituted. A common wording of this requirement is that the offender should 'lead an industrious life': perhaps more to the point is one that he 'should use his best endeavours to obtain and maintain himself in regular employment'.

Caution (pronounced 'kay-shun')

The probationer can be required to lodge a sum of money with the Clerk of Court within a stipulated period as a security for his good behaviour. On successful completion of the order the money is repaid to the probationer with accrued interest: the Clerk of Court will require confirmation from the supervising officer that the order has been completed successfully.

Caution cannot be paid by instalments, and the supervising officer will find the
question of collecting this money together integral to the treatment plan of the
early part of the probation period. This requirement can be seen as pertinent
to the question of the offender's motivation to co-operate with probation: it
literally ensures he has an investment in its successful outcome.

Compensation

Whilst the 1980 Criminal Justice (Scotland) Act has introduced the compensation
order as an additional penalty available in appropriate cases, section 58(1)(b)
of that Act expressly prevents the making of such an order in conjunction with
a probation order. However, compensation has featured as a requirement of probation orders in Scotland over the years, and remains available by virtue of the
general power to include extra requirements under sub-section 4 of sections 183
and 384 of the 1975 Act. In cases where compensation is ordered as a requirement
of probation, the supervising officer becomes responsible for ensuring that
receipts are obtained in order that the court may be satisfied that the requirement has been kept.

Associates

Whilst it is a regular requirement of after-care licences in Scotland that the
subject should choose his company carefully, the use of such a requirement in
probation seems to be less frequent. Such a requirement, whilst both reasonable
and enforceable, runs into some difficulties in regard to the practicalities of
its supervision. However, given a suitably co-operative relationship such a
requirement could be relevant to the probationer's rehabilitation.

Abstention from alcohol

A similar point could be made in regard to a condition concerning total absten-
tion from alcohol. A requirement to this effect might serve to assist the
probationer's own efforts, but could perhaps more usefully be expressed in an
emphasis on medical treatment as a relevant means towards rehabilitation or simply,
to co-operate with the supervisor in seeking ways to alter drinking habits.

Drugs

Special conditions may be inserted into probation orders to reflect the medical
and social possibilities of assisting the rehabilitation of those offenders whose
addiction to anything from 'hard' drugs to 'glue-sniffing' may have brought them
before the courts.

Requirements as to residence

The subject of residential care for offenders is a major one. The very possibility
indicates that whilst probation is treatment in the community, it is not simply a
business of contact, however frequent, between probationer and supervising officer.
There are considerations of the offender's need for treatment within the community,
but in a locus other than that of his home environment, as well as the relevance
of any non-custodial residential facility to the aims of the judicial system.
Probation can embrace all dimesnions of social work and practice.

Any legal requirement which seeks to govern a person's place of residence needs
careful definition, thus the occasion for a specific subsection (183(5) and
384(5)) of the 1975 Act relating to residence as a requirement of probation. The

probationer must not only consent to the general terms of probation but also to
the specific details of any requirement as to residence. Before making any such
requirement, the *court must* "consider the home surroundings of the offender",which
in practical terms means obtaining a social enquiry report. The person in charge
of any institution in which a probationer is required to reside must also receive
a copy of the order immediately after it is made and simultaneously with the
offender's actual admission.

The subsections dealing with residence were originally drafted (in the 1949
Criminal Justice (Scotland) Act) with the idea of a 'probation hostel' in mind.
Sections 59-61 of the Social Work (Scotland) Act 1968 empower and enable all
local authorities to establish or arrange for the support of residential facilities appropriate to any of their functions under that Act. Any supervising officer
contemplating a residential requirement for a probationer will need to obtain prior
assurance from his own or a relevant local authority that financial responsibility
will be accepted, and to advise the courts accordingly. It has been known for
Scottish courts to order residence in hostels south of the Border, but this is
rather unusual, but subject to availability and agreement to accept the probationer,
well within the competence of the Scottish courts.

Probation hostels were developed originally for the adolescent offender in
England and Wales with voluntary organisations working under the supervision of
the Home Office and receiving appropriate funding. This provision had already
been extended to adult offenders before a new thrust was given by the Criminal
Justice Act 1972, which only applies to England and Wales: probation committees
were given both power and encouragement to establish and run their own hostels.

The essential ingredients of any requirement relating to residence are:

>   The period shall not exceed 12 months, or go beyond the
>   date when the order expires.
>
>   and
>
>   The institution must be named in the order. The wording should
>   be as specific as "x hostel, known as y house, z street,
>   ABC town".

The requirement can be made:-

either, at the same time as the order is made

or, within 3 months of the making of the order by way of an application to
vary the original order for this purpose. Experience further suggests that the
wording of any such requirement shall further stipulate "and shall sleep there
each night unless permission has previously been obtained to absent himself".
Moreover, before any probationer can leave such a place of residence in advance
of the due time it is necessary for the order to be varied, so that this one
requirement can be removed.

In the absence of specific probation hostel provision, a requirement that the
probationer "shall reside where approved by his supervising officer" is quite
feasible.

However, the aim of such a requirement is more akin to that of those discussed in
'as to residence' above, rather than to a deliberate intention to provide
rehabilitation in a residential setting. A requirement "to reside where directed"
is not acceptable, potentially dangerous, legally dubious and is to be deprecated.
Equally if a social worker clearly intends a hostel placement, the procedure is
a condition drafted in the spirit of the discussion in this paragraph.

Requirement as to treatment for a mental condition

Many parallel considerations of both philosophy and practice applicable to
conditions of residence also apply to requirements that the probationer undergo
medical treatment. Sections 184 and 385 of the 1975 Act deal with such requirements:-

> The treatment must be for the offender's mental condition, i.e. these
> Sections do not deal with treatment for any purely physical condition.

> Only treatment specifically provided for by the subsection is
> permissable: any other condition purporting to relate to medical
> treatment is incompetent.

> The court must first obtain the evidence of a registered medical
> practitioner approved for the purposes by Section 27 of the Mental
> Health (Scotland) Act 1960.

A probation order can be made on the strength of such a medical report alone,
without further continuation for a social enquiry report, although the latter
is, as ever, to be recommended. If such an event does occur, however, it is
incumbent on the court duty social worker to take the fullest particulars
augmented by an interview and notify the relevant social work office: he should
expect to receive from the court a copy of the medical report.

That evidence must show two things:-

a)   the mental condition both requires and is susceptible
        to treatment

b)   the condition is not such as to warrant detention on a
        hospital order under Section V of the Mental Health Act,
        or under Section 175 of the Criminal Procedure (Scotland)
        Act - i.e. detention in the State Hospital.

The period of treatment shall not exceed 12 months or go beyond the end of the
order.

The treatment, which must be specified in the order, must be one of:-

a)   in-patient treatment in a hospital - i.e. a hospital within
        meaning of the Mental Health Act and _not_ the State Hospital
        at Carstairs.

b)   out-patient treatment at such institution or place e.g. a
        clinic as may be specified in the order.

c)   treatment by or under the direction of such medical
        practitioner as may be specified in the order.

Beyond that, the nature of the treatment shall not be specified.

The court shall not make a probation order containing a treatment requirement
unless it is satisfied that arrangements have been made for the intended treatment. If the treatment is to be undertaken as an in-patient the court must be
satisfied a bed is available and that arrangements have been made for the
probationer's reception and escort. Also, in this instance, the hospital will
require a copy of the probation order before it can admit the probationer. If

admission is direct from court, the escorting officer should have a copy of the order to give to the hospital authority.

Considerable scope is given to the medical practitioner in charge of treatment. He can, subject to the probationer's consent, arrange for a part of the treatment to be given in an institution or place not specified in the order, if he is of the opinion that such treatment can better or more conveniently so be given. He must give notice in writing of such an opinion to the supervising officer, in which event the treatment is deemed to be that specified in the order. Where the probationer is an in-patient, the duties of the supervising officer are confined to *"only such as may be necessary for the purpose of discharge or amendment of the order"*.

However the inclusion since 1975 of hospital social work within the functions of local authority social work departments makes for an enhanced social work contribution, particularly the possibility of hospital based social workers becoming directly involved in the supervision of probation cases, given that they are now 'officers of the local authority'.

The essential medical ethos is that successful treatment requires both the consent and co-operation of the patient, and that the doctor's responsibility for the purely medical aspects of treatment is sacrosanct. However, the real strength of this measure lies in the possibility of an inter-disciplinary, community-based approach to the mentally disordered offender: a whole range of health and social work resources is available. Classically those addicted to alcohol or drugs; compulsive offenders (e.g. gamblers, shoplifters); the sexually deviant; have all been considered relevant categories of criminal behaviour for medical intervention: in many cases the focus of social work intervention is on rehabilitation into the home community in a fashion more akin to after-care work in the medical social work field.

Requirement for unpaid work

The possibility of including in a probation order a requirement that the offender perform unpaid work in a specific Scottish provision, not available in England and Wales. It was introduced by the Community Service by Offenders (Scotland) Act 1978; section 7 of that Act created a new subsection, 5A, in section 183 and 384 of the Criminal Procedure (Scotland) Act, 1975, to make such a requirement possible. Prior to its enactment, courts in some areas had been including in probation orders a requirement that an offender should perform "community service", and had used the general powers available under subsection 4 for this purpose. Section 7 of the 1978 Act now applies all the criteria surrounding the new community service order (which it also introduced) to the inclusion of a probation order of a requirement that an offender should perform "unpaid work".

A full discussion of community service orders follows in the next chapter; briefly, a requirement in a probation order for unpaid work must specify:-

     i)   the number of hours to be worked, which must not be less than 40 and may not exceed 240.

    ii)   that the hours should be performed within 12 months of the start of the order, even if the order itself is for a longer period,

   iii)   that the offender report to an officer of the local authority specifically designated for community service purposes - this may or may not be the same person nominated to supervise the whole probation order.

It is implicit that the unpaid work should be for the benefit of the community at large, as opposed to the purposes of a private individual, and it is suggested that the wording of the requirement should be in terms such as:-

> "shall perform x hours of unpaid work for the benefit of the community within 12 months of the making of this order, as directed by the local authority officer designated for community service purposes".

However, it should be noted that the 1978 Act introduces a number of restrictions into the ordering of requirements for unpaid work, which do not apply to 'ordinary' probation orders:-

i)   no person under 16 can be made the subject of such a requirement,

ii)   no offender who resides or is to reside in England or Wales can be made subject to such a requirement - moreover an order containing such a requirement cannot be transferred to England or Wales without the requirement being withdrawn or otherwise nullified,

iii)   the court has to be notified that a proper community service scheme exists in the locality where the offender resides or is to reside,

iv)   the court must consider "a report by an officer of the local authority about the offender and his circumstances", together with an assessment as to his suitability for community service (1978 Act 1(2)(c)).

Moreover the 1978 Act gives the Secretary of State power to make rules by way of a Statutory Instrument about the performance of community service, whereas no other aspect of probation practice in Scotland is governed by any such rules.

Day training centre

The Criminal Justice Act of 1972 gave powers to Probation and After-Care Committees in England and Wales to establish and run Day Training Centres. These Centres were intended to provide a rehabilitation facility essentially for the petty recidivist offender by means of an intense social and vocational education and rehabilitation programme. The Act empowered courts to order up to 60 days attendance at such a Centre as a requirement of probation, and again, a new measure related to probation was directly coupled with financial obligations and procedures to make such a resource effective and available as a court disposal. No such power or obligation exists in Scotland, but it is consistent with the wide powers given to Departments by the Social Work (Scotland) Act, 1968 that such Centres could be established and used.

Breaches of Probation Orders

General

A breach of probation occurs either if the probationer fails to keep one of the requirements of probation, or if he commits another offence while on probation. There are thus _two_ types of breach of probation: in any reference to breach of

probation it is essential to be aware of which type is under consideration.   The
two types are commonly referred to simply as:-

    1.   breach of requirement

    2.   breach by further offence

In earlier days a breach of requirement was often known as a 'Section 5' breach,
and a breach by further offence as a 'Section 6' breach: these were the relevant
Sections of the Criminal Justice (Scotland) Act 1949, which set out the law in
relation to each type.   The relevant statute is now the Criminal Procedure
(Scotland) Act 1975, and therefore the Sections differ not only by type of breach,
but also according to whether the probation order was made by a court of solemn
or of summary procedure.   The Sections now are:-

Type of breach	Solemn procedure	Summary procedure
1. breach of requirement	S.186	S.387
2. breach by further offence	S.187	S.388

Hereafter reference is to the _type_ of breach, and only to the relevant Section as
may be necessary.

The subject of breach of probation is closely tied up with the question of 'which
court?'.   The various Sections of the Act talk about "the court which made the
order" and "the appropriate" court, but the answer to the question 'which court?'
is not thereby immediately apparent: the two are often, but not always, one and
the same court.

The two main aspects of the question relate to what level of court is involved
(High, Sheriff or District); and to where the breach occurs (in relation to the
probationer's home area).

The detail is easier to follow if the three following principles are borne in mind
at the outset.   These principles relate only to probation orders made and probationers resident in Scotland: the position in cross-border cases is decidedly
more complex and we deal with it separately.

    1.   The court with jurisdiction in the probationer's home
             area "holds" any order in relation to him and is the
             court to which the supervising officer relates for the
             purpose: it deals with any breaches of requirement
             relating to him.   Only the court of origin may deal
             with breaches due to further offences.

    2.   Sheriff Courts deal with orders made by Sheriff Courts
             whether on solemn or summary procedure: District Courts
             with District Court Orders.

    3.   The High Court deals with all probation orders made at
             any sitting of the High Court throughout Scotland.

Breach of requirement

Anything contained in the probation order to which the probationer should adhere is
a requirement of the order, and any failure on his part to do so constitutes a
breach of requirement.   Such a breach is not simply a mere detail, but an essential

ingredient of probation: it calls into question the whole contract with the court
into which the probationer entered by agreeing to the making of the order in the
first place. As noted earlier, all probation orders contain certain requirements
by definition: over and above that, other specific requirements may have been
inserted which will then appear on the order.

Any breach of requirement immediately entails a decision on the part of the supervising officer. Oversight or inaction represent a reaction, and the probationer
will draw his own conclusions about the importance of the matter and of the importance of probation. There are various intermediate possibilities, e.g. warnings of
varying severity, before a decision to take action in the court is reached:
consultation with senior officers in the Department, or possibly with the
Probation and After-Care Sub-Committee, may be appropriate. Considerations both
as to the letter and to the spirit of the probationer's breach and response
generally arise.

Action in the court occurs under either Section 186 or Section 387 of the 1975 Act,
depending on whether the order was originally made by a court of solemn procedure,
or a court of summary procedure.

Which court

The court which is to deal with the breach is as follows:-

1.   Any order made by the High Court is dealt with by that
       court. Wherever the probationer resides, that involves
       the supervising officer initiating action through the
       Justiciary Office in Edinburgh, although it may be
       possible for the hearing to take place when the court
       is on circuit in the appropriate area. The High Court
       has all the necessary powers to deal with the breach.

2.   If a Sheriff Court made the order, a breach of requirement
       is dealt with by the Sheriff Court in the probationer's
       and therefore the reporting officer's home area.
       The Clerk of Court will arrange for the court to be
       constituted as one of solemn or of summary procedure
       depending on the status of the original order. Even in
       the court making the order was in a different part of
       Scotland, the Sheriff Court in the probationer's home
       area has both power and responsibility to deal with the
       breach.

3.   Exactly parallel considerations apply in relation to a
       District Court order, only the procedure is always on the
       summary method (Section 387 of the 1975 Act).

Disposals

Taking action in this context means the supervising officer initiating proceedings.
In instituting such action, the supervising officer needs to be aware of the
possible outcome should the court be satisfied, either on admission by the
probationer, or after proof of the case, that a breach of requirement has occurred.
These possible outcomes are:-

i.   The court accepts that the probation should continue. In this
       case, the following possibilities exist:-

a)   Fine of up to £50. Note that this penalty
      is the same whether solemn or summary procedure
      is involved.

b)   Make a community service order: we discuss this
      in detail in relation to community service orders below.

c)   Vary the requirements of the order (e.g. add new
      ones), except that the order cannot be extended
      beyond 3 years from the date on which it was
      originally made. If the order is varied in any
      respect, the supervising officer will receive from
      the court copies of an amending order: these are
      legal documents having the same status as the
      original probation order, and need to be served
      on the probationer in the same way.

d)   Do nothing: in which event the disposal is
      recorded as one of "no order".

If anything else is announced (e.g. "admonish") that has the
effect of terminating the order. The point is that the court
can punish the breach of requirement without necessarily calling
the whole probation order into question, if the circumstances
justify it.

ii)   The court feels that the breach of requirement is of such
      gravity as to call the whole probation order into question.
      The *court of origin* then has power to deal with the original
      offence, as if the probation order had never been made: it
      simply proceeds to sentence. In the case of a probation order
      made by a court of summary procedure, it does now "proceed to
      conviction" and then sentences: a court of solemn procedure
      has already convicted, but now proceeds to sentence for the
      offence in respect of which the order was originally made.
      The accused is now a fully convicted person and faces the full
      range of possible penalties relevant to his offence(s). The
      imposition of a sentence for the original offence terminates
      the probation order. The supervising officer will need to
      close his case record accordingly and follow his Department's
      administrative procedures for closing cases. In respect of the
      copies of the Probation Order, or of any amending orders, he
      need do nothing, as the court proceedings terminate the legal
      order.

Action by Supervising Officer

The action which a supervising officer takes to bring a breach of requirement to
the attention of the court involves the laying of information alleging that a
breach of requirement has occurred. Thereafter he must swear an oath before the
appropriate judge (that is, of the High, Sheriff, or District Court) that the
information is true, before the administrative procedures for bringing the
probationer to court to face the allegation can be put into effect by court officials and the Police. The essential stages therefore are:-

i)   Laying information

The onus of proof in any criminal case is that the prosecution
must prove its case "beyond reasonable doubt".

At law the Procurator Fiscal has no direct responsibility for
breach of probation proceedings: the Morison Committee simply
recommend that supervising officers firstly discuss with him
the adequacy of their evidence in relation to this standard of
proof and secondly notify him of the fact that they were going
ahead. The Thomson Committee on Criminal Procedure re-examined
this matter and made different recommendations, to the effect
that Fiscal should be responsible in all respects, leading the
prosecution case in court, and facilitating the administrative
arrangements to bring the accused before the court. In some
areas, practice approximates that recommended by the Thomson
Committee, and the procedure we outline at this stage is in
accordance with those recommendations. Supervising officers
will need to ascertain the practice in their own area.

The supervising officer should prepare a document known as an
"information" which contains the grounds alleging a breach of
requirement. This document provides the basis of the allegation
(e.g. "failed to report") and is the essential starting point
of the subsequent proceedings. He should then take this to
the Procurator Fiscal and discuss the purely legal aspects of
the case with him. The Fiscal should countersign the Information.
In particular the Fiscal will be concerned with the availability
of corroborative evidence. - officer callers' book; information
from hostel; hospital report, copies of letters sent etc.

ii)   Deponing

The supervising officer's next step is to take the "Information"
duly signed by the Procurator Fiscal, to the court. Deponing
involves two things: first, the judge satisfies himself that the
breach is intrinsically sufficiently serious to merit court proceedings; secondly, the method of bringing the probationer before
the court is approved and authorised. There are 2 such methods:-

(a)   citation: this is the normal and preferable method, and
        is used when the probationer has a fixed residence. He
        duly receives a letter signifying that an allegation of
        breach has been made and that he must come to court on a
        specified date to plead to it. If he contests the allegation,
        the court may need to fix a later trial diet for a full
        hearing of all the evidence.

(b)   warrant: this is used when the probationer has left
        without trace. The court authorises the probationer's
        arrest and detention. When arrested (in whatever part
        of the United Kingdom) he is brought back to the court
        in the area of his normal residence to be dealt with
        for the breach. The supervising social worker must be
        ready to attend the court in person as soon as this
        happens. Occasionally, a probation period is completed
        before such a warrant is executed: in this event, the

supervisor needs to discuss the matter with both
Fiscal and court, as warrants, once issued, are not
lightly withdrawn.

Once the social worker has deponed, his immediate responsibilities
end. The court officials and the Fiscal's office arrange for the
necessary clerical procedure. However, any additional information
obtained by the supervising officer as to the whereabouts of the
probationer will need thereafter to be communicated to the Police,
with the minimum of delay.

Attendance at court

The supervising social worker must be ready to attend court in person, at any
hearing of a breach of probation case. His official functions will comprise:-

a)   giving evidence to support proof of the breach in any contested
        case. In this respect, he takes his cue from the leading of the
        Fiscal, but is liable to be cross-examined by the defence.

b)   assisting the court's disposal of the case. It will not always
        be possible to have a ready view as to the probationer's
        continued suitability for probation, especially if he has
        been out of touch for a period, and thus a continuation for
        reports may be necessary. In other situations, it may be
        possible to reach a view and prepare a report in advance of the
        hearing.

The supervising officer will continue to have casework functions in relation to
his client throughout the proceedings, and the usual post-sentence and through-
care consideration will arise pursuant to the imposition of any custodial sentence.

Breach by Further Offence

The commission of a further offence during the probation period is automatically a
breach of probation, which demands action by the court: it naturally calls into
question the whole probation order. An offence committed before the accused was
put on probation may not come, before a court until during his period of probation:
this does not count as a breach by further offence, even if the offence actually
occurred later than the offence for which the order was made. However, he may
come before a court for an offence committed during the probation period after the
probation has finished; this does constitute a breach of probation by further
offence. An accused person who is on probation at the time he commits an offence,
and who is convicted or found guilty of that offence, faces the prospect of
receiving two sentences: one for the new offence; and one for the offence in
relation to which the probation order was made - he is directly confronted with
this latter situation "as if the probation order had never been made".

The supervising officer is duty bound to notify immediately the court which holds
the order of the commission by the probationer of any further offence during the
probation period. There is no discretion or lee-way open to him in the duty to
report such an event. Among other things, this means that court duty social
workers need a list of all cases to be heard in any court in sufficient time to
check it for persons currently under supervision before the court sits. The
sections dealing with breach by further offence are 187 (solemn procedure) and 388
(summary procedure).

Which court

The question of "which court?" is occasionally more complex in breaches by further offence than in breaches of requirement.

In the situation where the court which is dealing with the further offence is identical in terms of both level and area with that holding the order, it can deal with both the new and the original offence at the same time. However, continuation of the case in regard to the new offence for a social enquiry report is inherently advisable and also allows both supervisor and court to form a considered view of the situation now revealed. In this breathing space, it is helpful if the supervising officer notifies the Clerk of Court about the breach, in order that the papers for the original offence can be looked out in time for the continued hearing. It is also worth commenting that, while the schedule of previous convictions will usually inform the court of the existence of a probation order, the duty social worker should be alive and alert to this situation in default. If the breach is *NOT* considered at this time, the procedure under heading "Disposals" below should be followed. Any imposition of sentence for the original offence terminates the probation order - even if a new probation order is made in respect of the later offence.

Where the courts are *not* identical, which they often are not, either in terms of procedure or of geography, the supervising officer's responsibility is much more to the fore. The court dealing with the new offence can sentence only in respect of that offence. It may well consider a social enquiry report which will comment on the accused's response to probation; and it may even express a view about the continuance of the probation; but it cannot deal with the original offence, nor can its view bind that of the court which holds the order. Nor, therefore, is the supervisor's responsibility thereby bypassed.

Disposals

The facts of any breach by further offence must then be notified to the court which holds the order. This court has the powers to deal with the breach, *and in this event, it will be dealing with the offence for which the order was originally made.* It is *not* possible to impose a sentence *and* let the probation continue: the *only* way the probation can continue is if the court takes *no* action; nor does it have powers in these circumstances to deal with the breach by varying the original order in any way. In notifying the facts of a breach by further offence, the supervising officer will need to have these limitations in mind. The court should welcome, along with the notification, his view as to the future of the probation order: he may well want to include this, especially if he *does* want the order to continue.

Action of Supervising Officer

Once a decision has been reached, either by the court or directly by the supervising officer, that the probationer should be brought back before the court which holds the order to be dealt with for the original offence, the essentials of procedure are as follows:-

   i)   The supervising officer should bring the matter to the
          attention of the Procurator Fiscal. He, in turn, will be
          concerned to satisfy himself that the commission of the
          further offence can be proved by reference to court records,
          which he may need to obtain for the purpose.

    ii)   Neither information on oath nor deponing are necessary
in the instance of breach by further offence. However,
the supervising officer does need to make his notification
of the breach by further offence available afresh to the
court officials, so that they, in co-operation with the
Procurator Fiscal's office, can put in motion the issue of
a citation or a warrant as may be necessary.

    iii)   Procedure in court is much as before. The supervising
officer needs to be present either to assist proof of
the matter, or more likely the court's disposal of the
case, by way of the advance preparation of a social
enquiry report. The sentence is for the original offence
and terminates the order. The situation is still full of
casework considerations, both short and long term.

Finally, it should be noted that a less complex procedure is available in
instances of breach by further offence when, in relation to the *new* offence which
constitutes the breach, a substantial custodial sentence has been imposed, which
in practical terms nullifies the continuance of the existing probation order. The
situation is one in which the procedure simply represents an administrative
tidying-up, which has become necessary only because the court dealing with the new
offence did not have power to deal with the order. In this situation the presence
of the erstwhile probationer is not necessary in court, and the court which holds
the order is simply invited to discharge it in the light of the new circumstances.

Breaches Involving Courts in England and Wales

An essential principle in Scotland is that the court which holds the order has all
the powers and responsibilities to deal with breaches of that order, whether they
be breaches of requirement or breaches by further offence. The system in England
and Wales makes much greater play of distinctions between both different levels of
court and between different areas. There are only two levels of court, Crown
Courts and Magistrates' Courts, and the basic system is that a Magistrates' Court
for the probationer's home area "supervises" on behalf of the court of origin,
whatever its level. In Scotland, we have seen that a probation order is "held" by
a court of the *same* level that made it, but in England, all Crown Court orders
are "supervised" by local Magistrates' Courts, whose powers are therefore limited
in some respects. The English system, however, contains powers to facilitate an
easy committal from one level to the other, whereas there is no cross-over point
between summary and solemn procedure in Scotland. Keeping these principles in
mind, the situations work out as follows:-

        Any probation order made in Scotland on a person resident in or who
goes to live in England and Wales will be "supervised" by a Magistrates'
Court for that area, whatever the level of the court making the order
in Scotland. Court areas in England and Wales are known as Petty
Sessional Divisions and the supervising officer will be a probation
officer for that Division. The National Association of Probation
Officers publishes a directory of officers and offices in each
area. Many of the larger areas have officers specifically designated
for court liaison purposes. The supervising Magistrates' Court has
powers in relation to breach of requirement, but not to deal with the
original offence, nor to discharge the order for any other reason.
The essential principle is that any discharge of the order, or the
imposition of any sentence for the original offence, is a function
of the Scottish court which made the order: Sections 188 and 389 of
the Criminal Procedure (Scotland) Act 1975 set out the arrangements

for bringing back a probationer before the Scottish court in such an event. The
supervising Magistrates' Court thus has powers only in regard to breaches of
requirement, and these are confined to:-

> i)   varying the order
>
> ii)   fine up to £50 (1972 C.J. Act)
>
> iii) take no action.

Should it decide that a breach of requirement is of such gravity that sentence
should be imposed for the original offence, it must follow the procedures for
sending the probationer back to the original Scottish court.

A similar situation exists in relation to orders made in England and Wales on
persons resident in, or who come to live in, Scotland. Such orders are
supervised by the Sheriff Court for the area of the probationer's residence,
acting in a summary capacity. Again the supervising Sheriff Court has no powers
to deal with the original offence, or a breach of requirement which in the court's
view necessitates such a course. Again, powers exist to send the probationer
back to the original English Court. The powers of a Sheriff Court supervising an
English order do include the fines and variation powers in the event of a breach
of requirement. The only difference is that a Scottish Court supervising an
English order *does* have power to discharge the order either on the grounds of
good progress, or in the event of the probationer receiving a substantial
custodial sentence in respect of some new offence.

Transfer, Variation, and Discharge of Probation Orders

Transfer. Transfers of probation orders are, or become, necessary in two main
sets of circumstances:-

Immediate transfer - when people offend away from their home area and are put
                     on probation by a court which does not have jurisdiction
                     in the area where they live, the order is transferred
                     directly by the court making it to the appropriate court
                     which does have that jurisdiction. Such a direct transfer
                     is also necessary when an offender, although appearing
                     before a court which does have jurisdiction in his home area,
                     is being made the subject of a requirement that he lives in
                     some other area.

Transfer during the currency of the order - such a transfer becomes necessary if
                     the probationer takes up residence in a place outwith the
                     jurisdiction of the court which made or which holds the order.
                     Such a move ordinarily arises from the domestic circumstances
                     of the offender, but equally could be the result of an appli-
                     cation by the supervising officer to vary the order by intro-
                     ducing a requirement of residence elsewhere.

i)   Immediate transfer

We dealt with the responsibilities of court duty social workers in these circumstances in context above. The formalitiies of transfer in such an event are
as follows:-

a) Probationer resident or to be resident in Scotland.

The court which makes the order will require the name of the
local authority area in which the probationer lives or will be
living. Copies of the order will be sent by the clerk of court
to the Sheriff or District Court (as appropriate) for the offender's
home area or area of residence, and to the Director of Social Work
for that area. In the case of orders made by the High Court, that
court holds all its own orders, and the clerk only requires the
name of the local authority area.

b) Probationer resident or to be resident in England and Wales

The court will require the name of the appropriate Petty Sessional
Division i.e. area of jurisdiction of a Magistrates' Court, and
will send copies of the order to the Clerk of the Justices for that
Division, and to the Chief Probation Officer for that area. The
order will require that the probationer will be under the supervision
of a 'probation officer appointed or assigned' to that Division. The
Magistrates' Court supervises on behalf of the Scottish Court.

ii) Transfer During the Currency of the Order.

A transfer of probation becomes necessary if the probationer moves residence
during the currency of the order, and in this instance the responsibility falls
on the supervising officer to initiate the administrative proceedings to put this
into effect. As a matter of good professional practice, the supervising officer
should first contact the relevant social work or probation office in the new area.
He needs to ascertain three things:-

- the probationer is or will be resident at the new address.
- transfer is acceptable.
- all the requirements at present in the order can be complied with
  in the new area, as, if this is not possible, a variation of the
  order will first be necessary.

The formalities of transfer are:-

Probationer moving within Scotland.

The supervising officer needs to apply to the court which holds the order
for a transfer to the new area, and needs to give the name both of the
court and of the local authority area to which transfer is to be made.
The probationer is not involved in this application or in any of the
ensuing administration, and has fulfilled his obligation by the initial
notification of a change of address. The clerk of the court in the new
area will issue an amending order, or will amend the existing order,
making the necessary changes, which he will then send to the Director
of Social Work for the new area. The arrival of this fresh or amended
documentation thus affords the new supervising officer an opportunity to
review and/or remake the probation contract.

Probationer moving to England or Wales.

The supervising officer must make the application as above, but only needs
the name of the Petty Sessional Division for the new area. The order will
be supervised by the Magistrates' Court for that area, and will require the
probationer to be under the supervision of a probation officer 'appointed or
assigned' to that Division.

iii) **Transfer to England and Wales of orders on person under the age of 17**

Courts in England and Wales cannot make probation orders on persons under the age of 17: instead they make supervision orders in terms of the Children and Young Persons' Act, 1969. However, in Scotland 16 year olds are regarded as adults unless they are already under supervision of a Children's Hearing, and frequently appear before the ordinary adult criminal courts; also children may occasionally appear before the adult courts, and are then also liable to be made the subject of a probation order by a Scottish court. To cope with the problem of 16 year olds and under who are put on probation by Scottish courts but who reside in or move to England or Wales, sections 189 and 390 of the Criminal Procedure (Scotland) Act 1975 together with schedule 5 of the English 1969 Act already referred to, permit of certain administrative steps to redress this rather anomalous situation.

In effect what happens is that the Scottish court makes a probation order in the ordinary way, or may already have made it and arranges that "three copies of the probation order, and any other documents and information as it considers likely to be of assistance" shall be sent to the Clerk of the Juvenile Court in the Petty Sessional Division in which the probationer resides or to which he has moved. This constitutes a referral to that juvenile court, the matter before it being that on which the probation order was made. The Juvenile Court has two courses of action open to it:-

      i) it can make a supervision order under the 1969 Act;

  or ii) it shall, if it does not make such an order, "dismiss the case".

Whichever course of action it adopts, the Scottish probation order ceases to have effect.

These arrangements provide a bridge between two systems which have taken different paths, with the result that the usual arrangements for reciprocosity are not possible. Occasionally the reverse situation occurs in that an offender made the subject of a supervision order under the 1969 Act moves to Scotland, and the court in England or Wales considers it appropriate to refer the matter to a Scottish court, rather than to the Reporter of a Children's Hearing. On receiving such a referral the Scottish court may "if it is of the opinion that the person should continue to be under supervision, make a probation order for the period specified in the (supervision) order," or *shall* dismiss the case.

Variation of probation order

A variation of probation refers to a change in one of the substantive requirements in the probation order, as opposed to the essentially administrative nature of transfers. A variation represents a change in the context of the order, and its importance approximates the making of that order in the first place. Accordingly, the probationer must be present in court and agree to the changes of requirement. Variations are ordered by the court which holds the order, and it is, therefore, necessary for arrangements to be made by the court officials for the probationer to be formally cited to appear.

Variations can be ordered in either of two situations:-

      i) On the application of the supervising officer. The procedure in
          this instance requires the preparation of a formal application
          for the purpose, and submission of this to the court: thereafter,
          the Court officials are enabled to arrange a hearing and issue
          the necessary citation.

ii) In a hearing for breach of requirement (see above).

The following variations are possible:-

i) cancelling any of the requirements in the original order.
In this instance the presence of the probationer is not
necessary as his consent is assumed. A variation to cancel
a requirement is necessary in the event of either successful
completion of medical treatment, or of residence in a specified
institution, in advance of the originally stipulated period. A
variation to cancel may also be necessary if the probationer is
moving to a new area in which compliance with a particular
requirement is not possible: such a variation should be done
before the transfer of supervision is effected.

ii) inserting any requirement, additional to or in substitution
of an existing requirement. However, it is necessary to
ensure that any such additional requirement could legally
have been inserted at the time the order was originally made.
The initiative for the inclusion of additional requirements
mainly rests with the supervising officer, either by making
his own application, or by way of a suggestion in a social
enquiry report at a breach of requirement hearing.

The following provisos apply to variations of probation:-

No variation shall reduce the period of probation.

No variation shall extend the period of probation
beyond three years from the date of the original order.

A probationer cannot be required to reside in an
institution or place for longer than 12 months.

The same rules apply to the insertion of requirements
as to medical treatment as would have applied at the
time the order was made.

Any additional requirement as to residence or to
medical treatment must be inserted within 3 months
of the date of the making of the order.

Once a variation has been ordered by the court, copies of orders also known as
amending orders will be issued by the Clerk of Court. These do require to be
served on the probationer, with the usual signing and countersigning as if the
probation order was freshly made. Should the variation represent the insertion
of a new requirement concerning either residence or in-patient medical treatment,
a copy of the order will be required by the named institution or hospital.

Discharge of Probation

The subject of discharge is, in some senses, only second in its importance to the
making of the order particularly since the possibilities of discharge seem to be
less widely known, let alone used: in any event, consideration of discharge is
integrally bound up with the basic meaning and purpose of probation.

Occasionally, discharge becomes necessary for purely administrative reasons. The
importance of discharge in these situations is simply that of avoiding untidiness .

Such situations are:-

1. The probationer is sentenced to a substantial period of custody
    by a court which does not have power to deal with the original
    offence. The supervising officer simply applies to the court
    which made the order for discharge in the light of this
    circumstance. Neither the presence of the probationer nor the
    serving of any discharge order is necessary.

2. The court which made the order, while dealing with a further
    offence, imposes a custodial sentence and omits through over-
    sight or non-preparation to deal with the original offence. A
    similar procedure to that outlined above is necessary.

3. The court which made the order, while dealing with a further
    offence, makes a new probation order in relation to that new
    offence.

    i)   It may discharge the original (first) order on the spot,
         in which event, no further action is necessary.

    ii) If it omits to deal with that original order, a similar
         procedure to that outlined above is necessary.

Much more important and relevant as the conclusion to this chapter on probation is
the possibility of discharging the order in advance of the due date, on the grounds
of good progress. The significance of this for the probationer is immediate: a
discharge of the order in these circumstances is equivalent to successful
completion of the order - he escapes both any possibility of punishment for the
original offence, and is no longer bound by the requirements of probation. For
the supervising officer, the importance extends well beyond the satisfactory
completion of one case into the whole area of work management: it becomes
possible simply to double the number of probation cases undertaken in a specified
period with the same input, if, say, two one year orders are both discharged at
the halfway stage on the grounds of good progress. Normally, the working
relationship with the court is such that half the probation period is usually
thought to be a minimum, but exceptional circumstances, or indeed a deliberately
adopted Departmental policy, for selected cases, for intensive supervision, agreed
with the court, may well justify an earlier approach.

A discharge of probation may be initiated in either of two ways. The authority
is paragraph 1 of schedule 5 to the Criminal Procedure (Scotland)Act 1975.

       The probationer may apply to the court. This is very rare, and
       there is some ground for thinking that probationers are less
       aware of their rights in the matter than might be the case. There
       is no reason why any person, subject to probation, should not be
       made aware of this possiblity without it being extended either as
       an offer or as a promise. However, he does have such a right, and
       may indeed need his supervising officer's assistance in approaching
       the court officials in pursuit of such an application. In this
       event, the supervising officer will be cited to attend a hearing
       convened for the purpose: the probationer must get himself to the
       hearing. The court has power to grant such an application in spite
       of any views expressed by the supervising officer.

    or The supervising officer may apply to the court. Before doing so,
       an independent check with the Police and/or Procurator Fiscal may

be in order: it is important to ensure that no outstanding matters
embarrass the application for discharge. In this event, the
probationer's presence is *NOT* necessary. If the application is granted
copies of an order discharging the probation order require to be
served on the probationer. Then the matter is complete.

Letters and forms for use in probation work

In view of probation's basis as a legal order, the letters and forms used in
connection with it need to be clear, precise, and accurate. The selection which
follows is designed to provide a readily accessible collection of forms and
letters which may be either unclear or unavailable within social work departments.

The probation order

The legal format of a probation order is determined by an Act of Adjournal, and,
as noted the legal responsibility for giving a copy of it to the probationer is
very frequently delegated by the clerk of court to the supervising officer. In
practice the habit of formally "serving" the order at a first or early interview
is often a useful opportunity to cement what was agreed in court by the probationer,
and then move into a discussion of how it is to be implemented by the supervisor.
It is suggested that copies of the order be endorsed by both the probationer and
the superviser, thus:-

"I have received a copy of the probation order and its contents have been
explained to me".

          Signed .... (by the probationer)

          Date ....

"I have given a copy of the probation order to (name of probationer) and have
explained its contents to him/her".

          Signed .... (by the supervising officer)

          Date ....

Example: of Probation Order

PROBATION ORDER

UNDER THE CRIMINAL PROCEDURE (SCOTLAND) ACT 1975, SECTION 384

IN THE SHERIFF COURT AT PEEBLES ON 3RD MARCH, 1980

The Court being satisfied that the offender   JOHN SMITH
has committed the offence with which he is charged/in view
of the conviction of the offender   JOHN SMITH

                    of Brown Street
....

                    BLACKTOWN
....

and being of the opinion that having regard to the circumstances,
including the nature of the offence and the character of the said
offender it is expedient to make a probation order under the
Criminal Procedure (Scotland) Act 1975 containing the under-noted

requirements:

And the Court having explained to the said offender the effect
of the order (including the requirements set out below) and
that if he fails to comply with the order, he may be brought
before the Court by his supervising officer for a breach of
probation and may be sentenced/dealt with for the original
offence, and that, if he commits another offence during the
period of the probation order, he may be dealt with likewise:

And the said offender, having expressed his willingness to
comply with the requirements of the order;

The Court therefore orders that for a period of ....2.years..
from the date hereof the said offender ..John Smith.........
who resides/is to reside in the Local Authority area of
.Seacliffe Region....... shall be under the supervision of an
officer of that Local Authority allocated for the purpose as
required by the Court at ....Blacktown......... in the said
Local Authority area: that the said offender shall be notified
in writing by the Clerk of Court of the name and official address
of the officer who is to supervise him and similarly if at any
time such supervision is to be undertaken by another officer
of the Local Authority allocated for the purpose; and that the
said offender shall comply with the following requirements,
namely:-

1.   to be of good behaviour;
2.   to conform to the directions of the supervising officer;
3.   to inform the supervising officer at once if he/she
      changes his/her residence or place or employment;
4.   to find caution of £50 within 6 weeks as a security
      for his good behaviour.

Date ...3.3.80.............

                                        Clerk of Court
                                   of High Street, Blacktown
                                        ....

NOTE: ...J. JONES.............

..Social Worker..........

                                   has been allocated as
                                   supervising officer in this case.

                                        Clerk of Court

Extra requirements

The subject of extra requirements was discussed above: many of these are possible
by virtue of specific sections of the 1975 or other Acts, and thus need to be
precisely worded in order to be legally competent; others have been expressed
in forms of words hallowed by practice and experience.

i.   Suggested Wording for Requirements of Probation Orders

      Work: "shall use his best endeavours to find and maintain
                   himself in gainful employment throughout the period
                   for which this order may be in force".

      Residental
      Control: "shall reside throughout the period for which this order

may be in force only at such address as shall have been approved in advance by his supervising officer".

Unpaid Work: "shall perform (number)........ hours of unpaid work of benefit to the community during the first 12 months of this order, as arranged and instructed by his supervising officer or by the designated local authority officer for community service purposes".

Drugs: "shall abstain throughout the period for which this order may be in force from taking prescribed drugs except in so far as they may be prescribed by a qualified medical practitioner".

Alcohol: "shall use his best endeavours to abstain throughout the period for which this order may be in force from the consumption of any form of alcoholic beverage".

Restitution   "shall make restitution to (named individual and address) of the sum of £... at the rate of £... per week OR at such weekly rate as may be required by his supervising officer".

Caution: "shall lodge with the Clerk of Court within .... weeks £.... caution for his good behaviour".

Variation of Probation

We noted above that the content of a probation order may need varying from time to time in circumstances where neither breach, nor discharge, nor the insertion of additional requirement, are contemplated.   One example would be that of a probationer, required to receive treatment as an in-patient for a mental condition, whose progress and response to that treatment prompts the doctor in charge of the treatment to the view that discharge from hospital would be appropriate before the twelve months has expired, but that nonetheless out-patient treatment should be continued.   The doctor cannot institute an application to the Court, and needs to work with and through the supervising officer.

Example:

The Clerk of Court,   Area Office: Blacktown
High Street,
BLACKTOWN.   Date: 3.3.80

Copy to Procurator Fiscal.

Dear Sir,

        Re: J. Smith, Brown Street, Blacktown.

The above-named appeared at Blacktown Sheriff Court on 5.9.79 for an offence of possessing drugs.   He was put on probation for 3 years.   It was an additional requirement of that order that he receive in-patient treatment at Blacktown hospital for 12 months.

I now apply in terms of Schedule 5 of the Criminal Procedures (Scotland) Act, 1975, that the order be varied as follows:-

1.   Delete the requirement that he receive in-patient
        treatment as noted above; and

2.   Substitute a requirement "that he receive out-patient
        treatment at Blacktown hospital under the medical
        supervision of Dr. Jones for the remainder of the
        first year of the order.

The reasons for this application are that Dr. Jones wishes to discharge Smith from
hospital as he considers that his original addiction to drugs is now sufficiently
reduced that it is appropriate to test him in ordinary society, but that he will
need continued psychiatric support which can be accomplished by seeing him as an
out-patient.

Yours faithfully,

C. Wood.
SOCIAL WORKER

Deletion of Requirement

Another instance of variation is the simple need to delete a requirement: an example
would be that of a probationer required to live in a hostel where progress justifies
his return home prior to the 12 month period of the original requirement.

Example:

The Clerk of Court,   Area Office: Blacktown
High Street,
BLACKTOWN.   Date: 3.3.80

Copy to the Procurator Fiscal.

Dear Sir,
            Re: J. Smith, Brown Street, Blacktown.

The above named appeared at Blacktown Sheriff Court on 5.7.79 when he was put on
probation for 30 months for offences of taking and driving away motor cars.   It
was an additional requirement of that order that he reside for 12 months in the
probation hostel known as Highfield House.

I now apply in terms of schedule 5 of the Criminal Procedure (Scotland) Act 1975
for that requirement to be deleted.   In the 8 months he has been at the hostel he
has done very well and also the situation at home has improved and he has been on
weekend leave quite successfully.   It is the view of both the hostel staff and
myself that the time has come to return him home permanently, and that is the
reason for this application.

Yours faithfully,

C. Wood
SOCIAL WORKER

Transfer of Probation

We have outlined the circumstances in which probation orders require to be transferred, and the action of the relevant social worker.

When a court makes a probation order on an offender resident in another area, the clerk of court sends all copies of the probation order to the supervising court in that area, and to the Director of Social Work or Chief Probation Officer as appropriate.   The only instances in which the court duty social worker needs a copy of the order are those in which the probationer is to be either an in-patient at a hospital, or the subject of a requirement of residence in a named institution: in these circumstances the escorting social worker needs a copy of the order before the probationer can legitimately be admitted to either.   Otherwise the only action the court duty social worker needs to make is to despatch a formal notification to the effect that an order has been made.

Example:

    The Director of Social Work)
or The Chief Probation Officer) as appropriate.

Dear Sir,
              Re: J. Smith, 12 Green Lane, Southbank, Blacktown.

The above named appeared today at Blacktown Sheriff Court when he was put on pro-bation for 18 months for an offence of possessing an offensive weapon.

Copies of the probation order will be sent to you by the clerk of court, but I enclose for your information copy of social enquiry report,
                              "   "   complaint (or indictment)
                              "   "   court referral form (if used)
                              "   "   the interview record.

Smith was provided with his fare and appropriate subsistence in order to assist him to return home.   He was given a verbal explanation of the requirements of probation and indicated that he understood them.   He was told to await reporting or other instructions, but to contact the nearest office in the event of either difficulty or a change of address or employment.

Yours faithfully,

C. Wood
SOCIAL WORKER

Transfer During the Currency of the Order:

Before formal transfer can be arranged through the court, the supervising officer needs to check the information provided by the probationer and to ascertain that transfer is both possible and acceptable.

Example:

The Director of Social Work.   Area Office: Blacktown.

                                        Date: 3.3.80

Dear Sir,
              Re: J. Smith, Brown Street, Blacktown.

The above named appeared at Blacktown Sheriff Court on 5.7.79 when he was put on probation for one year for fraud.

He has indicated his intention to move to 12 Green Lane, Southbank which I believe

to be in your area: I am led to believe this is the house of his sister-in-law,
with whom he now proposes to live. I would be grateful if the address could be
visited and the postiion ascertained. I should point out that the order contains
an additional requirement that he perform 60 hours of unpaid work of service to the
community, and to date he has performed 40 hours. Could you please indicate,
should the information prove to be correct, that you are prepared to accept supervision, and if so, the name and address of the supervising officer. Moreover I
would be grateful if you could confirm that arrangements exist in your area for him
to perform the remaining 20 hours unpaid work.

Yours faithfully,

C. Wood,
SOCIAL WORKER

It will be appreciated that the terms of the C.S.O. (S) Act do not permit the
transfer of such 'unpaid work' requirements to England and Wales, and if in this
instance the given address was outwith Scotland, the letter would reflect this
and indicate that on acceptance of supervision, that requirement would be deleted.
Subsequently the application to the court would be in a form such as the following:-

Example:

The Clerk of Court,   Area Office: Blacktown
High Street,
Blacktown.   Date: 3.3.80

Copy to: The Procurator Fiscal
           Future Supervising Officer

Dear Sir,
                  Re: J. Smith, Brown Street, Blacktown.

The above named appeared at Blacktown Sheriff Court on 5.7.79 when for an offence
of fraud he was put on probation for one year, with the additional requirement that
he perform 60 hours of unpaid work of service to the community.

Smith has notified me that he intends to live at 12 Green Lane, Southbank, which is
the home of his sister-in-law. This information has been verified. The appropriate court to which transfer should be made is the Southbank Sherriff Court, and
I have verified that arrangements exist in that area for Smith to complete the
remaining hours of unpaid work and to be supervised in terms of the order.

Accordingly, I apply in terms of paragraph 2 of the fifth schedule of the Criminal
Procedure (Scotland) Act 1975 that the probation order be amended to give effect to
the necessary transfer, and I enclose a copy of the existing order for the purpose.

Yours faithfully,

C. Wood,
SOCIAL WORKER

Transfer from England and Wales:

It can happen that probation officers in England and Wales, being unsure of arrangements in Scotland, either attempt to transfer orders direct to Scotland, or make
enquiries of social workers about their probationers who may become resident in
Scotland. A helpful response to them could be made along the following lines.

Example:

To: the probation and after-care officer.

Dear Mrs Black,
          Re: David Carmichael, Back Street, Blacktown

Thank you for your letter of 3rd inst. and I have been able to confirm that David does live at the address given, and I have established contact with him and arranged to see him.   I am able to accept transfer of the order, and all its requirements are enforceable in this area.

I would point out that in Scotland the structure and jurisdiction of the courts are different, and the procedure for transfer of probation orders is governed by the Criminal Procedure (Scotland) Act, 1975.

The Order will be supervised by Blacktown Sheriff Court, and the practice in this area is that the name and address of the supervising officer should appear on the order.   I would be grateful therefore if your Clerk to the Justices, when your court transfers the order, would either endorse or amend it, to the effect that:-

> "whereas the said David Carmichael will henceforward
> be resident at (new address), the court orders said
> David Carmichael to be under the supervision of
> C. Wood, Social Worker, Blacktown, in the Seacliffe
> Region."

The order should then be forwarded to The Clerk of Court, High Street, Blacktown. I should be grateful if your case records and/or other information could be sent directly to me as soon as transfer is effected.

Yours sincerely,

C. Wood,
SOCIAL WORKER

Breach of Requirement of Probation

Full details of the procedure to be followed are set out in the text. The supervising officer needs to complete the following two documents:-

i)   Information Document:

   This is the basis of the allegation that a breach of requirement has occurred.

   Example:

BREACH OF PROBATION
In terms of sections 186 or 387 of the
Criminal Procedure (Scotland) Act, 1975.

The Clerk of Court.

Copy to Procurator Fiscal.

INFORMATION

Whereas J. Smith (d.o.b.)
who resides at 12 Brown Street, Blacktown
appeared before the

Blacktown Sheriff Court
on 20th January, 1979

in respect of an offence of

assault to severe injury

and the Court, upon his expressed willingness to comply with the requirements thereof, made a probation order for a period of 2 years, placing him under my supervision,
I have to report to the Court that during the currency of the said order, the afore-
said J. Smith has failed to observe the requirements of the order in that -

He did fail to notify a change of address on or about
7th November, 1979.

Signed.

C. Wood,
SOCIAL WORKER

ii) Deponing:

The social worker and the appropriate judge before whom the deponing occurs
both need to sign the following document, as it authorises the citation or
arrest of the probationer, and his appearance subsequently before the court.
In the example, the section of the document authorising the summoning (i.e.
the citation) of the probationer has been deleted, as in the stated circumstances his whereabouts are unknown.   As the form of documentation used provides, on the same sheet, for either method some confusion can arise if the
social worker is not familiar with the procedure, although the handling of the
matter, once the social worker has completed his part, rests with the Court
Clerk.

Example:

Oath of social worker   dated: 3 March 1980.

Compeared: Christopher Wood, social worker

Within designated, who being solemnly sworn and examined depones that the said
John Smith has failed to observe the requirements of the foregoing probation
order in that he did:
                          fail to notify a change of address on or
                          about 7th November, 1979.

All of which in truth, as the deponent shall answer to God.

Signed: C. Wood,
        SOCIAL WORKER

Warrant to Summon

The Court grants warrant to officers of the law to summon the said accused to
appear for conviction and sentence on ... at ... o'clock.

Warrant to apprehend:

Eo die.   The court hereby grants warrant to apprehend the said accused.
Signed: P. M'Cann
(Judge of the appropriate Court)

Breach of Probation by further offence:

Any offence committed by a person on probation, during the currency of the order,
even if that offence only comes to notice after the date on which the order terminated, must be brought to the notice of the court which holds the order, by the
supervising officer.   The single exception to this rule relates to instances
where the court deals with the offence on which the probation order was founded at
the same time as it deals with the new offence.

Problems arise for supervisors when probationers appear in 'distant' courts for
offences, sometimes of a minor nature and that court disposes of the matter without
reference to the social worker holding the order, and the probationer then does not
declare this fact to the supervisor.   Where the supervisor does have knowledge of
the further offence then the formal procedure takes the following form:

Example:

To the Clerk of Court.

Copy to Procurator Fiscal
  "   " S. W. Departmental file.   Dated: 3 March 1980

BREACH OF PROBATION
In terms of section 187 (or 388) of the
Criminal Procedure (Scotland) Act, 1975.

INFORMATION

        Re: John Smith,
            12 Brown Street,
            Blacktown.

The above named appeared before this court on 5.4.79 when he was placed on probation
for a period of two years, for an offence of causing death by dangerous driving.

He is under my supervision.

On 28th February, 1980 Smith appeared before the District Court at Elgin on a
charge of being drunk and incapable.   He was fined £5 which was paid at the bar.
The offence occurred following a wedding party at which Smith was a guest, and
involved two other persons also guests at the wedding.

The offence for which he was placed on probation had no connection with alcohol:
Smith's response to probation has, until this matter arose, been very good and in
all respects he is functioning within the terms of the order.   Because of this,
the view which is now presented for the consideration of the court is that no
further action should be taken in respect of the order, beyond a warning letter
which would be sent out over the signature of the Director of Social Work.

I would be obliged for the court's instructions on this matter.

G. More,
SOCIAL WORKER

The above enables the view of the supervisor to reach the court about this offence.
It is entirely a matter for the court's decision as to what action should thereafter be initiated, and beyond telling the probationer what steps have been taken
the supervisor should await instructions from the court before introducing any
measures, whether formal or informal respecting the breach of the order.

The rather exceptional circumstances used in the example enable a reasoned approach for the continuation of the order to be made.   It is an entirely different matter when the further offence is of the same or similar kind to the original one, and the time between the two is, perhaps a matter of weeks or a few months.   In such cases supervisors would be required to make a fuller statement about his social situation and response to the order, as the circumstances would appear to call for the order being called into question by the court which made it.

Discharge on the ground of bad behaviour

Dear Sir,

> Re: J. Smith,
>   Brown Street, Blacktown

The above named appeared at the Blacktown Sheriff Court on 10.12.79 when he was put on probation for one year for an offence of theft.

I have to inform the court that Smith appeared before the Sheriff Court at Ayr yesterday, and was sentenced to 2 years imprisonment.   In view of this I apply in terms of paragraph 1 of schedule 5 of the Criminal Procedure (Scotland) Act, 1975, for the probation order to be discharged.   Should the court not grant such an application, Smith is by virtue of this further offence in breach of his probation order, and the court may wish separate proceedings to be initiated against him on that account.

Yours faithfully,

C. Wood
SOCIAL WORKER

Discharge on the grounds of good progress

We suggested in the text that greater use might be made of this provision.   The procedure is brief and straightforward.

Example:

The Clerk of Court,   Area Office: Blacktown
High Street,
Blacktown.   Date: 3.3.80

Copy to Procurator Fiscal

Dear Sir,

> Re: J. Smith,
>   Brown Street, Blacktown

The above named appeared at the Blacktown Sheriff Court on 4.2.79 when, for offences of assault and breach of the peace he was put on probation for 2 years.

I apply in terms of paragraph 1 of schedule 5 of the Criminal Procedure (Scotland) Act, 1975 that the order be discharged ahead of time on the grounds of good progress.   I have ascertained that no further offences have been committed by Smith Since the order was made, and that no matters are outstanding against him.

Briefly the offence was a domestic dispute involving his wife, and as a result of my involvement with both of them during the past months I consider that the circumstances which produced that offence are unlikely to occur, and that the couple would be likely to contact me voluntarily in the event of any future difficulty.

Yours faithfully,

C. Wood,
SOCIAL WORKER

Termination of Probation where a Requirement for Caution has been included.

Reference has been made to the possible inclusion of a requirement in probation orders that the accused finds caution as a security for his good behaviour.   Before this can be redeemed by the probationer, the court will need confirmation from the supervising officer that he has been of good behaviour, and an initiative in this matter by the supervising officer would not be out of place.

The Clerk of Court,   Area Office: Blacktown.
High Street,
Blacktown.   Date: 3.3.80

Copy to the Procurator Fiscal.

Dear Sir,
            Re: J. Smith,
                  Brown Street, Blacktown

The above named appeared at the Blacktown Sheriff Court on 4.3.78 when, for an offence of breach of the peace, he was put on probation for a year.   It was an additional requirement of the order that he lodge £20 within 4 weeks as a security for his good behaviour.

The probation order terminates today in the ordinary course of events.   I have ascertained that the sum of £20 was lodged within the stipulated period, and that Smith has committed no further offence while on probation: I also regard his response to supervision as satisfactory.

In my view the security of £20 may therefore be refunded.

Yours faithfully,

C. Wood,
SOCIAL WORKER

Chapter 7

Community Service and Unpaid Work

The power of courts to order offenders to perform unpaid service for the community is relatively new. It first became available to courts in England and Wales in 1972: the relevant legislation for those countries is now the Powers of Criminal Courts Act, 1973. In Scotland, the relevant legislation is the Community Service by Offenders (Scotland) Act 1978. Community Service as a disposal is unique in that both these Acts allow for the variable and gradual implementation of its use according to the availability of resources.

The existence of an unacceptably high number of people in prison was a crucial factor behind the introduction of community service as a disposal available to criminal courts. In England and Wales, the 1967 Criminal Justice Act had introduced the suspended sentence as an alternative to direct imprisonment, and in 1970 the Advisory Council on the Treatment of Offenders was commissioned with the task of suggesting additional measures. The publication of its report "Non - and Semi-custodial penalties" (generally known as the Wootton Report) was the chief stimulus to development South of the border.

The Wootton Report discussed the possible introduction of community service either as a requirement of a probation order, or as a separate new disposal in its own right. In the circumstances of the time, it was decided that the latter course had greater merit. The task of administering the new order was given to the Probation Service, and the Home Secretary has been able to notify courts across England and Wales that they can use such orders as soon as the probation services in the relevant areas have been able to establish schemes which meet his criteria.

In England and Wales community service for offenders is only available as a disposal in its own right - the community service order. In Scotland developments have taken a different course. In 1975, "experimental" schemes of community service for offenders were announced by Government and four areas invited to initiate them. There was no separate or new legislation available, and in all four areas the probation order was used as the means of introducing community service into the range of disposals available to the courts. Opinions and approaches had varied about the merits of using probation in this way, but now the 1978 Community Service by Offenders (Scotland) Act has made two methods of disposal possible. The new Act has introduced a separate community service order, virtually on the English model; but has also introduced specific legislation for "unpaid work" to be made a requirement of a probation order.

Even with only the one disposal method as available in England and Wales, community service schemes have shown varying characteristics and emphases, both in regard to how courts use orders from a sentencing point of view, and also in regard to the management of placements and work performance. Even so the situation had some advantages of simplicity: the offender's obligation was simply to do unpaid work for the community as an alternative to imprisonment; and the public at large might regard such orders as having strong retributive and punitive elements, administered more cheaply and perhaps more humanely than sentences of imprisonment.

The introduction in statute of a specific requirement in a probation order to perform "unpaid work" is a departure from the accepted formula that probation is intended to provide advice, assistance and befriending to the offender. This departure may open the way to an enlarged concept of probation which combines "get help" with "give help". This could in turn provide a fresh focus for work with probationers, such that the community service/unpaid work placement is taken up into the overall "contract" made with the offender, whereby not only may the community's awareness be encouraged and used in the intervention, but the offender also encouraged to re-examine his general attitudes to and participation in society. However it remains that the whole of the probation order, what we have referred to as the probation "contract", is greater than any one of its parts, and under the arrangements introduced by the 1978 Act is not intended as the probation order merely the adopted or disguised vehicle for the ordering of unpaid work if that is all that is intended.

The Community Service Order

The objective of introducing community service into criminal justice legislation has been to extend the range of non-custodial disposals available to courts as alternatives to imprisonment. The first consideration, therefore, for any social worker or report writer contemplating suggesting such a disposal to a court is to adjudge the likelihood of the offender receiving a custodial sentence. The possible benefits of the offender's performance of community service to himself or even to the community are secondary considerations; of themselves they do not necessarily warrant a recommendation for a community service disposal per se, if other existing non-custodial measures seem appropriate. The Government have been at pains to emphasise their intention that the community service order should be used as an alternative to imprisonment.

One of the attractions to courts of the community service order is said to be its adaptability to a variety of sentencing considerations. In common parlance it is described as an alternative to "short" sentences of imprisonment without any accompanying definition of what constitutes brevity in this context. It is important that social workers familiarise themselves with the particular aims and interpretations of the scheme in the area where the offender resides or is to reside, and with the mind of the court which is to deal with him.

Community Service Orders are made in Scotland under Section 1 of the Community Service by Offenders (Scotland) Act 1978. They can be made on any person "of or over 16 years of age convicted of an offence punishable by imprisonment, other than an offence for which the penalty is fixed by law". The order must specify the number of hours of community service which the offender must perform, but this number may not be less than 40, and may not exceed 240. The hours are normally to be completed within 12 months of the making of the order, but the order remains in force until the hours have been completed, or the order revoked.

A number of provisos apply to the making of orders under S.1 of the 1978 Act:

    i)   The offender must consent to the making of the order.

    ii)   The court must have been notified by the Secretary of State
         that a scheme exists in the area in which the offender
         resides or is to reside.

    iii) The court must have considered a report "by an officer of a
         local authority" about the offender and his circumstances,
         together with an assessment as to his suitability for
         community service.

In England and Wales, community service orders are made by virtue of Section 14 of
the Powers of Criminal Courts Act 1973. The differences are:

    i)   The offender must be 17 or over.

    ii)   The court must consider a social enquiry report.

    iii) The "officer" will be a probation officer appointed or assigned
         to a Petty Sessional Division.

When S.6 of the Scottish Act is activated, community service orders can be made
by a court in either country on offenders resident in either country, subject to
all the relevant provisos, and appropriate transfer arrangements exist if an
offender moves during the currency of an order.

The community service order, of which the offender will receive a copy will
contain a number of detailed requirements to which he must adhere (S.2 of the 1978
Act). The central one is that he must perform the number of hours of service
ordered by the court and stated in the order. Others derive directly from this,
and simply have to do with the mechanics of making arrangements for the service to
be performed:

they are:

a)   report to or as instructed by the officer appointed for community service
      purposes.

b)   notify at once any change of address or employment.

Over and above these standard conditions in any community service order a
Scottish Court (but not an English one) may also order:

    i)   the offender to find caution
and/
 or ii) impose any disqualification appropriate to the offence.
and/
 or iii) make an order for forfeiture in respect of any article used
         in the commission of the offence

The order does not contain any generalised commands to "be of good behaviour" or
"conform to the directions of the supervising officer" familiar from probation
orders. Nor is there any legal duty on the "officer appointed" for community
services purposes to "advise, assist and befriend" persons under his charge.
Indeed, the criteria developed for the making of community service orders have
stressed the point that an offender in need of counselling or assistance with

personal problems may be unsuitable for this disposal method. The community
service order, notwithstanding that the offender must consent to it, represents a
conviction.

Unpaid work as a requirement of probation: The Community Service by Offenders
(Scotland) Act 1978, has now introduced to Scotland specific legislation for
offenders to perform unpaid work as a requirement in a probation order. Prior to
its enactment, courts had used probation as a means of ordering community service
but there had been a degree of unease in some quarters at its use for something so
specific and substantial as community service. Section 7 of the new Act now
regularises the position by creating a new subsection, 5A, in sections 183 and
384 of the Criminal Procedure (Scotland) Act 1975. We deal with this subject in
detail in the context of the probation order.

Community Service Orders made on a breach of probation: Not only has the
Community Service by Offenders (Scotland) Act made available two different
methods for the ordering of community service or unpaid work, it has also introduced a new possibility in relation to a breach of requirement of probation.
Section 8 of the Act makes it possible for a community service order to be made on
a breach of requirement of probation, without prejudice to the continuation of the
order. Previously the only substantial penalty available in such circumstances,
if the order was to remain in force, was a fine not exceeding £50: otherwise the
only possibilities were to vary the order or to terminate it.

Even without Section 8's inclusion it would have been possible for a court in such
a circumstance:-

either   i)   to vary the probation order by the inclusion of a requirement
                  that the offender perform unpaid work

or   ii)   to sentence for the original offence, and make a community
                  service order in respect of that offence.

What Section 8 allows for is that an offender who has breached his probation
order, either in respect of one of its standard requirements (e.g. failure to
keep in touch), or in respect of any extra requirement (e.g. hostel residence,
or *even* of unpaid work), may now become the subject *both* of the original probation
order, which remains in force, *and* of a community service order. Even with
Section 8's inclusion the courses of action already outlined above as being available without it both remain as possibilities.

It seems that the intention of section 8 is to emphasise the availability of a
community service order in a situation where imprisonment might otherwise serve.
It is not to suggest that a community service order should be used as an alternative to a £50 fine where some relatively modest breach of probation has occurred.
The reason that the order is made to run concurrently with the existing probation
order is that the social work support originally considered necessary might still
be as or more needed in the circumstances of the breach that has occurred.

Terms of Service and Administrative Arrangements: Some details governing the
actual performance of community service are set out in the Act, and apply to both
community service orders and requirements for unpaid work in probation orders.

The court has to concern itself with detail in that:-

                                                                    Section

     1   The offender must consent   1(2)(a)

2   The number of hours must be specified   1(1)

3   It must satisfy itself that the offender is a   1(2)(c)
    suitable person to perform community service,
    and to that end consider certain reports, and/or
    hear the relevant officer of the local authority

4   It must satisfy itself that provision can be made   1(2)(b)
    under the arrangements made by the local authority,
    or in England and Wales, the probation service, in
    the locality in which the offender resides or is to
    reside

5   It must explain in ordinary language the offender's   1(4)
    obligations and liabilities

6   It must provide copies of the order for both the   2(3)
    offender, and the Director of Social Work. It
    must also be desirable for the placement agency
    to receive a copy, although that is not obligatory.

In his performance of community service, the offender has to relate to persons
other than a supervising officer, and it is therefore important that all concerned
in dealing with him are clear about the arrangements, and about accountability.
The Act says that the offender must "perform for the number of hours specified in
the order such work at such times as the local authority officer may instruct".
(Section 3(1)(b)).

However, Section 3(3) says that the instruction shall "so far as practicable avoid
any conflict with the offender's religious beliefs, or interfere with his normal
schooling or work".

A number of points arise:-

The offender consents to do work rather than do any particular type of service of
his choosing. This forms a background to whatever attempts are made to meet his
wishes, use his skills, or secure his motivation under the various approaches used
in the different schemes.

Under a separate community service order, the instructing local authority officer
will in the larger authorities probably be the designated community service
organiser or a member of his staff. Even so, schemes may delegate de facto
supervision of the offender's work performance to a voluntary agency or individual
not directly controlled by the Department. The offender is thus entitled to a
clear explanation of how the accountability is structured, and what his rightful
expectations of both the placement and of the local authority officer are.
Equally, there needs to be a clear contract between any voluntary agency or
individual, and the Department, particularly in view of community service's
status as a court disposal.

There is an additional dimension to this situation under a requirement for unpaid
work in a probation order. A supervising officer will be appointed for the
probation order who has overall responsibility for its implementation. Although
the wording of the requirement for unpaid work may not specify the involvement of
the community service organiser, these two will need to be clear about their
respective obligations and objectives. There is thus extra need that both the

placement agency and the offender should understand the position also. There is
nothing inherently unworkable in all this, even if it does appear to require a
high standard of practice skills.

The community service is an extra ingredient in the offender's life, to be fitted
into the normal rhythm of his work or education. This may be even more true if
the offender is unemployed, but in this instance care needs to be taken that his
performance of community service does not render him "unavailable for work" in the
eyes of the Department of Health and Social Security.

An offender performing community service under a separate order discharges his
responsibilities to the court immediately he satisfactorily completes the required
number of hours. The offender performing unpaid work as a requirement of a
probation order still faces the continuing constraints and supervision it entails.

The 1978 Act gives the Secretary of State power to make rules by way of a Statutory
Instrument to govern the arrangements for the performance of community service.
Such rules might usefully clarify the offender's rights and expectations on
community service, and make for a certain uniform minimum standard of practice
which would introduce a degree of equity in the administration of justice. No such
rules have been made at the time of going to Press. In England and Wales, the
whole range of probation and after-care services is governed by the existence of
such rules. In Scotland, the whole tenor of the Social Work (Scotland) Act made
for a separation of responsibilities between central and local government in
practice matters, and Section 27 abolished the whole administrative set-up which
had characterised - as it still does in England and Wales - the provision of social
work services for offenders. In the 1978 Act then, we have not only a new court
disposal, but new administrative and financial arrangements, relating only at
present to community service, but with a possible future significance beyond their
present importance.

Breaches of Orders

Some of the differences between community service orders and requirements for
unpaid work in probation orders become particularly apposite when the question of
breach arises. The two need separate consideration.

i)   Community Service orders. An offender who commits a further
                offence while subject to a community service order is not in
                breach of that order per se - even though action may need to
                be taken in relation to that order as a result of the sentence
                he receives for the further offence. As far as the community
                service order itself is concerned, the *only* breach proceedings
                to be initiated relate to a breach of requirement of the order
                (Section 4 of the 1978 Act). A breach of requirement may be
                constituted by:-

                i)   failure to perform the work as instructed

                ii) failure to complete the number of hours in 12 months

                iii) failure to perform the work satisfactorily;

                iv) failure to report any change of address or employment

                The decision about breach proceedings is the responsibility
                of the supervising officer. A breach of requirement cannot
                be prosecuted before a court without proceedings being
                initiated by him. Once the decision to initiate proceedings
                is taken, the actual procedure is the same as for a breach of

requirement of probation. Information has to be laid; the
officer has to "depone"; and the court arranges for the
offender to be brought before it. If the case is proved the
court can do one of four things (Section 4 of the 1978 Act):-

It can:

Impose any penalty in respect of the original offence it
might have done had it not made a community service order.

or   Fine not exceeding £50 and let the order continue.

or   Vary the number of hours, except that the overall total
ordered may not exceed 240 hours, and let the order continue.

or   Take no action, and let the order continue.

ii)   **Requirements for unpaid work in probation orders.** An offender
who commits a further offence while subject to a probation
order with a requirement for unpaid work is by definition in
breach of the whole order of which that requirement is a part.
Should the court which deals with the new offence not be
competent to   deal with the original offence for which the
order was made, the supervising officer must inform the court
which made the order of the new offence. The responsibilities
and procedures are precisely those for a breach of probation by
commission of a further offence, and reference should be made,
under this head, for the procedures which require to be followed.

An offender who fails to perform his unpaid work as instructed,
or satisfactorily, or within 12 months, is in breach of a
requirement of probation, and proceedings may be taken against
him on that account, if that is the decision. The responsibility
for initiating action in this case is with the officer supervising
the whole probation order, even if the evidence to support the
allegation is provided by the community service organiser or a
member of his staff, and the procedures are identical with
those for a breach of requirement of probation, set out at that
reference above. As the law now stands any offender who
breaches a requirement of a probation order for unpaid work
is equally liable to be dealt with for the original offence
in respect of which that order was made; or to have the probation
order varied: the requirement for unpaid work might be the one
to be varied.

iii)   **Community Service Order made on a Breach of Probation.** We
mentioned above,in context, that it is possible, under Section
8 of the 1978 Act, to make a community service order in respect
of a breach of requirement of probation without prejudice to the
probation order remaining in force. The question of breach proceedings
becomes very complex in this situation.

If the offender fails to perform, or to perform satisfactorily,
a community service order which has been made in this way, he
becomes liable to any of the penalties listed above
without prejudice to the continuation of the community service
order, or of the original probation order.

However the "original offence" in the context of a community

service order made under Section 8 is a breach of requirement
of probation. If the community service order thus made is not
to remain in force once a breach of its requirements (i.e. only
in regard to work performance) has occured, the penalties open
to the court are those available at the stage at which the
breach of requirement of probation was originally proved. If
the probation order is to remain in force, those penalties
are a fine of up to only £50, together with any variations in
the other contents of the probation order.

It would appear that the original offence in this context is
the breach of requirement of the Probation order and in dealing
with it, the original Probation order should be allowed to
continue. This situation is both unclear and unsatisfactory
and significantly the equivalent provision in the powers of the
Criminal Courts 1973 Act has never been activated.

In our view this complex duality of orders is to be avoided.

Revocation and Amendment

Section 5 of the 1978 Act gives courts powers to revoke and amend Community service
orders. The Section is particularly designed to cater for circumstances which
arise after orders are made. As with breaches of orders, community service has
to be considered as a disposal in its own right. The considerations which apply
to requirements in a probation order are quite different.

Community Service Orders. The possiblility of revocation applies only to community
service orders. An application for revocation can be made either by the supervising officer or by the offender. These are the possible outcomes of such an
application:-

i)   The court may finish the order ahead of time, without the
            offender suffering any penalty.

ii)   The court may vary the order by changing the number of hours
            or by extending the 12 month period.

iii)   The court may deal with the original offence in any way it
            could have done at the time had an order not been made.

iv)   The court may take no action.

If the third course of action is anticipated or intended, it seems to us important
that the procedures are such that the offender is heard by the court, and the
rules of natural justice observed. This detail is not set out in the Act.

The provision for revocation is designed to cover the following possible
situations:-

            To reward good progress ahead of time. For an example, an
            offender may find a deep commitment to the service he is
            performing such that either reducing the hours or finishing
            the order completely may enhance his standing as a more
            willing volunteer with the agency.

            By virtue of changed personal circumstances - for example,
            a new job - the offender cannot be found suitable community

service work, and it is not considered in the interests of
justice that he should be penalised for this change. In this
instance, termination or appropriate variation is sought, not
a penalty nor a sentence for the original offence.

The offender moves to an area where no scheme exists. This
is a delicate situation, in that a judgement as to the
offender's motive for such a move is involved. If it is judged
that he is trying to evade the order, he cannot be breached if
he notifies the change of address, but an application for
revocation can be made, with a sentence for the original offence
being a likely outcome. If his move is not so motivated, the
situation is akin to a simple change of personal circumstances
as suggested above.

Requirements for unpaid work in Probation Orders. There is no separate power to
"revoke" probation orders. They can be discharged as the grounds of good progress,
and it may well be that successful commitment to a requirement for unpaid work
would justify such an application if all the other objectives of the order were
also attained. Probation orders can also be varied to take account of personal
circumstances, and one possible such variation is the deletion of the requirement
for unpaid work if it becomes impracticable for the offender to perform it.

The offender subject to a requirement for unpaid work who moves to an area where
there is no community service scheme with the intention of avoiding that requirement presents a problem. Breach of requirement proceedings are not possible if
he notifies the change of address. The only solution is that the probation order
as such, with all its other requirements, can be transferred but before that is
done it must also be varied to delted the requirement for unpaid work. The
offender continues to be subject to the sanction of the court if he either commits
a further offence or breaches any of the other enforceable requirements, and in
the meantime, the new supervising officer will be seeking to reinforce the
offender's commitment to avoiding further trouble.

Transfers and Cross-Border Problems

Community Service Orders. Following Commencement Order No.2 (April 1980)
courts in Scotland are now able to make community service orders on offenders
resident in England and Wales provided they are aware that a scheme exists in the
area concerned. Such a scheme, however, being established in connection with the
Power of Criminal Courts Act, could not accommodate 16 year olds, even though a
community service order would be competent for a Scottish court had the 16 year
old been resident in an area of Scotland where a scheme existed.

Transfers within Scotland are entirely straightforward, provided a scheme is
available. The procedures adopted should ensure that some certificate is also
transferred showing the number of hours already worked by the offender, in the
event of such transfer being made during the currency of an order.

Requirements for unpaid work in Probation Orders. That part of the Community
Service by Offenders (Scotland) Act 1978, which empowers courts to include in
probation orders a requirement for community service extends only to Scotland.
Courts in England and Wales cannot include in probation orders made by them
requirements for unpaid work, even though the offender may be resident in Scotland.
Scottish courts cannot make probation orders with requirements for unpaid work on
offenders resident in England and Wales, and if the community service were the
chief consideration would have to make a community service order.

Any offender resident in Scotland who is the subject of a probation order which includes a requirement for unpaid work who moves to England or Wales during the currency of the order but before the requirement is completed poses a problem. Revocation proceedings are not available for probation orders, and no breach of requirement occurs if he notifies the move.   The probation order is transferable if the requirement for community service is first deleted: the best that could be hoped for is that the offender could be persuaded to perform work voluntarily in England, and negotiations with the new supervising officer would also be necessary to see if this was a practical possibility.

Breaches of Community Service Orders.   Courts in England and Wales which are dealing with either breaches of requirement or with applications for revocation in respect of an order originally made in Scotland cannot deal with the original offence.   They can take any of the other measures (fine up to £50 or variation) which allow the order to continue without making any reference to Scotland but must remit the case back to the original Scottish court if their decision is that sentence for the original offence is appropriate.   The Scottish court would not be bound by that decision, and might let the order continue, and transfer it back again to the jurisdiction of the court for the area in which the offender resides. We sense that such a course is unlikely.   Authority is to be found at Schedule 1. of the 78 Act,(which is dependent on the implementation of S6 of the Act).

Breaches of requirements for unpaid work in Probation Orders.   There are no cross-border problems under this heading because neither is it competent for an English or Welsh court to make a probation order with such a requirement; nor for a Scottish court to make a probation order with such a requirement on an offender who resides or is to reside in England and Wales.

PART FOUR: CUSTODIAL MEASURES

Chapter 8

Prison Sentences; Sentences for Young Offenders;
Detention of Children; Residential Training for Children

The courts have power to order various custodial measures in respect of crimes and
offences. A number of factors influence the length and type of any custodial
measure imposed - the level of court; the nature of the offence; the extent of
previous criminality; the age of the offender; the specific penalties or provisions
of any relevant statute. Whatever sentence a court may impose in respect of a man,
it may also impose in respect of a woman, except that there is no Detention Centre
for female young offenders; however, the sentences will be served in single-sex
institutions. No person can be admitted as an inmate to any penal establishment
except by express sentence or order of the court, or by administrative decision
under certain statutory orders where the court does not specify the type of
institution in which the offender is to be held. All penal establishments are
under the control of the Secretary of State, who exercises his control through
Prisons Division of the Home and Health Department.

(1) Sentences of Imprisonment

   i) Powers of Courts.   The powers of courts to impose sentences
       are governed mainly by the type of procedure being used, and
       by the level of court hearing the case. Sheriff Courts cannot
       impose sentences of imprisonment of more than 2 years in cases
       on solemn procedure: and generally cannot impose sentences
       of more than 6 months imprisonment in cases on summary
       procedure. District Courts cannot impose prison sentences
       in excess of 60 days. Occasionally, a particular statute
       may give a (Sheriff) summary court powers in excess of
       6 months (e.g. the Police (Scotland) Act 1967 allows for
       sentences of 9 months imprisonment for assaults on police
       officers). Within these general boundaries, courts have
       discretion to adapt the length of sentence to the circumstances
       of the individual offender and of his offending, past and
       present. Increasingly, the tendency is towards individual-
       isation of sentences, with the hope that the use of imprison-
       ment will be considered only as a last resort.

  ii) Consecutive and concurrent sentences.   Offenders who face
       the court on a number of charges may receive sentences of
       imprisonment in respect of each charge. It is important
       to determine whether these sentences are imposed consecutively

or concurrently. Also, such sentences may be imposed
consecutively to, or concurrently with, a sentence which
the offender may already be serving.

Examples

a) Y receives two sentences, one of 18, the other of 15
   months imprisonment, to run consecutively: that means
   he receives a total of 33 months imprisonment.

b) Z receives two sentences, one of 3, the other of 6
   months imprisonment, to run concurrently: that means
   he will serve in effect, a 6 month sentence.

c) X, who has already served 2 months of a 6 month sentence,
   receives a further sentence of 6 months imprisonment:

   if imposed concurrently, he will serve 6 months,
   starting from the later date;

   if imposed consecutively, he will commence serving
   the new 6 month sentence on the day after he would
   otherwise have been released from prison in respect
   of the earlier sentence.

   It should be noted that the Sheriff Summary Court, which
   only has power to order a sentence of 6 months, cannot,
   when dealing with an offender who faces more than one
   charge, impose sentences which *in total* amount to more
   than 6 months. It is further worthy of mention that
   courts of solemn procedure have the power to order that
   a prison sentence shall take effect as from the date that
   the accused was first committed for trial - though the
   date on which sentence is imposed may be some weeks later:
   alternatively, the court may indicate, in passing sentence,
   that any pre-trial period of custody has been 'allowed for'
   in determining the actual length of sentence to be served.

iii) Determinate sentences. The great majority of prison
     sentences are determinate - that is of fixed length. All
     such sentences automatically carry a period of 'remission':
     this period is equivalent to one third of the period of
     sentence, and is dependent on the offender's good conduct
     in prison. However, there is no remission on sentences of
     less than 31 days. Prison Governors have power to order up
     to 14 days loss of remission if the prisoner offends against
     discipline: for more serious breaches of prison discipline
     the offender can be referred to the Visiting Committee
     (there is one for each penal establishment) who can award
     forfeiture of remission up to the maximum amount which can
     be earned on the sentence being served. The majority of
     offenders leave prison having retained their full remission:
     once thus discharged, they are no longer under the control
     of the prison or the court in respect of that offence, and
     their sentence is at an end.

iv) Other sentences. There exist a number of other sentences
    which the courts may impose:-

    a) Life Imprisonment. Life imprisonment is the fixed

penalty for any offence of murder committed by an
adult. The sentence is also available as one of the
penalties in some very serious cases. Young Offenders
convicted of murder receive sentences where technical
designation is slightly different, but where substantive
effect is virtually identical.

Judges have power, when imposing a sentence of life
imprisonment, to make a recommendation as to the
minimum length of time which they consider such an
offender should serve in custody prior to release on
licence.

The release from prison of persons sentenced to life
imprisonment is a matter for the Secretary of State.
His powers in this respect were originally laid down
in the 1949 Criminal Justice (Scotland) Act at Section
57: he was empowered to release such persons "at any
time . . . subject to compliance with such conditions,
if any, as (he) may from time to time determine". There
is also power to recall any such person to prison at any
time, but this does not necessarily preclude the person's
subsequent release under the same original sentence.

Since the enactment of the 1967 Criminal Justice Act, the
Parole Board can recommend to the Secretary of State that
a person serving a life sentence should be released on
licence. Before doing so, the Secretary of State is required to consult with the Lord Justice General and with
the Trial Judge, if available. In practice, the cases of
persons serving life sentences are reviewed and considered
by the Parole Board in a fashion akin to normal parole
cases. The arrangements for social work supervision of
such persons work similarly. Although, in the nature of
the sentence, the person will be subject to licence for
life, it is possible for the reporting and supervision
requirements to be reviewed and amended, as appropriate,
in such a licence, if the progress of the offender over
a sufficient period of time justifies it.

b) Corrective Training. Section 21 of the Criminal Justice
(Scotland) Act 1949, empowered Courts to pass a sentence
of corrective training in certain circumstances. The
pre-conditions were:-

the offender is 21 or over

the offender is appearing before a court of solemn
procedure and is convicted of an offence punishable
with imprisonment for 2 years or more; and

he has on at least two occasions since attaining
the age of 17 been convicted of offences similarly
punishable; and

the court must be satisfied that such a sentence
is expedient with a view to his reformation and
the prevention of crime.

A sentence of corrective training could then be passed

in lieu of any other sentence, and would be for a period
of between 2 and 4 years determined by the court.   The
'corrective' element refers to the type of regime the
offender would experience in prison in comparison with
an ordinary prison sentence of similar length.   Moreover,
the offender sentenced to corrective training was subject
to supervision on release, under conditions determined by
the Secretary of State, and in accordance with the Prison
Rules.

c) <u>Preventive detention</u>.   Section 21 of the 1949 Act also
allowed for preventive detention.   The pre-conditions
were:-

the offender was age 30 or over; and

the offender was convicted in the High Court of an
offence punishable with imprisonment for a term of
2 years or more; and

he had been convicted on indictment on at least three
previous occasions since attaining the age of 17 of
offences similarly punishable;

on two of those three occasions he received a sentence
of borstal, imprisonment, or corrective training;

the court was satisfied that it was expedient for the
protection of the public that the offender should be
detained in custody for a substantial time.

A sentence of preventive detention would be of not less
than 5 and not more than 14 years.   The intention of such
a sentence was to protect the public, as opposed to the
aim of corrective training to provide a particular regime
for the offender.   The length of a sentence of preventive
detention would be fixed by the court, but may well have
exceeded the length of sentence that would ordinarily have
been imposed simply in relation to the particular offence:
the sentence was intended for the persistent serious
criminal.   The sentence was also followed by supervision
on release.

Corrective Training and Preventive Detention

It is important to have a knowledge of these sentences, as
occasionally they crop up as C.T. or P.D. in lists of previous
convictions and also in respect of the provisions of the
Rehabilitation of Offenders Act, 1974, which relate to them.

These sentences were abolished in England and Wales by the
Criminal Justice Act of 1967, but in their place was introduced the Extended Sentence of Imprisonment: it seems to
combine elements of both the earlier concepts, and the new
sentence does involve supervision on release.   In Scotland
the sentences of corrective training and preventive detention
do not appear to have been specifically repealed: provision
for them is not contained within the consolidating Criminal
Procedure (Scotland) Act 1975, but nor does schedule 10 of
that Act actually repeal section 21 of the 1949 Act.   The
sentences do not appear to have been used in Scotland in

recent years, but the Extended Sentence of Imprisonment
is not available to Scottish courts.

v) <u>Prison regimes</u>.   The running of prisons is governed by
   Prison Rules: in the words of Rule 5, "the purpose of
   the training and treatment of convicted prisoners shall
   be to establish in them the will to lead good and useful
   lives on discharge, and to fit them to do so". A related
   point is expressed in the saying that offenders go to
   prison "as" punishment and not "for" punishment.

   a) <u>Types of Prison</u>.   Prisons are of various types. Courts
      commit directly to 'local' prisons which therefore receive
      all categories of prisoner in the first instance. There
      are only two 'open' prisons in Scotland, one at Penninghame,
      near Newton Stewart, which caters for about 80 prisoners,
      and one at Dungavel in Lanarkshire. Most prisoners serve
      their sentences in 'closed' prisons. Apart from factors
      such as length of sentence, prisoners will also be grouped
      according to the degree of security risk they represent to
      the public. Any one institution may contain a variety of
      sections, variously termed 'wings' or 'halls', dependent
      on the physical nature of the building: there may be
      remand sections; training sections; secure sections; and
      so on. For the convicted prisoner, factors such as
      proximity to family, employment skills and other individ-
      ualised factors are less likely to be determinate of where
      he will serve his sentence than sheer availability of
      cells and hard facts about the nature and location of
      Scotland's prisons.

   b) <u>Women prisoners</u>.   Women offenders serve their sentences,
      and are held on remand, at Cornton Vale, near Stirling.
      This new prison also acts as a young offenders'
      institution for all female prisoners in Scotland so
      sentenced.

   c) <u>Letters</u>.   All the incoming and outgoing mail of
      prisoners will be censored by the prison authorities.
      All prisoners can receive an unlimited amount of in-
      coming mail, but may only write one free letter out per
      week: any other letters they may wish to write have to
      be paid for out of the earnings they receive for the
      work done in the prison. However, all prisoners may
      ask for additional free letters in order to write to
      agents or social workers. 'Special' letters may be
      granted in exceptional circumstances at the discretion
      of the Governor, and prison social workers may be
      involved in the determination of such cases.

   d) <u>Visits</u>.   Prisoners serving sentences of less than 3
      months are allowed two 20-minute visits during their
      sentence and may choose when to have them. Prisoners
      serving 3 months or more are allowed two 20-minute
      visits during the first two months; and three visits
      during each additional two months. 'Special' visits
      may be granted in exceptional circumstances at the
      Governor's discretion: these may be suggested on
      welfare grounds by social workers working either

within or without the prison. All visits will be
supervised by prison officers.

Prisoners are normally allowed three adult visitors,
but if children accompany adults, the number is usually
reduced. If circumstances allow (e.g. pressure of
numbers of people visiting at any one time) visits may
in practice exceed the stated period. Also a prisoner
whose family live some distance away can be allowed to
accumulate visits. The Department of Health and Social
Security are empowered to pay a wife an extra lodging
allowance to allow her to stay overnight near a prison.

No visitor will be allowed into a prison without a pass
previously sent out by or on behalf of the prisoner
concerned. Social workers visiting for official
purposes should be aware of the visiting hours, and
have a means of identification on them.

(2) Custodial Sentences for Young Offenders

A whole range of separate and special provisions apply to young offenders
aged 16 but under 21 years. These provisions are now to be found in the
1980 Criminal Justice (Scotland) Act, but that Act has made some significant
changes to the previous arrangements; because of the recency of these changes,
it is necessary to consider the situation which applied for quite a number of
years prior to the enactment of this legislation.

i) Sentences prior to the 1980 Act. Prior to the 1980 Act
    there were three quite separate custodial sentences available
    for young offenders, and prison service institutions reflected
    the nomenclature, concepts, and aims, of these disposals.
    Briefly the sentences were:-

    a) Detention Centre training. The sentence of Detention
       Centre Training was introduced to Scotland by the Criminal
       Justice (Scotland) Act 1963, two years after its intro-
       duction in England and Wales. The sentence was a fixed
       one of 3 months: one month's remission for good conduct
       was available to inmates, but release was followed by a
       12 month period of statutory after-care licence. It was
       not competent to sentence offenders to Detention Centre
       Training if they had previously been in Borstal,
       Detention Centre or Young Offenders' Institution.
       Colloquially the sentence was referred to (following
       W.S.Gilbert) as a "short, sharp shock": the official
       HMSO handbook "The Sentence of the Court" said,
       "Detention Centres provide a means of treating young
       offenders for whom a long period of residential
       training away from home is not yet necessary or justified
       by their offence, but who cannot be taught respect for
       the law by such non-custodial measures as fines or
       probation. The regime is unsuited to those who are
       seriously handicapped physically or mentally.
       Reconviction statistics have disclosed a relative
       lack of success in dealing with such offenders."
       No detention centre for females ever existed, in
       Scotland, and all offenders sentenced to Detention

Centre Training served their sentences at Glenochil,
near Stirling - indeed until the recent opening of a
Young Offenders' Institution at the same location,
"Glenochil" was synonymous in Scotland with Detention
Centre Training.

b) <u>Borstal training</u>.   Borstal Training has a much longer
   history, and the sentence took its name from the village,
   in Essex, where the first institution designed to give
   effect to the concept was located. Whilst the concept
   has found varieties of expression in the different
   borstal institutions subsequently established, and has
   indeed changed over the years, the handbook on the
   Sentence of the Court described its objectives and
   working thus: "it is designed to achieve recovery from
   established criminal habits, and, since . . . this is
   for many young offenders a slow and difficult process
   . . . the period of supervision after release is regarded as an important and integral part of borstal
   training. The emphasis. . . is on remedial and
   educational treatment based on close study of the
   individual. The system of training seeks the all round
   development of character and capacities. . . and is
   based on progressive trust demanding increasing personal
   decision, responsibility and self control". It was this
   "treatment" concept which formed the basis of borstal's
   indeterminancy as a sentence: no offender could be
   detained for more than 2 years, but his release date was
   determined by the Governor, in conjunction with the
   Visiting Committee, in the light of the offender's
   response to training. The period of ensuing after-care
   was 12 months, with recall for 3 months being the
   available sanction in the event of a further offence,
   or of a breach of requirement of the after-care licence.
   Three borstal institutions for males, Polmont, Noranside
   and Castle Huntly, had been established in Scotland,
   with the majority of offenders serving their sentence at
   Polmont; all female borstal trainees served their sentences
   latterly at Cornton Vale. The average length of stay within
   the institution was of between 9 and 12 months. It is worthy
   of note that the sentence of borstal training was available
   to Sheriff Summary Courts in Scotland, whose custodial
   powers do not normally exceed 6 months.

c) <u>Young offender's institutions</u>.   Young Offenders'
   Institutions were also created by the 1963 Criminal Justice
   (Scotland) Act, in that it required that any offender
   who was not considered suitable for either detention
   centre or borstal training should serve his sentence
   in a Young Offenders' Institution. The length of any
   such sentence would be fixed by the court in accordance
   with its ordinary powers, as far as the duration of the
   sentence was concerned. The prime objective was to
   avoid young offenders having to serve their sentence
   in the same institutions as adult prisoners. The
   handbook on "The Sentence of the Court" suggests that
   elements of both borstal and detention centre training
   should be included in the regime: "the emphasis is

on a brisk tempo and a high standard of discipline,
and on personal attention of the kind given in borstals."
Sentences of between 6 months and 18 months carried a
12 month period of statutory after-care licence
comparable to borstal after-care in its sanctions.
Sentences of 18 months and more rendered offenders
eligible for parole, and liable to a different set of
after-care arrangements in the event of not being
released on parole. Young offenders institutions were
also the place in which fine defaulters, aged 16 but
under 21, served their period in default. Their
objective was further constricted by the absence in
some parts of Scotland of Remand Centres for this age
group, with the result that young people were held on
remand in adult prisons.

It is important to conclude this review of the arrangements which existed prior to the 1980 Act by remarking
that, subject to review, in England and Wales the
situation still approximates that which obtained in
Scotland until only recently. Borstal Training is
identical there except that it extends to include
15 year olds, and can only be ordered by a Crown Court;
Detention Centre Training is the same, except that it
is possible to send an offender for 6 months training
in such an institution; and young offenders not so
sentenced are kept in separate wings of adult prisons,
though sentences of between 6 and 18 months are not
available to English courts in relation to young
offenders. A knowledge of these sentences is also
necessary, as they all occur on the schedules of previous
convictions relating to offenders who have experienced
them.

ii)   The Arrangements Introduced by the 1980 Act

The two main changes for custodial sentences introduced by the 1980 Act are:-

- the abolition of Borstal Training as a sentence.

- the extended availability of Detention Centre
   Training.

The changes are effected by section 45 of the Act, and
are achieved by amending section 207 of the 1975 Criminal
Procedure (Scotland) Act, which had in general terms
simply stated "no court shall impose imprisonment on a
person under 17 years of age." Subsection 3 of section 45
specifically repeals the sections of the 1975 Act which
previously had made available both Borstal Training
(i.e. sections 204 and 414) and Detention Centre Training
(i.e. sections 209 and 418). Subsection 1 of section 45
of the 1980 Act considerably extends section 207 of the
1975 Act in the following detailed ways.

Subsection 1 of section 207 C.P(S)A.75, now S45 of the
C.J.(S)A.80 precludes courts from ordering imprisonment

on any person under 21 years of age. The significance
of this is that any person in this age group cannot
serve a sentence in an adult prison, but has to be
the subject of a period of "detention" - the use of
the different word is deliberate - in accordance with
the subsections which follow.

Subsection 2 restricts the maximum period of detention
which a court can order on a young offender to the
same period of maximum imprisonment it can order on
an adult offender: i.e. Districts Courts cannot order
more than 60 days detention; Sheriff Summary Courts
cannot order more than 6 months detention; and so on.

Subsection 3 imposes the requirement that detention
cannot be ordered unless the court is of the opinion
that no other method of dealing with him is appropriate;
and obliges all courts except the High Court to state
its reasons for that opinion, and to enter them in the
record of proceedings.

Subsection 4 legislates the compulsory obtaining by
all courts of a social enquiry report to help in the
formation of this opinion as to disposal. There is
no substantive change here, but there is the same
change of wording from the 1975 Act's "shall obtain
such information as it can . . .". Again it will be
noted that the term "social enquiry report" still
does not appear in criminal justice legislation.

Subsection 5 makes the most crucial statement about
the arrangements: it says two things:-

"(a)   in a case where a court by way of sentence
       imposes detention... for a period of at least
       28 days but not exceeding 4 months the court
       shall order that the detention be in a detention
       centre; and,

 (b)   in any other case it shall order that the
       detention be in a young offenders institution."

Subsections 6 to 11 deal with a number of detailed
situations requiring specific resolution.

Subsection 6 allows a court to determine that a period
of between 28 days and 4 months may be ordered not to
take effect in a detention centre by virtue either of
the physical or mental unfitness of the offender, or
if, for any special reason, it considers a young
offenders institution more appropriate, but in this
latter instance it must, unless it is the High Court,
state and record its reasons for this opinion.

Subsection 7 allows that if a person is already in a
detention centre and receives either a further sentence
of less than 28 days or a period of detention imposed
other than by way of sentence (for example for fine

default) then that sentence or period shall also take
effect in the detention centre.

Subsection 8 orders that periods of detention imposed
at the same time and ordered to be consecutive shall
be treated as a single period of detention.

Subsection 9 rules that where a period of detention
is ordered consecutive to, or concurrent with a period
of detention already being served and the ensuing total
is more than 5 months, the offender shall be transferred
to a young offenders institution to serve the remainder
of that total period. Example: A is sentenced to
4 months detention and accordingly begins to serve it
in a detention centre: however, 2 months into his
sentence he appears at court and receives a 3 month
sentence of detention consecutively to his present
sentence. Ordinarily the latter sentence would also
take effect in a detention centre, but as a result of
its being ordered consecutively the total becomes
7 months, and thus A will be transferred to a young
offenders institution, even before completing the
first 4 month sentence.

Subsection 10 allows the Secretary of State to transfer
an offender from a detention centre to a young offenders
institution if he is satisfied that an offender is
physically or mentally unfit for detention centre training as it can occur that such unfitness may only become
apparent subsequently to the preparation of reports and
the sentence of the court.

Subsection 11 extends the ordinary remission arrangements
applicable to adult offenders to young offenders; and
ensures that the parole provisions of the 1967 Criminal
Justice Act, shall also continue to be extended to young
offenders who may be eligible.

All these eleven subsections are added to section 207 of
the 1975 Act, which previously had no subsections at all,
by subsection 1 of section 45 of the 1980 Act, and that
subsection 1 rounds off by extending all these provisions
which it has set out to cases on summary procedure by
making the appropriate extensions and/or substitutions to
section 415 of the 1975 Act, which defined the powers of
imprisonment for summary jurisdiction.

It is however possible, and important to highlight one
aspect of advising the courts under these new arrangements.
The cutting back on the so-called 'treatment' ethic which
characterised the Borstal system means that before venturing opinion about the advisability of custody, the report
writer must now be able to satisfy the court that all other
non-custodial measures have been reviewed. Under this
legislation sentence is now a matter for decision as to
the length of time to be spent in custody. Advising the
court about the range of alternatives is crucial so that
if a custodial sentence is imposed the amount of knowledge

and advice is at a level which makes that a rational
choice. It is not any part of the social work function
to be seen to be speculating about the length of the
sentence, nor any longer a question of pointing courts
in one of three specific but separate directions if
custody is contemplated.

The whole subject of dealing with young offenders was
the subject of a major government report "Young Adult
Offenders - Report of the Advisory Council on the Penal
System" (the Younger Report 1974 HMSO) which drew
attention to the high reconviction rates of all custodial
institutions for the young offender, and desired to
achieve a major shift away from such institutions
towards treatment in the community. In the wake of
reactions to the Younger Report's publication, the
government has only produced a Green Paper (i.e. a
consultative document) for England and Wales, but has
proceeded to legislate for Scotland, as outlined above.

The availability of detention centre training is now
extended in three important ways:-

  i) instead of being a fixed sentence of 3 months,
     a much wider range of sentences (28 days to
     4 months) will be served in detention centres.
     The inference is that nearly all short sentences
     will be of the "short, shock" kind by definition.
     Whether or not the existing designated institution
     at Glenochil will continue to be the only such
     centre remains to be seen,

 ii) the restriction on repeated use has been lifted,
     so that offenders may repeatedly be sent to these
     institutions. The inference must be that a second
     or third attempt might be more successful if the
     first fails,

iii) a direct consequence of extending the range of
     this sentence downwards is that the District
     Courts now have this sentence available to them,
     in that sentences of between 28 days and 60 days
     are within their powers, and now take effect in
     detention centres: the repeated use of the
     sentence is also available to these courts.

In all these changes introduced by the 1980 Act no
previous consultative or policy document is available
to social workers from which to derive rationale,
guidance or interpretation for operating under the
present arrangements. Nor has sufficient time yet
elapsed for it to become clear how prisons division
will allocate, treat and train those young offenders
not sentenced to detention centre training, and how
they will utilise those institutions known until only
recently as borstals. At the time of writing the
situation is too fluid for us to do other than describe
the previous practices as we have done, and define the
changes which the Act has made.

Young Offenders Convicted of Murder

The 1980 Act has also made some changes to the arrangements for young offenders convicted of murder. Until its enactment, life imprisonment was the sentence passed on any person aged 18 and over convicted of murder, whereas offenders under 18 were sentenced to "Detention during Her Majesty's Pleasure."

Section 43 of the Act has amended section 205 of the Criminal Procedure (Scotland) Act, 1975, which had previously governed the situation. The effect of section 43 is that:-

    i) life imprisonent is the sentence on offenders aged 21 and over convicted of murder,

    ii) offenders under the age of 18 are sentenced to be detained in such places and under such conditions as the Secretary of State may direct. The place need not be a penal institution, especially initially, but there may well be various changes and transfers according to the progress and maturation of the offender. It will be noted that the Act has dropped the title "Detention during Her Majesty's Pleasure" in favour of "Detention without limit of time". The release and supervision arrangements for such offenders are operated as for a sentence of life imprisonment, and the Secretary of State is advised in relation to these matters by the Parole Board,

    iii) offenders aged 18 but under 21 are sentenced "to be detained in a young offenders institution and shall be liable to be detained for life." This is a titular and not a substantive change.

Detention of Children

There are circumstances in which children - i.e. persons under 16, or aged between 16 and 18 but under the supervision of a Children's Hearing, can be prosecuted for crimes and offences before the courts, rather than being referred to the Children's Hearing System. In extremely serious cases a child may thus become liable to prosecution by the solemn procedure method, although the cases tend to be few and far between. Section 44 of the 1980 Act makes provision for the detention of such children, by making amendments to section 206 of the 1975 Criminal Procedure (Scotland) Act which had previously set out the law. Section 44 allows that "where a child in convicted and the court is of the opinion that no other method of dealing with him is appropriate, it may sentence him to be detained for a period which it shall specify in the sentence; and the child shall during that period be liable to be detained in such place and on such conditions as the Secretary of State may direct." We discussed above the obligation on courts to consider reports when dealing with children, and to have regard to their welfare. This wording again allows that the place of detention need not be a penal institution, though it is quite possible that the sentence will be of a duration such that the child may pass into the young offender, or even adult, age group during sentence and thus may be the subject of various transfers which may then include detention in penal institutions. The rest of section 44 deals with the detail of release under supervision from this sentence, and we consider this below.

Residential Training for Children

When children are prosecuted summarily before the Sheriff Court, the court may order a period of residential training of not more than two years, and must specify the period of such an order. An order for Residential Training is made in terms of section 413 of the 1975 Act. The place and conditions of such detention are determined by the Secretary of State: there is no remission as of right, but the offender may be released to supervision in the community, and will remain subject to such supervision for the unexpired portion of the original sentence.

Social Work Departments are much more actively involved in orders under section 413 than in either of the other two measures discussed above. The Parole Board is not involved in section 413 orders and accordingly, the views and continued involvement of the social worker are even more crucial to the effective discharge of the Secretary of State's functions under this Section.

Rarely, if ever, will a child be appearing before the court with such a disposal in prospect without a Children's Hearing having recently considered his case. It requires careful consideration as to whether any advantage will be gained by the court's imposition of such an order as against any course of action open to the Children's Hearing under residential supervision requirement (Section 44(1)(b) of the Social Work Act. The use of a section 413 order is the only means if the case is on summary procedure by which a child can actually be detained in any establish-ment, but it is no necessary guarantee of such detention in, nor necessarily of the availability of, a particular place in a List D School or other type of institution.

The main additional involvement for social workers, over and above both the report-ing and after-care functions in relation to these orders, is the responsibility imposed on the Social Work Department to arrange for the offender who is made the subject of one of these orders to be detained in a place of safety organised by the Department pending the Secretary of State's decision as to where the offender will commence his period of training. Circular SW13/1971 deals in detail with such matters, but it is chiefly of importance to note that a considerable amount of advance planning is necessary to arrange such a place of interim detention if the making of such an order is anticipated. In particular, the social worker may feel that the offender should be detained in penal custody until the Secretary of State's decision. An arrangement to this effect can be made in conjunction with Social Work Services Group, but the necessary warrant authorising such detention needs to be obtained prior to the court's making of an order, because the court's powers to order custodial remand lapse once the order is made. Social Work Services Group take the view that a period of interim detention in custody should only be suggested in very exceptional circumstances: the simple non-availavility of a place of safety within the Local Authority's own institutions does not of itself justify such a course.

Chapter 9

The Mentally Disordered Offender

The Criminal law applies certain special considerations, and in some instances
particular disposals, to offenders who may be suffering from mental disorder.
Social workers, therefore, have a two-fold concern with these provisions; both in
respect of their duties under Section 27 of the Social Work (Scotland) Act; and
equally so, (since the local government reorganisation effective from May 1975), in
view of the inclusion of medical social work within the responsibilities of Social
Work Departments. In the mental health field generally, the governing Act is the
Mental Health (Scotland) Act 1960: this replaced the earlier Lunacy (Scotland)
Acts and the Mental Deficiency (Scotland) Acts, by making fresh provision for "the
reception, care and treatment of persons suffering from or appearing to suffer from
mental disorder, and with respect to their property and affairs. . ." The powers
of the criminal courts in respect of the mentally disordered offender were also set
out in that Act, but are now located in the Criminal Procedure (Scotland) Act 1975.
This chapter discusses the powers and procedure of courts in relation to the
mentally disordered offender. Mental disorder is defined (in the Mental Health
(Scotland)Act)as including mental illness, severe subnormality, subnormality, and
psychopathic disorder.

The provisions of Part V of the Mental Health (S) Act 1960 are concerned with the
use by the Courts of the provisions and facilities afforded by the Act in respect
of persons diagnosed as suffering from mental disorder. To this end it adopted the
Part IV provisions to meet the requirements of the administration of justice in the
criminal courts, so that certain safeguards are inbuilt and the scope of the provisions extended beyond the age limitations outlined in Part IV.

The procedural aspects, formerly located at Part V of the 1960 Act, are now to be
found at S.174-178 (Solemn) and S.375-379 (Summary) of the 1975 Act. The sections
of Part V repealed by the 1975 Act are: SS.54,55,57(1) to (4),59(1),60(1)(2) and
(4), 62, 63 and in Schedule 4, the entry relating to the 1949 C.J.(S) Act.

Hospital and Guardianship Orders

The purpose of a hospital order is to enable an offender to be admitted and compul-
sorily detained in hospital for as long as is necessary in his own and the public
interest: the purpose of a guardianship order is similarly for him to be under
guardianship. Normally Part IV of the Mental Health (Scotland) Act 1960 is the

basis for the compulsory admission of a person to hospital, or his reception into guardianship: it allows that a person who is suffering from any mental disorder that requires or is susceptible to medical treatment may be admitted to hospital or received into guardianship, "but (excepting emergency admissions) no person over the age of 21 shall be admitted or received except where the mental disorder from which he suffers is:-

> i)   mental deficiency such that he is incapable of living
>   an independent life or of guarding himself against
>   serious exploitation

> or ii) in a mental illness other than a persistent disorder
>   which is manifested only by abnormally aggressive or
>   seriously irresponsible conduct."

The availability of hospital or guardianship orders to the criminal courts allows for mentally disordered offenders to receive the resources of the health services if appropriate, and subject to the conditions and arrangements outlined in this chapter.

In the case of a guardianship order, an offender is not admitted to a hospital, but is under the care of a guardian, who may be:-

> i)   the Local Health Authority

> ii)   a person chosen by that Authority

> iii) any other person who has been accepted as a suitable
>   person to act in that capacity by the Local Health
>   Authority. Guardianship may well involve the patient's
>   residence in an institution or establishment run by a
>   Local Authority Social Work Department or other
>   appropriate organisation.

In respect of hospital and guardianship orders made by a court:-

> i)   The nearest relative has no power to order the patient's
>   discharge.

> ii)   There is no limitation (as there normally is) on the
>   continued detention in hospital or retention under
>   guardianship of psychopathic or sub-normal patients
>   beyond the age of 25.

> iii) Such orders can be made in respect of a sub-normal or
>   psychopathic person who has attained the age of 21.

Before making a hospital or guardianship order, the court must satisfy itself that the medical evidence justifies such a course: we deal with the requirements as to medical evidence below. The following requirements also apply:

> i)   The penalty for the offence is not fixed by law.

> ii)   The offence is punishable with imprisonment.

> iii) The court is of the opinion, having regard to all the
>   circumstances, including the nature of the offences
>   and the character and antecedents of the offender, and
>   to the other available methods of dealing with him,
>   that the most suitable method of disposing of the case
>   is by means of such an order.

iv) a) a hospital bed is available within 28 days of the
         making of an order (hospital order)

     b) the local authority, or other person involved, is
         willing to receive the offender into guardianship
         (guardianship order).

The court makes a hospital or guardianship order in terms of Section 175 or 376 of
the Criminal Procedure (Scotland) Act, dependent on whether the case is on solemn
or on summary procedure. The order must specify the form of mental disorder from
which the accused is found to be suffering. A hospital order can include directions for conveying the patient to and retaining him in a place of safety pending
the hospital bed becoming available during the 28 days period: however, no direction for conveying a patient to a residential establishment provided by a local
authority under Part IV of the Social Work (Scotland) Act can be made unless the
court is satisfied that the local authority is willing to receive him therein. A
hospital order shall not specify the State Hospital (Carstairs) as the place of
detention unless the court is satisfied on the medical evidence that:-

     i) the offender requires treatment under conditions of
         special security because of his dangerous, violent,
         and criminal propensities,

and ii) he cannot suitably be cared for in a hospital other than
         the State Hospital.

A hospital or guardianship order cannot be combined with a sentence of imprisonment (or other sentence of detention), or with a fine, or with a probation order.

A hospital or guardianship order is not made to run for any specified period, but
the patient may be made subject to special restrictions (see below).
Otherwise, the order lapses after 12 months, unless it is renewed because the
patient still needs to be detained in hospital, or retained in guardianship. Such
a renewal will in the first instance be for one year, thereafter for 2 year periods.
Renewal does not involve the court, but on each occasion a fresh medical examination is made and a report submitted to the managers of the hospital or to the
guardian. If restrictions have not been imposed, a hospital order can be discharged at any time by the responsible medical officer or the hospital managers;
and a guardianship order can be discharged by the responsible medical or Local
Health Authority. Also, in either case, the patient himself has the right to apply
to the Mental Health Review Tribunal who may order his discharge: such an application must be made within the first 6 months after the making or any renewal of the
order.

Restriction Orders

In making a hospital order, but not a guardianship order, a court may make a further
order restricting his discharge from that hospital. Such an order is made in terms
of Sections 178 or 379 of the Criminal Procedure (Scotland) Act, dependent on the
method of prosecution(solemn or summary) being used. The following additional
requirements apply before a restriction order can be made:-

     i) The doctor, approved for the purposes of Section 27 of
         Mental Health (Scotland) Act, who gives evidence in the
         case, gives his evidence orally before the court.

     ii) It appears to the court, having regard to the nature of
         the offence, the antecedents of the person, and the risk
         that as a result of his mental disorder he would commit
         offences if set at largè, that it is necessary for the

protection of the public to make such an order.

The restriction order can be for a specified period or more usually, (as the course of mental illness can rarely be accurately predicted) without limit of time.

The effect of a restriction order is that a patient may not be granted leave of absence, transferred to another hospital, or to guardianship, or discharged, except with the consent of the Secretary of State. Neither the patient nor his nearest relative can apply to the Mental Health Review Tribunal, though the Secretary of State can request the tribunal's advice. While a restriction order is in force, patients are reported on as regularly to the hospital managers as those not subject to restriction.

The discharge of patients subject to restriction orders is controlled by the Secretary of State. The legal and social work considerations parallel in many respects the discharge of an offender on parole from a penal institution, and the responsibility of the social worker involved in such supervision is similar. There are two forms of discharging a person subject to a restriction order:-

    i)   Conditional Discharge. The conditions involved in any discharge will always include residence at an approved address and specific arrangements for supervision. These arrangements involve the appointment of two supervisors: one will be a doctor; the other often a social worker.

    ii) Absolute Discharge. A conditional discharge lapses either if the fixed period of restriction expires or if it is converted by the Secretary of State into an absolute discharge. Rarely is the patient actually released from hospital absolutely: the absolute discharge, especially where there is no time limit on the restriction order, depends on the patient's progress.

Inquiries into Mental Condition

The Act lays upon prosecutors a general duty in respect of persons who may be suffering from mental disorder: "Where it appears to the prosecutor in *any* court (emphasis added) before which a person is charged with an offence that the person may be suffering from mental disorder, it shall be the duty of such prosecutor to bring before the court such evidence as may be available of the mental condition of that person". An immediate consideration here is that, in contra-distinction to the ordering of social enquiry reports, such reports may well be obtained pre-trial; or occasionally prior to any hearing of the case at all. The outcome of a medical examination of a person charged by the police can be a decision not to proceed at all in the courts. Hospital based social workers may, therefore, be aware of court proceedings before their colleagues in the field, and the point illustrates the importance of close liaison between the two. The submission or input of social work information at this stage is governed by the same considerations applicable to pre-trial reports prepared at the social worker's own initiative, i.e. essentially that the accused consents and that the information is useful to the court.

The Act also gives the courts specific powers to order medical reports over and above the general power to make enquiries, (already discussed in the section on social enquiry reports; see above). Sections 180 and 381 of the Criminal Procedure (Scotland) Act empower courts to make enquiries into the physical or mental condition of an offender before determining the method of dealing with him, provided:-

    i)   the court is satisfied he did the act or made the omission
charged

   ii)   the offence is punishable with imprisonment

  iii)   the court thinks such an inquiry ought to be made.

The sections allow a court to continue the case either in custody or on bail for
the purposes of the necessary medical examination, and to this end to arrange that
the bail requirement under the Bail Act should include requirements of residence
in or attendance at a specified institution. The period of any single continuation
shall not exceed 3 weeks, but further continuations may be ordered, if necessary.

The law also requires that a court gives to any institution or place in which or
at which the offender may be required to reside or attend a statement of its reason
for thinking such an inquiry necessary, *and* any information (e.g. a social enquiry
report) already before it about his physical or mental condition.

In practice, it often happens that social enquiry and medical reports are ordered
by courts simultaneously (especially as the court's ordering of a medical report
does follow a hearing of the case), and the opportunities for cooperation between
both report writers are clearer and easier. Whilst the author of a social enquiry
report will need to be aware of the specifically medical considerations and disposals outlined in the rest of this chapter, his chief concern is the provision of
information to the court, and secondly, to see that the levels of cooperation
necessary with the medical authorities are sufficient to provide a measure of assistance to both the offender and his family throughout any sentence and after discharge.

A remand or committal for trial of any person who 'appears to the Court to be suffering from mental disorder' may be to a hospital, provided that it is available for
his admission and suitable for his detention (S.180 '75 Act) instead of to a penal
establishment. This is subject to the institution being named on the warrant and
the responsible medical officer being satisfied that such course is reasonable in
the circumstances of the case.

Requirements as to Medical Evidence

Before the court can make any of the specific orders, other than probation, in
regard to mentally disordered offenders, certain stringent requirements as to the
medical evidence must be met:-

    i)   The court must be satisfied on the evidence of <u>two</u>
doctors that the offender is suffering from mental
disorder of a nature or degree which in the case of a
person under 21 years of age, would warrant his admission
to a hospital, or his reception into guardianship under
Part IV of the Mental Health (Scotland) Act 1960.

   ii)   Both the doctors must agree that the offender is suffering
from the same form of disorder, whether or not either of
them thinks he is also suffering from some other form of
mental disorder.

  iii)   One of the doctors must be a practitioner approved for
the purposes of Section 27 of the Mental Health (Scotland)
Act by a Health Board as having special experience in the
diagnosis or treatment of mental disorder.

   iv)   Whilst the evidence may be either written or oral, the
doctors concerned can be required to attend court to
give evidence and be cross-examined. Further, the law

           allows the defence to arrange an independent medical
           examination of the accused, even if he is already
           detained, for the purpose of rebutting the existing
           medical evidence.

v)   Copies of any reports submitted other than by or on
      behalf of the accused shall be given to his counsel
      or solicitor. If he is not so represented, the sub-
      stance of any report shall be disclosed to him, or, if
      he is a child under 16, to his parent or guardian, if
      present in court.

vi) The court must adjourn the case if it considers further
      time is necessary, in the interests of the accused, for
      the consideration of such a report.

vii) The evidence must indicate that a bed in a specific
      hospital is available within 28 days; or that a Local
      Health Authority, or other person approved by a Local
      Health Authority, is willing to receive the patient into
      guardianship.

Insanity

Sections 174 and 375 of the Criminal Procedure (Scotland) Act 1975 make provision
for dealing with persons who are insane at the time of their trial or who were
insane at the time of the commission of the act or omission constituting the
offence. The concept of insanity is a complex one and the various issues connect-
ed with it fall outwith the scope of this work. It is unlikely that social workers
will be involved in the determination of such an issue: however, any information
held by the social worker can be shared with the prosecutor and/or medical authorities to assist their consideration of the matter. A person who is found to be
insane either at the time of the trial or of the offence is not convicted and
sentenced in the normal way.

A finding of insanity may be made either before a trial actually gets under way
(so that, in fact, it cannot then proceed) or during the course of a trial. The
accused is then formally acquitted by reason of insanity, but he becomes the subject of an order under Section 174 of the Act if the case is on solemn procedure,
or Section 375 of the Act if the case is on summary procedure.

A person, sane at the time of the offence, may become insane before being brought
to trial, in which event an appropriate order would be made as just described.
Conversely, if an offender, insane at the time of the offence, regains his sanity,
the trial may be able to go on in the normal way.

It can happen that such an order can be made in the accused's absence, if it is
not practicable to bring him before the court for the purpose of determining
whether he is insane, provided that no objection is raised by him or on his behalf.

The effect of an order made under either of these sections is equivalent to that
of a hospital order, together with an order restricting discharge, made without
limitation of time (see above). The order will specify that the accused will be
detained either in the State Hospital which is located at Carstairs, in Lanarkshire,
or at such other hospital as the court may for special reasons specify.

The social work contribution to patients care: it will be seen that this is a
specialised field, largely the province of qualified medical practitioners. It may
be, however, in individual cases, that social workers are called upon to submit
reports; it should be a cardinal point that such reports are supportive in the

provision of social background information and it is quite inappropriate for
writers to venture opinion as to the suitability of this type of disposal.

There is, however, a range of activity associated with such orders to which social
workers should be alert. Matters such as securing premises, informing landlords
of absence, acting for the patient in respect of the protection of goods and
property, as agent for the collection of wages, employment documents etc. all
suggest work requiring involvement and the fullest possible cooperation with the
hospital authorities.

So far as guardianship is concerned, the nomination of a named social worker,
designated as 'Mental Health Officer' may in certain cases be a possibility. Such
duties under Part V of the 1960 Act are the same as those accruing under Part IV
except as noted the age range is increased.

Guardianship involves acting for and with the individual and with and for the
medical authority in any treatment or support role. As this relates to persons
who are deemed to be incapable of exercising normal controls, restraints and
judgment, the responsibility is a heavy one and importance is attached to securing
all necessary safeguards when property, money etc. are entrusted or about which
authority has to be exercised in respect of the discharge of duty.

S.29 of the 1960 Act confers 'on the authority or person named . . . as guardian,
to the exclusion of any other person, all such powers as would be exercisable by
them or him in relation to the patient as if they or he were the father of the
patient and the patient were a pupil child', so that in the context of criminal
law provision, the exercise of guardianship should be regarded as being well beyond the kind of authority position associated with court orders such as probation
or licence under the Criminal Procedure or Justice Acts.

Discharge of hospital or guardianship orders are, in the nature of things, not a
social work responsibility but require the professional judgment of the medical
practitioner in the case. There is, however, valuable input to be made by the
supply of relevant social information, the provision of social supports and the
securing or maintaining of a community base for the patient. This latter assumes
a particular urgency when the patient has been hospitalised for a lengthy period
and the processes of re-socialisation are seen to be tasks which necessitate both
the display of skills and the provision of secure and undemanding accommodation.

Transfers from Institutions of Mental Health Cases. The Mental Health (Scotland)
Act (1960) provided a procedure at S.65, whereby persons committed to custody,
whether for sentence or trial could be transferred to hospital, on order of the
sheriff if they are found, while in custody, to be suffering from a mental disorder. This procedure is specific to situations where the condition only becomes
apparent after the committal to custody. A sheriff may make 'a transfer order'
if he is satisfied on the evidence of two duly qualified medical practitioners
(as described) that the person is suffering from a mental disorder which would
warrant his admission to hospital under Part IV of the Act and that such a course
is desirable.

Section 66 lays down the conditions under which a person serving a custodial
sentence may be so removed to hospital. Custodial sentence in context includes
children under S.206 or S.413 orders. Broadly the considerations indicated
earlier as to medical evidence and the advisability of the transfer appertain, and
of course once this has been accomplished the sentence length ceases to have effect
and the prisoner, now patient, becomes subject to the release and discharge procedures under Part V of the Act. Any transfer order so made must be affected
within 14 days of its being made, otherwise it lapses and if transfer is still

desired, a new order has to be sought.

If having been so transferred to hospital, and a restriction order is in force, and the Secretary of State is notified by the responsible medical officer before the expiry of sentence that the person no longer requires treatment, then the Secretary of State may order his removal back into the penal system, or in the case of a child, back to an appropriate residential establishment or exercise his power to release on licence, subject to the considerations of the necessary advice available to him via the hospital authorities and the parole board. The provisions of S.69 are thus brought into line with the present arrangements under the Criminal Justice (Scotland) Act.

S.71 provides for the transfer from a List D school to guardianship of children suffering from mental disorder and while the exercise of these provisions is rare, instances may arise where social workers have to be aware of the needs of persons concerned and be prepared to advise those holding the primary responsibility for care of the community aspects of the case, and also be aware of the potential for a social work responsibility, post discharge.

Chapter 10

Parole and After Care

A system of parole came into being in Scotland on 1st April, 1968, following the enactment of the Criminal Justice Act, 1967. Sections 60 and 61 of that Act deal with the release of persons on parole licence, and they apply to Scotland as well as England and Wales.

The concept of parole licence is fundamentally different from that of after-care. Whilst the latter is an integral part of the sentence to which it applies, it nonetheless represents a period of supervision after the custodial part of the sentence has been served. A period of parole, on the other hand, involves release before the normal date of discharge, and represents a period during which the offender is regarded as still serving his sentence, albeit under open supervision in the community.

The approach of the supervising officer, therefore, has to reflect a more active awareness of his responsibility, as a direct agent of the Secretary of State, for aspects of public protection and crime prevention, over and above his endeavours to assist the rehabilitation of the particular offender who is his immediate client. The arrangements for consultation with Prisons Division in regard to any possible breach of requirement are designed to facilitate this need for close co-operation.

Eligibility and release.   Any offender sentenced to more than 18 months imprisonment, or detention in a young offenders' institution, is eligible for parole. The offender must himself express a willingness to be considered for parole, and is given an opportunity to state his own reasons, attitudes, and views both orally and in writing. An offender must serve 12 months in custody, whatever the length of the total sentence. Some special arrangements apply to young offenders, and we discuss these below

Examples

> i)   A receives a sentence of 21 months imprisonment. He
>   would normally serve 14 months if he gains full remission:
>   thus one third of his sentence is 7 months but he cannot
>   be released on parole until he has served 12 months.
>   The maximum period he could be on parole is 2 months.

> ii) B receives a sentence of 3 years imprisonment. He could
>   be released at any time after serving 12 months of his

sentence, and would remain under parole supervision until
2 years of his sentence had expired.

It should be noted that the actual date of release occasionally depends on a
number of circumstantial factors, e.g. the availability of work, accommodation,
and the actual period of parole is rarely of as fixed duration as a period of
after-care licence. Moreover, the date of release can occasionally be arranged
and/or notified at rather short notice and the supervising officer's involvement
in the practical aspects of release arrangements is crucial in such instances.

Consideration of a prisoner for parole begins about 4 months before his first
potential release date. The first request made of the community based social
worker is for a home circumstances report. The preparation of this differs from
that required prior to a period of after-care in that release is only a possibility.
The potential arrangements that a supervising officer can himself make on behalf
of a potential parolee are likely to be of great importance. Moreover, the use-
fulness of such a report is likely to be all the greater if its contents arise out
of ongoing contact between supervisor and offender, thus making attitudinal and
emotional comment more pointed. In the cases of life sentence prisoners a review
for parole is initiated by Prisons Dept., usually after about 6 or 7 years of the
sentence has been served.

The first consideration of a prisoner's circumstances will be undertaken by a
Local Review Committee. Each establishment housing eligible inmates is serviced
by a Committee, which comprises both lay and professional elements. One of its
members will interview each prisoner, and reports from a variety of sources will
be available to the Committee. However, an actual decision to release a prisoner
will not be made without a subsequent consideration of his case by the Secretary
of State and the Parole Board. The Board only considers those cases in which the
Secretary of State is prepared to contemplate release and which are referred by
him to it for possible release.

Section 61 of the 1967 Act authorised the Parole Board to review all cases of life
imprisonment; all cases of young offenders and of children convicted of murder;
and all cases of children sentenced to detention under section 413 of the Criminal
Procedures(Scotland) Act,1975. The concept which applies to any offender released
to supervision under one of these sentences is that of parole, and similar
considerations and arrangements apply in regard to recall. In the nature of these,
intermediate or special sentence notices of "thirds" of a sentence do not apply.

Those prisoners who are refused parole are not given any reasons for the Board's
decision, but all cases are reviewed and reconsidered annually. The consideration
of life prisoners is also undertaken annually unless the Board decides at a review
not to undertake a further review for a period in excess of a year.

The Parole Licence

Offenders will be given, and supervising officers will receive, a copy of the
licence. The licence will indicate the period for which it is effective and the
name of the supervising officer, together with the arrangements for first contact.
Parole licences may, and frequently do, include specific extra requirements,
especially in regard to work and/or residence, and indeed can be regarded in this
respect as having even more of the possibilities applicable to probation orders.
All licences include requirements on the parolee to keep in touch with his supervisor; to be of good behaviour and lead an industrious life; and to inform his
supervisor at once of any change of address or employment.

Parolees released from determinate sentences remain under supervision until the expiry of two-thirds of their original sentence. There is in the nature of the conception no possibility for early discharge. However, a supervising officer may feel, especially in regard to life sentence cases, that the social work contract agreed with the offender in terms of his individual rehabilitation may have been completed before the supervision expires. Such a decision requires great certainty of judgement, but it may in such circumstances be in order to request that the requirement to report be written out of the licence. Voluntary contact is always a continuing possibility, and reporting can be written in again if a sufficiently serious change of circumstances appears to justify it. It is certainly better that the offender is not seen because of a decision to that effect properly and professionally arrived at, than that he is not seen due to apathy, oversight, or other non-relevant reasons.

Recall and Reconviction

The supervising officer has _no_ discretion in regard to reporting either any further offence or any suspected breach of requirement committed by a person on parole: he may offer a view about the continuation of supervision but he must report the facts for the Secretary of State's consideration. Such reports should be treated as a matter of extreme urgency.

The normal arrangements for recall of a parolee who has breached a requirement of his licence involve the submission by the supervising officer of a written report justifying and requesting such a course. In any case of great urgency, especially one involving potential danger to the public, a report may be made initially by telephone, supported later in writing. Prisons Division can arrange for almost immediate recall.

The parolee can make representations to the Parole Board against a decision to recall him made in regard to an alleged breach of requirement. Although the matter is not triable by a court or by its standards, it is possible for him to be re-leased again either immediately, if some clear misunderstanding arose, or at a future date, if the Parole Board so decides.

Any court other than a District Court can in regard to a person who is on parole and who is either convicted or found guilty of an offence punishable with imprison-ment, order the revocation of the parole licence. It can do this in addition to imposing any other sentence it can competently impose, although it need not do so. A person whose licence is revoked in these circumstances cannot make represent-ations against the recall to the Parole Board. Indeed, a person recalled in these circumstances is not eligible for release on parole until a further 12 months has elapsed, or before the expiration of one-third of the period during which the licence would have remained in force, whichever is the later. Any parolee who makes an appearance before a District Court while under supervision should be reported on immediately by the supervising officer to Prisons Division, as the Secretary of State may consider that the circumstances justify recall under the procedures mentioned earlier.

Social work practice aspects of parole.   The Parole Board, in its annual report for 1973, essayed a definition of its expectations of social work practice and supervision in parole cases, substantial parts of which are reproduced here:-

> "Supervision is not only to help an individual released from
> prison to resettle into the family and community but also to
> help offenders particularly, to assume their responsibilities.
> It means building up strong family units able to withstand
> pressures and to provide an adequate and stable base from
> which members of the family may contribute positively to

community life.

The word supervision may not convey the wide range of
support, service and control which prisoners may need when
released from prison. What is desirable is that each prisoner should come out into what may be termed a social network
which will provide not only a living place and employment
but will meet the parolee's need for friendship and support.
Some parolees will come out to a supportive environment and
all the supervising social worker need to do is to see a
parolee sufficiently frequently to establish a relationship
which can be used if he needs advice, emotional support or
control which his own family and friends are temporarily
failing to provide. Other parolees have an inadequate or
non-existent social network and for them the social worker
must make good the gaps or even create a whole new situation
in which to live. It will assist him to do this if he
appreciates the rehabilitation measures already attempted
during the custodial part of the sentence and if he has been
actively involved in them.

Supervision should start with contact inside the prison or
at the very latest at the prison gate when the parolee is
released. When few personal or social resources are available the supervising social worker will need to accompany
him through the intricacies of applying for Social Security,
finding a job and settling into a hostel or lodgings. Those
released from prison feel like foreigners in a strange land
for a while and a guide is essential at first.

Wives and children may have learned to do without the prisoner
and, despite their longing for his return, he may be felt to
be an intruder as well as being welcomed when he arrives
home. The social worker must engage the family in understanding the problems of re-entry both for the parolee and
for themselves. There may be relatives who cannot believe
that the ex-prisoner has matured and changed and their
expectations that he will prove a failure once again may
contrive to bring about such a failure. Such situations
require family discussions led by a supervisor skilled in
the understanding and use of family relationships.

Accommodation is hard to find for many parolees. What is
required is a range of facilities, which includes small
hostels, as well as specially selected landladies. For
some parolees facilities should include a setting involving
a more communal life where living and working take place
with the same group of people. For others who want a more
independent way of life bed-sitting rooms or flatlets may
be required.

Employment is a major factor for a prisoner on parole and
it is not enough simply to direct a man to the Department of
Employment or to tell him to read the employment vacancies
advertised in the press. The Board realises that parolees
are particularly vulnerable to national employment trends and
to pressures related to the taking and keeping of a job: it
still hopes that the Trades Unions may become more involved

with the employment problems of parolees as well as of
prisoners. It hopes to see social work departments developing contacts with employers and also themselves offering
employment to parolees, for example, as trainees in their
own establishments.

Accommodation and work are important parts of a parolee's
social network, but so too is the use of leisure time.
Many parolees have past patterns of heavy drinking often
amounting to alcoholism. These people need help in developing drinking habits less dangerous to themselves and society.
Similarly many aggressive young offenders need help in
channelling their aggression constructively. The supervising
officer must be concerned to introduce parolees to clubs of
all kinds to arrange for them to attend classes and to engage
in sports. Such activities may build on interests developed
in prison and offer the parolee a chance to make friends in
a less deviant social group. For some parolees the most
important thing the supervising officer can do is to provide
them with an opportunity to help other people."

After-Care Licence

Section 27 (b) (ii) of the Social Work (Scotland) Act, 1968, required every local
authority to provide a service for 'the supervision of and the provision of advice,
guidance, and assistance for ... persons in their area who, following on release
from prison or any other form of detention, are required to be under supervision
under any enactment or by the terms of an order or licence of the Secretary of
State or of a condition of requirement imposed in pursuance of any enactment."
Whilst this statutory definition is such that the obligation to supervise only
officially commences with the offender's release, it is an integral part of professional practice that service provision in this area of work necessitates a continuing involvement with the offender, his family and home community from the moment
that sentence is pronounced in court. The prevailing philosophy, as expressed by
the 1963 Report of the Advisory Council on the Treatment of Offenders, is that
'after-care begins at the moment of sentence': the point is also apparent in the
use of the term 'through-care' to describe social work involvement.

In May, 1976 the S.W.S.G. and S.H.H.D. of central government issued a document entitled 'Guidance for Social Workers in relation to the administrative provisions
for the supervision of persons released on licence or parole from penal establishments,' which set out all the legislative framework and administrative details
relating to after-care licences; the document was colloquially known as the 'after-
care notes.' Statutory after-care relates entirely to children and young offenders,
with only parole, extending to include adult prisoners. Therefore, the changes to
sentences for young offenders introduced by the 1980 Criminal Justice (Scotland)
Act have brought in their train changes to after-care, and, by the same token, made
considerable sections of the 'after-care notes' obsolete.

Before the 1980 Act the following sentences on young offenders each carried a statutory 12 month period of after-care licence:-

        Detention Centre Training
        Borstal Training

Sentences of 6 months and more, up to 18 months detention, in a Y.O.I..

Sentences of 18 months detention and over passed on young offenders made the offender eligible for parole, and different considerations applied.

The 1980 Act's abolition of Borstal Training as a separate sentence also meant the cessation of borstal after-care licences.   Borstal after-care was originally conceived as an integral part of the whole concept of Borstal Training.   The idea compulsory after-care was later extended to the sentences of Detention Centre Training and of Detention in a Young Offenders Institution when they were introduced in 1963.   However, the 1980 Act does not legislate for any after-care on those sentences which now take effect in a detention centre, i.e. sentences of between 28 days and 4 months, and repeals section 11 of the 1963 Act which previously governed detention centre after-care.

Thus we are left with a residual situation whereby only sentences of 6 months or more in a Young Offenders Institution carry any period of statutory after-care.

Administrative Arrangements and Procedures in After Care

Preparations for Release.   The official responsibilities of a supervising officer begin prior to the offender's release, and initially involve the preparation of further reports.   As the institution begins to plan for the anticipated release of an offender on after-care, it will request of the community based social worker a 'Home Circumstances Report.'   It will already have received a copy of the social enquiry report prepared at the time of sentence, but the home circumstances report needs to reflect the changes which have taken place since sentence which can affect work with the offender on establishing a programme of rehabilitation: it needs to provide an up to date assessment of the home situation which is relevant to the major issues of resettlement of the offender within the community.   This objective needs to be kept in mind, whatever the format the actual request for the report may take.   In turn the institution will in due course send a pre-release report which will include information on the person's response to training, work record, any particular aptitudes revealed in the institution, and so on.

Some institutions, particularly in the case of offenders serving longer sentences, may afford the opportunity of a few days home leave shortly prior to release.   A report as to the feasibility of such leave may be requested by the institution, and a further report as to its outcome is vital to the assessment of its use and validity.   The purpose of home leave is to provide the offender with an opportunity to acclimatise himself to the environment to which he will be returning, and it should help him renew or establish new contacts which are helpful to his resettlement.   In particular the prospects of employment demand exploration.

Release Arrangements.   Institutions hope to inform social work departments of proposed release dates about 2 months in advance, and require the name of the allocated supervising officer as an essential ingredient in the preparation of the licence to give to the offender prior to his release.   The supervising officer will receive his own copy of this licence, showing any extra requirements that may have been included.   Although there is no "serving" of the order comparable to probation, that by no means precludes a discussion of the licence's requirements, and the establishing of a specific contract for the social work aspects of its implementation.   The offender will also be given a travel warrant, subsistence money, and a letter of introduction to the Departments of Employment and of Social Security.   The institution's notification of a release date will also require of the future supervising officer a date and time for the offender's first contact with him on release.   Only in exceptional circumstances should this not be on the actual date of release, and the supervising officer needs to complete the "notification of safe arrival form", which will have been included in the papers sent to him by the institution, confirming that contact has been established: the failure of an offender to make this first contact should be reported immediately.

Supervision.   Once the offender is released, the social worker, in implementing an after-care licence is an agent of the Secretary of State, and is accountable to him. The Secretary of State does not control the manner in which social workers carry out the day to day supervision of persons released from custody, as this is a matter of sound social work practice for which social work departments are responsible. It is necessary, however, to the exercise of his own responsibility that the Secretary of State receives information about an offender's return to society, his progress during supervision, and the ultimate outcome of the process.

The "notification of safe arrival" is the first item of such information to go direct to Prisons Division at St. Margaret's House, Edinburgh, as opposed to the pre-release communication with the individual institution. Thereafter any change of supervising officer also needs to be notified to Prisons Division, as it will be recalled that the statute required the name of a "specified officer" to appear on the original licence.

During supervision the commission of any further offence by the offender needs to be notified to Prisons Division immediately, whatever the outcome of any court appearance. There is no leeway at all in this matter, and the situation is akin to that of a probationer committing a further offence, in that it calls the whole business of his release and licence into account. Greater flexibility obtains and more initiative is required, in the event of the offender not complying with the general requirements or with any specific condition of his licence. It is possible to arrange for a progress report to be submitted to Prisons Division, with a view to their sending a "warning letter" without either a further offence having been committed, or without as yet initiating proceedings for recall.

Should it prove necessary to initiate recall, the procedure involved is the writing of a report to Prisons Division setting out the circumstances of the breach and requesting recall. While no court proceedings are requested, the supervising officer should satisfy himself in his own mind that all reasonable opportunities have been afforded to the offender, and that his evidence affords an adequate basis on which to proceed. It has to be borne in mind that the offender will have to be released in the not too distant future, and may well continue to be under supervision under the original licence.

More positively, it is open to a supervising officer to submit a report to Prisons Division suggesting either the cancellation of any of the conditions or requirements of the licence, or its total discharge in advance of the due date on the grounds of good progress. In any event Prisons Division require a report on the ordinary termination of any after-care supervision, which is submitted on a form originally included in the papers sent to the supervising officer by the institution at the time of the offender's release. There is no objection to amending the layout of this form if the objectives of the final report are thereby enhanced.

Forms of Communication used in After-Care Work. The following are examples of forms in current use by Prisons Divisions for the after-care of young offenders: they are presented here in the usual sequence of arrival and use.

Request for Nomination of Supervising Officer. This form is issued at the stage in an offender's sentence at which the institution is making its official plans for release. In the event that it may not have been preceded by through care involvement, or an earlier request for home circumstances reports, it represents for the area social work office an urgent need to allocate a case, as release will be relatively imminent. If the offender is not known in the area to which it is proposed to release him, the area social work office needs from the institution all the background information as well, so that allocation can be undertaken properly.

To: The Director of Social Work   H.M.   Y.O.I.
       (Area Office or Divisional Address)   (Address)

Name   Date of birth   Address on release
David Williams   1.4.60   25 Simon Square
                                                      Eastville.

I write to inform you that the above named was sentenced to a period of 12 months
in a Young Offenders' Institution on 14th October, 1979, and that it is proposed
to release him to your area on 13th June, 1980.

Please nominate a Supervising Officer and return the tear-off portion of this form
to the above address indicating the Reporting Instructions and if the inmate can
return to the above address.

The tear-off portion should be returned not later than (date).

                         Yours faithfully

                         Governor.

To: The Governor,   Area Office
    HM. Y.O.I.   Date........

Name: David Williams (1.4.60)
      No. 2006/79

The Supervising Officer for the above named will be:

Name: Mrs L Smith, Senior Social Worker

Address: 43 High Street
         Eastville
         Telephone 73241

He will report to his Supervising Officer at the above address on 13th June, 1980
at 9.0 am.

He can return to the above address: Yes.

                    Signature: Mrs L Smith.

The Documents in the Case: Subsequently the institution will send to the nominated supervising officer the relevant papers for use in supervision.

To: Mrs L Smith   HM. Y.O.I.
         Senior Social Worker   Date........
         43 High Street
         Eastville

Name: David Williams (1.4.60)
         No 2006/78

Date of Release: 13th June 1980

Address: 25 Simon Square, Eastville.

I enclose herewith documents and A.C. forms required for supervision of the above
named person.

ACF 4 Should be completed and returned to AC HQ immediately after the initial release interview.   The completed ACF 6 (principal plus one copy) should be submitted at the termination of the supervision period.

                                        Yours sincerely,

                                        Governor

Enclosures: Copy of supervision order: pre-release report and
               copy of ACF 3: ACF4 (1 copy): ACF 6 (3 copies):
               Governor's report: copy of letter to parent.

Copy of After-Care Licence.   This is the document which the offender signs prior
to release, and of which a copy is sent to the supervising officer.   It is the
"Notice of the Secretary of State" referred to in the legislation: its status is
akin to that of the probation order in a probation case.

               PRISONS (SCOTLAND) ACT, 1952 (c.61)
               CRIMINAL JUSTICE (SCOTLAND) ACT, 1979 (c.44)
               Glenochil Young Offenders' Institution.

Name: David Williams   Date of Sentence: 14th October, 1979.
Date of Release: 13th June, 1980.   Supervision expires: 12th December 1980.

The Secretary of State in exercise of the powers conferred upon him by section 33
of the Prisons (Sctoland) Act, 1979, has determined that the person named above
shall, after release until the date herein stated, be under the supervision of Mrs
L Smith, Senior Social Worker, 43 High Street, Eastville, unless the Secretary of
State makes an order for recall, or orders supervision to cease before that date.

               REQUIREMENTS

Until the date of expiry of supervision, the person named above-

          shall not, except for any period spent in HM Forces, have a
          change of address without first obtaining the consent of the
          appointed supervising officer:

          shall obey the appointed supervising officer's instructions
          and shall be punctual and regular in attendance at employment;

          shall abstain from violation of the law and shall not associate
          with persons of bad character;

          shall, if returning to civil life from the Forces during the
          period of supervision, report at once by letter to the appointed
          supervising officer.

                           ———

ATTENTION IS DIRECTED TO THE PROVISIONS OF THE PRISONS (SCOTLAND)ACT 1952 AND THE
CRIMINAL JUSTICE (SCOTLAND)ACT, 1979

Failure to comply with any of the requirements listed above may lead to the Secretary of State issuing a recall order on a person who is under supervision after
release from a young offenders' institution;   failure to comply with the order of
recall may lead to arrest by a constable or prison officer without warrant and
return to the place where the person named above is required in accordance with

the law to be detained.

The period not exceeding 3 months in total for which a person under supervision is liable to be detained after recall shall commence from the date of being taken into custody under the order of recall.

Where a person sentenced to detention in a young offenders' institution, being under supervision after release from such an institution, is convicted of an offence punishable with imprisonment, the court may, instead of dealing with the case in any other manner, make an order for recall.

I hereby acknowledge that I understand the above requirements, which have been explained to me, and my liability to recall if they are not complied with.

Governor: Signed: (Inmate)

                                   Date:

Release Instructions   Form ACF 3.
                                             HM. Y.O.I.
                                             Glenochil

Release Instructions

Name: David Williams   Earliest date of release
Address on release: 25 Simon Square   13th June 1980
                    Eastville.

Supervising Officer: Mrs L Smith, Senior Social Worker
                       43 High Street
                       Eastville.
                       Telephone 73241

1. Travel Arrangements: You will need to travel by 'bus.

2. Other Instructions: To report to Mrs Smith at the above address at 9.0 am on
                         13th June.

3. You will have in your possession Form B79 (which should be presented at the
   local office of the Department of Health and Social Security on the day of your
   release).

                                   Governor.

Notification of Safe Arrival   Form ACF 4

To: Prison Divisions   43 High STreet,
    AC HQ   Eastville
    St. Margaret's House   13th June 1980
    Edinburgh.

Dear Sir

Name: David Williams (1.4.60)
       No. 2006/79

Released from HM Institution: Glenochil Y.O.I.   Date of Release 13 June 1980

Address: 25 Simon Square,   Supervision ending
          Eastville.   12th December, 1980

I write to confirm that the above named did report as instructed to me at 9.0 am this morning.

                                              Yours faithfully,

                                              Mrs. L. Smith,
                                              Senior Social Worker.

Termination of Supervision   Form ACF 6

To: Prisons Division   43 High Street,
    AC HQ,   Eastville
    St. Margaret's House,
    Edinburgh   13th December, 1980

Name: David Williams (1.4.60)
       No. 2006/79

Released from: HM YOI Glenochil.   Date of release: 13th June, 1980

Address: 25 Simon Square,   Supervision expires
          Eastville   12th December, 1980

Response to Supervision and Assessment

        Fairly ordinary: little change in outlook but kept the
        formal requirements.

Record of Employment: During Supervision Period.

        3 or 4 casual jobs of short duration. There is a good deal
        of unemployment in this area.

Any Further Convictions During Supervision Period:

        No.

                                              Signed: Mrs. L. Smith,
                                                       Senior Social Worker.

There are no other forms in standard or regular use. Any other sort of progress report, or applications for matters such as recall, warning letters, or early discharge, can be presented as an ordinary letter to Prisons Division, giving the sort of identification details common to all the forms shown above, but being set out according to the circumstances and needs of each case or situation. Similarly notification of changes of supervising officer, further offences, or transfers of supervision can be presented in ordinary letter form. Such letters might take the corresponding models from probation practice as illustrated.

Social Work Practice in After-Care

Although the "after-care notes" issued by SHHD and SWSG were primarily concerned with administrative provisions, as their full title indicates, they do nonetheless afford practice guidelines of a general kind, which clearly central government, as authors of the document, wish to support, without in any way usurping the autonomy of local social work departments and their responsibility for standards of professional practice. These practice guidelines afforded by the "after-care notes" may have more lasting significance than some of the now outdated administrative methods contained within them. Section II of these notes is entitled "Some Comments on Practice Procedure", and is reproduced here.

"The goals of social work service with offenders are similar to those for other client groups and include helping people to enhance and more effectively utilise their own problems solving capacities; linking people with systems that provide them with resources, services and opportunities; and promoting the best use of these. For this client group however it is important to recognise the particular need to modify attitudes and behaviour and to act as an agent of social control. This means reconciling the restrictions which might be necessary for the protection of society with the freedom of the individual which is essential if an offender is to take his place as a member of the community.

Social work with offenders and their families is a continuing process which may span a number of situations brought into being either by statutory orders or by voluntary referral. Former practices which divided for example, probation supervision from 'after-care' are inappropriate to modern social work practice. It has been said that 'after-care' should be fully integrated with the work of penal establishments, conceived as a process which starts as soon as sentence has been passed, developed during detention and available thereafter for as long as necessary".

1.   It is essential that all prisoners should be seen following conviction and sentence to a penal institution, before leaving the court building. This can be done by arrangement with the holding authority, usually the police but in the High Court, with prison staff. These arrangements should be made by Social Work Departments and should constitute a standing prodedure in working with offenders. It is quite common for many people sentenced to imprisonment to be unprepared for the realities of the situation. Early contact with the offender provides an opportunity to deal with matters of immediate concern to him and possibly his family. These can include a range of feelings about his sentence or practical domestic affairs such as advising a spouse or parents about the nature of the sentence and how to resolve urgent financial problems. The importance of this initial contact cannot be over-stressed. The offer of help at a time when the offender is being segregated from the community is a positive demonstration of concern for him as an individual and forges a stable link with systems within the community which he can use. It is possible that this experience will enable the offender to think of the relevance of social work contact during and after sentence and he is more likely to make constructive use of supervision on release than someone who considers he has been ignored after conviction and during sentence.

A brief note of the post-sentence interview and of action taken and proposed, together with a social enquiry report - if available - and any other relevant information should be forwarded with the minimum of delay to the social work unit in the receiving penal establishment. This will identify the community social workers' interest and involvement and lay the foundations for collaborative action with institutional staff.

2. A primary aim of penal policy is to enable the inmate on release to lead a
useful and industrious life. This cannot be accomplished in isolation at the
institution. It requires work to be undertaken by social workers during the
period of custody, in relation to social problems which may in fact be
contributory causes of the offenders criminality and affect the likelihood of
subsequent offending.

Invariably there are problems associated with the offenders separation from the
community and his future return to it. His ability to deal with his affairs in
the outside world is very limited. The extent to which a wife or relative can
give support depends not only on their personal abilities but also on the quality
of services and facilities which enable them to function in a supportive way.
The problems of a wife and children of a prisoner can be as acute as those of
single parent families. A custodial sentence is an event to which offenders and
their relatives adapt. Some of the adaptations can be seen as part of a positive
process of maturation, others are less favourable and some can exacerbate and
reinforce previous inappropriate patterns of social behaviour.

The social worker - both in the community and in the penal establishment - has
opportunities of organising intervention at a number of levels with a variety of
people and with the various systems in which they operate.

3. It is expected that there is continuity of contact from the point of sentence
with the social worker responsible for the prisoner. At the time of discharge
therefore the social worker will in fact be dealing with a current case, but one
in which the focus has shifted to a phase where the social worker himself or
herself is responsible for more direct action with the offender. During the
period within the prison there will already have been an exchange of information
between prison staff and social workers in the community. However, at the point
of release Prisons Division will formally provide details about the offender
relating to his response to custodial treatment, family situation, employment
possibilities, associates etc. The months immediately after release are crucial.
Many of the post-release problems should have been anticipated and as much action
as possible taken for their resolution before actual discharge. It is, however,
essential that there is close contact at the point of discharge in order that the
offender recognises the social worker's readiness to give appropriate help,
particularly in settling him in accommodation and employment and the work which
enables this to be done.

Speed is essential. There could be important immediate situations with which the
offender is faced and he will be adjusting to these, but the manner in which he
does so and the decisions which he makes, will affect the likely success or
failure of the period of supervision and the extent of risk to the community.
Contact at this critical point in time should be prompt, definite, and positive
and seen as having a priority in the competing demands for social workers' time.
The extent and nature of attention given during supervision should vary according
to the indiviual offender and not to any general labelling, but it is self-evident
that without appropriate contact the social worker and the offender cannot
discharge the responsibilities they each have in relation to the terms of
supervision. <u>Without contact there can be no work with the client</u>.

Considerations respecting Young Offenders

    i)   Parole

        Young offenders who are sentenced to periods of detention
in excess of 18 months are eligible for parole, but there
is a degree of overlap with adult considerations arising
from the fact that some of them may reach the age of 21
during their sentence: as a result there is a greater
range of possible eventualities. Schedule 5 of the 1980
Act, sets out the arrangements which apply.

        Sentences of detention on young offenders are pronounced
as " X years detention in a young offenders institution"
even when it is inevitable in view of the length of
sentence that the offender will become an adult during
it. The variety of possible outcomes stems first from
a degree of flexibility available to the prison system
to arrange for the transfer of young offenders to adult
prisons at any point between the ages of 21 and 23 while
they are serving their sentence, and secondly from whether
or not parole or ordinary after-care arrangements will
apply on release. A young offender can be transferred to
an adult prison as soon as he reaches the age of 21, but
need not be: one reason for keeping him in a young offenders institution, particularly if his release is fairly
imminent, may well be to ensure that he is released under
supervision.

        However, no one can be detained in a young offenders
institution beyond their 23rd birthday, and no parole or
after-care licence on a young offender can extend beyond
'.1s 23rd birthday (subsection 4 of Schedule 5 of the
1980 Act.) Once a young offender is transferred to an
adult prison, all the ordinary adult considerations apply
to him, and for parole and after-care purposes he is
deemed to be an adult.

        A young offender who receives more than 18 months detention,
but who does not get parole, is released on an ordinary
after-care licence, which will run for 12 months, except
that it may not continue past his 23rd birthday. We noted
above that young offenders who receive sentences of between
6 and 18 months detention are released on after-care licence
of only 6 months duration, and subject to the same restriction.

        A young offender who receives more than 18 months detention
and who does get parole is subject to that parole licence
until the expiry of the period of 12 months from the date
of such release, or until the expiry of the licence, whichever is the later, (1980 Act, Schedule 5, subsection 2.)
This arrangement replaces section 60(3)(b) of the 1967
Criminal Justice Act, 1967, which previously dealt with
young offenders, and which had the effect of continuing
their parole licences for a good deal longer in many cases.
Subsection 4 of the Schedule, which decrees that no licence
on a young offender shall remain under supervision beyond

his 23rd birthday has the effect of reducing periods of
after-care and parole on people sentenced as young offenders, and to make the periods of parole comparable to those
of people who are adults when sentenced.

Some examples will illustrate these details:

A, who is 17, is sentenced to 3 years detention. If he
does not get parole, he will be released, assuming he
earns full remission, after serving 2 years, but will be
under after-care supervision for 12 months. If he gets
parole and is released immediately after serving 12 months,
he will be on parole licence for a year, and it will expire
exactly at the two-thirds point of his sentence. However,
if he gets parole and is only released, due to various
circumstances, after serving 18 months, the effect of
subsection 2 is that his parole licence will still run
for 12 months, and will not expire at the two-thirds
point.

B, who is $18\frac{1}{2}$, is sentenced to 6 years detention. If he
does not get parole, he will be released, assuming he
earns full remission after serving 4 years, at age $22\frac{1}{2}$.
If he has not to be transferred to an adult prison, he
will be released on an after-care licence which would
ordinarily last for 12 months, except that in this case
it will expire after 6 months on his 23rd birthday - the
effect of subsection 4. If, however, he has been transferred to an adult prison, he will be released after
4 years, but the only after-care possible would be
voluntary after-care. If B gets parole, the earliest
point at which he could be given parole would be after
serving two years. At this point he would still be in
a young offenders institution. The 1980 Act's qualification
of section 60(3)(b) of the 1967 Act means that his parole
licence will expire at the two-thirds point of his sentence:
he will be on parole for two years. This is also the point
at which parole would expire, either if he got parole some
time after the two year point and/or if he was transferred
to an adult prison, and paroled from there.

C, who is 20 gets 6 years detention. If he does not get
parole he will have to serve 4 years, but would have had
to have been transferred to an adult prison because he
will be 24 years old by then: the only after-care will
be voluntary. He could be released on parole any time
after serving 2 years, but if he had not been transferred
to an adult prison prior to release, the parole licence
would have to terminate on his 23rd birthday. However,
if he is transferred to an adult prison any parole licence
would expire when he reaches the 4 year stage in his sentence
and by then he would be aged 24.

ii) Statutory After-Care

The statutory basis of young offender after-care was
originally set out in section 12 of the 1963 Criminal
Justice (Scotland) Act, but section 45(2) of the 1980

Act redefines that original section by setting out amended arrangements in its Schedule 5. Paragraph 2 of Schedule 5 makes the following arrangements in Substitution of S12 of the 1963 Act.

a) Young offenders sentenced to a period of, or periods totalling, 6 months or more detention in a young offenders institution may be required by notice of the Secretary of State given to them on release from that detention, both to be under supervision of such officer as may be specified in the notice, and to comply, while under the supervision, with such conditions as may be specified.

b) Young offenders whose period of detention does not exceed 18 months will be subject to supervision for 6 months after release. This replaces the period of the 12 months licence which applied prior to the 1980 Act.

c) Young offenders whose period of detention does exceed 18 months, but who are not released on parole, will be under supervision for 12 months after release.

d) No period of after-care supervision of a young offender shall continue past his 23rd birthday.

e) There is power for the Secretary of State to order young offenders sentenced to less than 6 months detention in a young offenders institution, but not less than 3 months, to be under after-care supervision. An identical power had existed since 1963, but instances of its use appear to be rare, or even non-existent.

f) There is power for the Secretary of State to modify or cancel any of the requirements or conditions of an after-care licence. This includes the power to discharge it early on the grounds of good progress.

g) Offenders released on after-care are liable to be recalled by the Secretary of State if they fail to conform to the requirements of after-care, or to comply with any specific condition which may have been inserted. The period of recall may not exceed 3 months but the offender can be released prior to such a period. Any remaining period of the original licence continues to be effective after release from recall, and thus the offender may become liable to a further recall. In this latter event the actual period spent on recall the first time has to be deducted from the overall 3 month liability, and so if the full period has been served the first time, no further sanctions remain and the licence becomes a dead letter.

The introduction of the 1980 Act does not affect the court's power to order recall to a young offenders' institution in cases where a person under supervision commits a further offence. The court's powers are set out at Section 212 for

cases on solemn procedure, and Section 421 for cases on
summary procedure, of the Criminal Procedure (Scotland)
Act, 1975. These sections allow that "where a person
sentenced to detention in a young offenders' institution,
being under supervision after his release from such an
institution, is convicted of an offence punishable with
imprisonment, the court may, instead of dealing with
him in any other manner, make an order for his recall."
The sections go on to determine that the court's order
for recall has exactly the same effect as one made by
the Secretary of State for a breach of requirement of a
licence. It should be noted that the court can only
order recall in cases where the offence in punishable
with imprisonment; for example a young offender under
supervision appearing before a District Court for plain
drunkenness could not be recalled by the court, though
he *could* be recalled by the Secretary of State. It
should also be noted that a court's order for recall is
instead of any other disposal.

iii) Children Sentenced to Detention

In respect of children ordered to be detained for residential
training under S413 of the C.P.(S) A. 1975, there is scope
for their return to their home community, by arrangement
between the manager of such institution and the local Social
Work Department, with the agreement of S.W.S.G. before the
expiry of the ordered period. Such children are technically
under the control of the stated institution to which they
may be returned at any time during the period of sentence,
with a minimum of administrative consultation.

The position regarding children sentenced by courts of
solemn procedure is somewhat different. S.44 of the 1980
Act substitutes a new form of the governing S.206 Criminal
Procedure (Scotland) Act 1975 which, in its original form
had suffered from a lack of clarity and definition. S.S.2
of the original is now extended to S.S.2-7 incl. and makes
specific arrangements for release and licence.

It provides for release on licence for children sentenced
for periods exceeding 18 months; it must be clearly understood that at the point of consideration, all such cases
will be subject to consideration by the Parole Board for
Scotland.

Further provision is made for the Secretary of State to
consult the Board regarding the inclusion or subsequent
insertion of conditions in the licence, or variation
or cancellation of such condition.

A licence issued under the new S.206 (section 44 of the
1980 Act(remains in force until either the expiry of
the original sentence or 12 months from the date of release
under licence whichever is the later. Thus a child who is
sentenced to 5 years detention and is released after 3 years
will be on licence for 2 years; whereas if he is not released
until after 4½ years of his sentence, he will be on licence

for 12 months, thus extending the effect of the court's
sentence beyond the originally specified 5 years.

Subsection 5 gives the Secretary of State power to
revoke a licence and recall the child to a place which
he directs. He can use this power on the recommendation
of the Parole Board or at his own instance, "where it
appears to him to be in the public interest to do so
before consultation with the Board is practicable."
Any person recalled under subsection 5 has to be informed
of the reasons for recall so that he can make representation
in writing to the Parole Board: the latter may, on receipt
of such representation, require the Secretary of State to
release him on licence forthwith. If a person is not released immediately after recall as a result of his represent-
ations, he remains in detention either until the expiry of
the original sentence, or for 3 months from the date of his
recall, whichever is the later. However, the Secretary of
State may, in spite of all this, release him again on
licence before the period of recall expires.

CUSTODIAL SENTENCES, AFTER-CARE, AND PAROLE

Age	Length of Sentence	Designation	Period served or remission	After-Care		Parole		Recall	
				Basis	Period of Supervision	Basis	Period of Supervision	By S of S	by Court
Under 16	Fixed sentence No limit Solemn Procedure	Detention in a YOI and liable to be detained for life. S43 CJ(S)A 80.	Indeterminate within original limit	N/A	N/A	S.44 CJ(S) A79.S of S plus Parole Board.	Rest of original sentence	Rest of sentence or 3 months: further release possible	N/A
	Fixed sentence 2 years max. Summary Procedure	Residential Training S413 CP(S) A '75	Indeterminate within original limit	N/A	N/A	S of S SWSG	Rest of original sentence	Rest of original sentence	N/A
Under 18 for murder	Life	Detention without limit of time.S43CJ (S)A.80	Indeterminate	N/A	N/A	S61 CJA 1967 S of S plus Parole Board	Life	Revocation Review in 12 months	Revocation Review in 12 months
16 to 21	28 days up to 4 months	Detention Centre Training	One-third remission available	Voluntary	Voluntary	N/A	N/A	N/A	N/A
	Less than 28 days; or 4 mths. to 6 mths.	Young Offenders Institution	No remission One-third remission	Voluntary	Voluntary	N/A	N/A	N/A	N/A
	6 months to 18 months	Young Offenders Institution	One-third remission available	Section 45 & Schedule 5 CJ(S)A 80	6 months	N/A	N/A	3 months	3 months
	18 months and over	Young Offenders Institution	One-third remission or Parole	Section 45 CJ(S)A 80 + Schedule 5					

CUSTODIAL SENTENCES, AFTER-CARE, AND PAROLE

Age	Length of Sentence	Designation	Period served or remission	After-Care Basis	After-Care Period of Supervision	Parole Basis	Parole Period of Supervision	Recall By S of S	Recall by Court
18-21 for murder	Life	Detention in a YOI and liable to be detained for life. S42 CJ(S)A 79.	Indeterminate	N/A	N/A	S61 CJA 1967 S of S & Parole Board	Life	Revocation 12 months review	Revocation 12 months review
21 and over	Up to 18 months	Imprisonment	One-third remission	Voluntary	Voluntary	N/A	N/A	N/A	N/A
			OR						
	18 months and over	Imprisonment	One-third remission	Voluntary	Voluntary	N/A	N/A	N/A	N/A
			Parole	N/A	N/A	S60(1)CJA 67 S of S & P.B.	Up to two-thirds point of sentence	Revocation 12 months review	Revocation 12 months review
21 and over for murder	Life	Life	Indeterminate	N/A	N/A	S61 CJA 67 S of S & P.B.	Life	Revocation 12 months review	Revocation 12 months review

Chapter 11

Rehabilitation of Offenders Act

This short Act is of considerable complexity: in essence it intends to enable
offenders to put their past behind them, by erasing their criminal records after a
suitable crime-free period. Its aims are expressed by the Act thus:

> "to rehabilitate offenders who have not been convicted of
> any serious offence for periods of years; to penalise the
> unauthorised disclosure of their previous convictions; to
> amend the law of defamation".

The provisions of the Act apply equally to Scotland, England and Wales, except
Section 3 which is specific to disposals made by the Children's Hearings under the
Social Work (Scotland) Act 1968. The Act is qualified by a Statutory Instrument
(1975, no.1023: Rehabilitation of Offenders Act 1974, (Exceptions) Order, 1975)
which gives "exceptions and interpretations" to the Act. The provisions in the Act
are contained within 11 Sections.

Important principles of the Act are:-

1. Some sentences are outwith its provisions and may never be
    erased.

2. The periods of rehabilitation vary, according to sentences.

3. A further conviction during the rehabilitation period may
    render null and void the rehabilitation consideration for
    the original sentence.

4. Disclosure of convictions can be part of the official duties
    of officials in social work, Police, etc: moreover, entry to
    such professions may necessitate the disclosure of *all* (if any)
    convictions of the applicant.

The Act takes into account offences committed before and after its enactment, 31st
July 1974. Throughout the Act the word 'spent' is used to describe convictions
which have been 'lived down' and which, therefore, may not be disclosed without
specific authority.

The Effect of Rehabilitation

The act says that *with some exceptions*, a rehabilitated person "shall be treated for all purposes in law as a person who has not committed, or been charged with, or prosecuted for, or convicted of, or sentenced for the offence or offences which were the subject of that conviction". This means that a rehabilitated person can regard himself as a person of good character who has no criminal convictions to disclose. The Home Office booklet of guidance gives examples of situations in which the rehabilitated person *need* not disclose his spent convictions:-

a)   filling in forms (e.g. for a job, to join a union) or at interviews

b)   refusal of or dismissal from employment because of a spent conviction

c)   making an agreement for hire purchase or insurance

d)   giving evidence in civil proceedings.

The important qualifying factor in all the above remarks (including the examples given) is the fact that there are exceptions to these general rehabilitative provisions. These are listed in the Statutory Instrument already mentioned. The chief exception is that the Act does *not* apply to any subsequent criminal proceedings, whether the rehabilitated person appears as witness or as a result of a further charge. However, the practices of Procurators Fiscal in the quotation of previous convictions can take account of the spirit and intentions of the Act in the compilation of schedules of previous convictions submitted to the court.

Exempted Sentences

Under Section 5 of the Act, the following convictions can never be expunged. While, in the course of time, an offender may incur convictions subsequently to those listed, and in due course the later convictions may be expunged, there are some major penalties which remain on the record for all time and which never become 'spent'. These sentences must for all purposes be considered to be outwith the scope of the Act:-

1.   Sentence of life imprisonment.

2.   Sentence of detention during Her Majesty's Pleasure; this sentence is imposed on persons under 18 convicted of murder: Section 206(1) Criminal Procedure (Scotland) Act 1975.

3.   Sentence of corrective training. Corrective training was a form of imprisonment imposed under Section 21(1) of the Criminal Justice (Scotland) Act 1949, on offenders under 30 years of age who had a number of previous convictions.

4.   Sentence of preventive detention. Preventive detention was a form of imprisonment imposed under Section 21(2) of the Criminal Justice (Scotland) Act 1949 on persistent offenders.

5.   Sentence of detention for a period in excess of 30 months, under Section 206(2) of the Criminal Procedure (Scotland) Act 1975 or under the equivalent English Act: (Persons under 18 convicted of serious crimes on solemn procedure).

6.   Any sentence of imprisonment in excess of 30 months.

Rehabilitation Periods

With the above exceptions, any other conviction is subject to the terms of the Act.
The Act's complexities begin with the calculations necessary to work out the
rehabilitation period for the various sentences, together with the age of the
accused at the time of conviction.   The tables given at Section 5(2) in the Act
have here been extended, and examples given, in the interests of clarity.

Table A   Standard Sentences

Table A refers to a standard list of convictions, none of which is a sentence
exceeding 30 months in duration.   The rehabilitation periods are 5, 7 and 10 years:
these periods, in relation to offenders under 17 at the time of conviction, are
half of the period given for adults.

Sentence	Rehabilitation Period
A sentence of imprisonment (or of corrective training) for a term exceeding 6 months but not exceeding 30 months.	10 years
A sentence of imprisonment for a term not exceeding 6 months.	7 years
A fine.	5 years

Any fine imposed, irrespective of amount, or of such matters as fine supervision
orders, or imprisonment in default, is, for the purposes of this Act, deemed to be
a 'spent' conviction 5 years from the date of conviction.

For persons aged under 17 at the time of any such conviction the period is halved.

Example: A, aged 25, for an offence of theft is given a sentence of imprisonment
           of 12 months on January 3rd, 1974.   Provided he commits no further
           offences, he would be rehabilitated and the conviction spent on
           January 2nd, 1984.

           B, aged 16, jointly charged with A, was sentenced to 3 months
           detention.   Again provided he commits no further offence he
           would be rehabilitated and the conviction spent on
           July 3rd, 1977.

Table B   Sentences Confined to Young Offenders

Sentence	Rehabilitation Period
Borstal Training	7 years
A sentence of detention for a term exceeding 6 months but not exceeding 30 months:	5 years
i.e. under Section 206(2) of the Criminal Procedure (Scotland) Act 1975, or in England and Wales, under Section 53 of the Children	

Sentence	Rehabilitation Period
and Young Persons Act 1933.	
A sentence of detention for a term not exceeding 6 months: but only under either of the same Sections; i.e. not an ordinary sentence of imprisonment imposed on a young offender - in which event Table A above applies.	3 years
Detention Centre Training	3 years

There is no cross reference to adult rehabilitation periods, as this table is confined to certain specific sentences which can only be imposed on young offenders. Young offenders may receive ordinary prison sentences, but in this event Table A above applies.

It is important to note that these periods can be extended if a person is convicted of a further offence within the rehabilitation periods of a previous conviction (see S.H.H.D. Circular 26/1975 and below).

Table C   Other Court Orders and Requirements

This is a compendium table covering a range of orders made both by Courts (including Juvenile Courts in England and Wales) and by Children's Hearings in Scotland, except that decisions taken by the Reporter *alone* are *not* convictions. There is no difference in the rehabilitation periods according to the age of the offender at the time of conviction. The important point about this table is that there are *alternative* rehabilitation periods depending on the length and nature of the orders concerned. The period is calculated from the date of the conviction, or finding of guilt.

Nature of Order	Rehabilitation Period		
	I	OR	II
Absolute Discharge	6 months		(not applicable)
Discharge of referral by Children's Hearing	6 months		(not applicable)
Conditional Discharge Bound over to keep the peace Bound over to be of good behaviour Caution Probation	1 year		OR to the end of the order whichever is the longer period
Supervision Order under the Children and Young Persons Act 1969 in England and Wales.	1 year		OR to the end of the order whichever is longer.
Supervision Order under Section 44(1)(a) OR (b) Social Work (Scotland) Act 1968.			
Residential Training as arranged by the Secretary of State ordered under Section 413 of Criminal Procedure (Scotland) Act 1975 - previously	1 year		OR to the end of the order whichever is longer.

Nature of Order	Rehabilitation Period

Section 58(a) Children and Young Persons
(Scotland) Act 1937:

Fit Person Order	1 year	OR to the end of the order
Approved School Order		whichever is <u>longer</u>

These two disposals were available under
earlier Children's Acts in both Scotland
and England and Wales, but have now been
superseded. However they are included
here both for completeness and because
the convictions may not have become
spent in view of later offences on the
part of the offenders concerned.

Fit Person Order: Section 61, Children
and Young Persons (Scotland) Act 1937
<u>or</u> Section 57, Children and Young Persons
Act 1933 (England and Wales). Approved
School Order: Section 61, Children and
Young Persons (Scotland) Act 1937 <u>or</u>
Section 57 Children and Young Persons
Act 1933 (England and Wales).

28 days in Remand Home

1 year after the date on which the order ceased to have effect   OR   (not applicable)

Under the earlier Children's Acts
already referred to it was possible,
on a finding of guilt, for Juvenile
Courts to order detention in a remand
home. This was a discreet disposal:
it constituted a sentence and is not to
be confused with remands for the purpose
of investigation and report compilation.
(Section 54, Children and Young Persons
Act 1933).

Attendance Centre Order

1 year after the date on which the order ceased to have effect   OR (not applicable)

Under the Criminal Justice Act
(England and Wales) 1948, Section 19
These centres were designed to occupy
offenders on Saturday afternoons:
sentences could not exceed 24 hours
and the sentence was performed in a
number of 2 hour periods. The centres
are staffed by the Police, but this
has never been a Scottish Court disposal.

Examples: i) Y is required to find caution of £30 for his good
                behaviour for a period of 6 months, on March 10th,1975.
                The conviction is spent on March 9th, 1976 (i.e. a year
                from the date of conviction).

           ii) On the same date, Z was put on probation for two years.
                The rehabilitation period in this case is the same as
                the duration of the order, and the conviction would be
                spent on March 9th, 1977.

iii) On the same date, Q was also put on probation for 2 years;
      however, a year later, the order is discharged on the
      grounds of his good progress. In this case, the
      rehabilitation period is only <u>one</u> year.

Breach of Probation

iv) Assume Z breaches his probation order 4 months later by
     the commission of a further offence:

a) If the court proceeds to deal with the original
    offence, the probation order is terminated and the
    conviction for the original offence remains until
    both it and the later conviction (which constitutes
    the breach) have been expunged following the normal
    guidelines of this Act.

b) If the court does not deal with the original offence
    the original conviction will stand, not spent until
    the rehabilitation period for the <u>new</u> offence has
    been completed, even though the probation order may
    have expired well before then.

Table D   Orders Under the Mental Health Acts

Table D is concerned with hospital orders made, on conviction, under the Mental
Health Act 1959, and the Mental Health (Scotland) Act 1960. Subsection 7 of the
Section 5 states the rehabilitation periods.

Order under Part V of the Mental Health (Scotland) Act 1960 with or without an order restricting discharge	5 years	OR until 2 years <u>after</u> the order ceases to have effect, whichever is the <u>longer</u> period.

Examples: i) A is made the subject of a hospital order on June 14th, 1970:
               no restrictions are imposed.
               Hospital Orders are not specified by the court as being
               for a fixed period: if no restrictions are imposed, they
               lapse after 12 months unless reviewed and renewed by the
               medical authorities. Assuming A's order actually lapses
               before 5 years, his conviction, whatever the period of his
               actual detention, will be spent on 13th June 1975.

ii) B is made the subject of a hospital order on the same day,
     but a restriction on discharge is imposed without limit
     of time. His actual discharge is, therefore, determined
     by the medical authorities, but the discharge of the order
     may not follow for some time after his release. His con-
     viction becomes spent 2 years after the order ceases to
     have effect i.e. after it is discharged, not after he is
     physically discharged from the hospital.

Table E   Miscellaneous Provisions

i) Any sentence, not otherwise   5 years
    covered in the above provisions,
    which is open to rehabilitation.
    For example no mention is made

in the Act of Community
Service Orders: these
would be covered by this
5 year rule.
It is worthy of note that
in Scotland, unpaid work as
a requirement of probation
would be subject to the
probation considerations
and, therefore, carry a
much shorter rehabilitation
period.

ii) Any order disqualifying,   To the end of the order
     prohibiting, or imposing
     any other penalty.

This means, for example, that driving disqualification or
endorsement may have the effect of extending the rehabilitation
period for an offence beyond what it otherwise would have been.
X, aged 16, is fined and disqualified from driving for 3 years:
the fine would normally result in the conviction being 'spent'
after $2\frac{1}{2}$ years in view of X's age, but the driving disqualification
ensures that X must wait the full 3 years before his conviction
is spent.

iii) Deferred Sentence.   This is an interim measure, not of
      itself constituting a conviction. The decision made at
      the subsequent hearing and the penalty imposed thereat will
      be the operative factors under this Act.

iv) Suspended Sentence of Imprisonment.   This sentence is
     treated as a sentence imposed on the original date, even
     though the actual serving of the sentence may not take
     effect unless a further offence is committed during the
     operational period of the suspension. Even if the sentence
     is varied, should it be put into effect (e.g. only 6 months
     of an original 12 months sentence are ordered to be served),
     it is the original length of sentence that counts for the
     purposes of this Act (i.e. the 12 months ordered and not
     the 6 months served in the terms of the example, which
     therefore attracts a 10 year period, and not one of 7 years).

v) Consecutive and Concurrent Terms of Imprisonment.   Consecutive
    terms of imprisonment, and terms which are wholly or partly
    concurrent, shall be treated as single terms for the purpose
    of this Act, so that, for example:-

    a) two consecutive sentences of 6 months imposed on
        the same occasion shall be counted as a single
        term of 12 months (thereby attracting a 10 years
        rehabilitation period).

    b) two concurrent sentences of 6 months imposed on
        the same occasion amounts to one 6 month period
        spent in custody (thereby attracting only a
        7 year rehabilitation period).

Offenders Abroad.

i) The Act does not apply to Northern Ireland: however, certain orders made under British legislation but having an effect in Northern Ireland are within the scope of the order. (For example, under Section 72(2) of the Social Work (Scotland) Act 1968, children made subject to a supervision requirement by a Children's Hearing who subsequently move to Northern Ireland can become subject to a probation order in lieu of the original order once they move, and the rehabilitation considerations applicable to the original order apply).

ii) Convictions recorded in foreign courts are regarded as coming within the scope of the Act, providing that the foreign conviction would also have been a crime here.

iii) The Act is not valid outside Great Britain, and spent convictions here are not necessarily so regarded elsewhere.

Convictions in the Services. The Act also applies to those convictions in the services which were:-

either for offences against the ordinary criminal law or for 'service' offences which carry some serious moral blame.

However, if the offence was a purely 'service' one of a kind which most people would not consider criminal (e.g. failure to salute), the Act only applies if the sentence was 3 months detention or more. The Home Office booklet gives the following example:-

On 30th March 1971, a sailor was convicted by a Naval Court Martial of indecency with another sailor and sentenced to 1 month's detention. Being an ordinary crime in civilian law, the usual rehabilitation considerations do apply (i.e. it becomes spent on 30/3/76). On 9/4/72 he receives 7 days detention from his C.O. for swearing: this is too trivial either to attract the attention of the Act or to extend the period in relation to the first offence.

The rehabilitation periods are:-

Sentence of cashiering, discharge with ignominy or dismissal with disgrace	10 years
Sentence of dismissal	7 years
Any sentence of detention	5 years

Further offences during the rehabilitation period.

i) In general terms, when a further offence takes place during the rehabilitation period, the period applicable to the earlier offence is considered to be extended for the duration of the later one. An offender would need to quote both if obliged to do so, even if the rehabilitation period for the first one would otherwise have expired.

For example, in June 1964, J was sentenced to 3 months imprisonment for theft: that would normally be spent in June 1971. In

In April 1970, he is again convicted of theft and fined
£50: that becomes spent in April 1975. However, if
required in applying for a job in August of 1971, he
would have to give details of both convictions.

ii) If the rehabilitation period for the later offence is
shorter than that for the earlier one, it nonetheless
continues until the expiry of that earlier conviction.

Example: D is fined in May 1972: in January 1973, he
is put on probation for a year, which he completes
satisfactorily. Although the conviction in respect of
which the probation order was made would normally have
been spent in January 1974, it stays with him until May
1977 when the fine becomes spent.

iii) There are some minor offences which do not carry imprisonment as a possible penalty (e.g. drunkenness, various
bye-law offences, and others typically tried by District
Courts) which represent exceptions to the above
considerations. Similar convictions in foreign courts are
also subject to the same exceptions.

Example: G is put on probation for a year for assault;
he subsequently appears before the District Court for
being drunk and incapable and is admonished. Although
the 6 months rule relating to the admonishment may
extend beyond the expiry date of the probation, the
offence of assault does become spent on successful
completion of the probation.

Disclosure of spent convictions. The second aim of the Act is to "penalise the
unauthorised disclosure" of previous convictions. To underline the importance of
this, the Act creates a new offence for which the maximum fine is £200. Another
new offence, created by the Act carries penalties of £400 or 6 months' imprisonment, or both, for a person convicted of obtaining specified information from
official records by means of fraud, dishonesty, or bribe. Those in possession or
receipt of information concerning a person's previous convictions should, therefore, exercise great care.

Such information is termed by the Act "specified information" and is defined in
Section 9(1) as "information imputing that a named or otherwise identifiable
rehabilitated living person has committed or been charged with or prosecuted for
or convicted of or sentenced for any offence which is the subject of a spent conviction". The wide scope of this definition should be noted - it embraces not
simply police lists of convictions, but also suggestions or implications of crime
("information imputing"): in practical terms this covers outcome such as verdicts
of not guilty or not proven; references to No Action decisions or other matters
referred to the Reporter of a Children's Hearing which did not result in a formal
disposal by a Hearing.

Disclosure of previous convictions is *not* an offence if it is part of a person's
"official duties". The meaning of this phrase is not defined in the Act, and it
is possible that its interpretation will only ultimately be tested in a court case.
However, SHHD Circular 26/1975 does offer useful guidance along these lines:

i) "The term has a wide meaning, and is not, for example,
confined only to duties imposed by statute . . .
The purpose . . . is to prevent deliberate disclosure

to a person who has no right to the specified information
and would have no lawful use for it". We discussed above,
respecting social enquiries, the appropriateness of social
workers providing the court with information about the
totality of a person's previous convictions in a social
enquiry report, over and above the more limited or edited
list of convictions that might have been submitted by the
prosecution in the spirit of this Act. In any event,
Section 7 of the Act excludes further criminal proceedings
from the scope of the Act, and thus the comment in the
Circular only serves to emphasise the propriety of this
particular aspect of the report writer's official duties.

ii)   Disclosure in the following circumstances should not be
      regarded as contravening Section 9(2) of the Act:-

      a)   disclosure in accordance with a statutory duty

      b)   disclosure to persons or authorities, who by virtue
           of the exceptions provided for by Order of the
           Secretary of State, have a lawful use for information
           about spent convictions.

      c)   disclosure to persons or authorities who, though not
           exempted, will continue to have a proper use for such
           information (e.g. Local Authorities assessing the
           suitability of a person to have care of children).

      d)   disclosure for official purposes between officers of
           the same organisation (e.g. different departments of
           a local authority), or officers of related organisations
           (e.g. social workers and police).

iii) Special care should be exercised in disclosing information
      about previous convictions to those who require the
      information to assess a person's suitability for employment.
      The chief exception here is that some professions listed in
      the Statutory Instrument (1975, no.1023) require full inform-
      ation about *all* the convictions of a potential applicant
      (e.g. social work, police, prison service). It has also been
      ascertained that candidates for social work training courses
      are included in this rule which requires total disclosure of
      spent convictions.

There are other more general circumstances in which disclosure of
spent convictions can lawfully be made:-

I.   Disclosure can be made to the rehabilitated person. It
     would not be an offence to draw the attention of the person,
     if official duties so demanded, to any or all of his
     previous (including spent) convictions. A social worker
     would be within his rights to make reference to past
     criminality in pursuance of his efforts to help the client
     if necessary in the context of the immediate supervising
     relationship (e.g. if discharge of probation was requested
     by the probationer, or more generally in helping the
     client face reality, to prevent a further lapse into crime).

II. Spent convictions may be disclosed to any other person
     at the express wish of the rehabilitated person.

Situations may arise where the rehabilitated person
positively wants it known that he has been crime-free for
a period of years (e.g. person previously on probation
wishing to enter a particular employment, or the armed
forces). It is important that the official concerned is
absolutely sure that he acts on an express and not an
implicit wish of the rehabilitated person, and written
confirmation may be advisable.

<u>Limitations on rehabilitation</u>. There are certain limitations imposed by the Act
(Section 7) which qualify the guiding principle set out in the preamble. Nothing
in the Act shall affect:-

  i) The Royal Prerogative to grant free pardons, to quash
     convictions, or to commute sentences.

  ii) The enforcement of any process to enforce fines or any
      other sum to be paid under a Court Order. For example,
      even if the conviction is spent by virtue of the time
      elapsed, the penalties for non-payment can still be applied.

  iii) The issue of process in respect of breach of any condition
       or requirement of a Court Order. For example, a breach of
       requirement of a probation order may still be prosecuted
       even if the order has terminated - it may be that a
       further offence comes to light, or an actual arrest is
       made in regard to a previously existing warrant. It may
       well be that the penalty imposed for the breach attracts
       a different rehabilitation consideration, even though
       probation is normally spent on the date the order terminates.

  iv) Any prohibition, disqualification, disabling or other penalty
      which extends beyond the rehabilitation period of the
      associated conviction.

      <u>Examples</u>:

      a) A is admonished for careless driving, but disqualified
         for 3 years: the conviction becomes spent well before
         the disqualification ceases to apply.

      b) B is sentenced to a period of imprisonment for possessing
         fire-arms, and the court orders a prohibition on the
         possession of fire-arms for life, the prohibition applies
         for life, even if the conviction becomes spent.

Section 7 also provides certain safeguards to protect the public welfare, and that
of individuals who might be placed in 'jeopardy' by the operation of the rehabilitation clauses (Subsection 2). In certain circumstances, spent previous convictions can be referred to without penalty, and in some situations persons can be
required to admit them. The following situations can include such reference:-

  i) Any criminal proceedings, including any appeal.

  ii) Any service disciplinary proceedings or appeal therefrom.

  iii) Any proceedings relating to adoption, guardianship, wardship,
       marriage, custody, care or control, or access to any minor
       (i.e. child under 18), or the provision of care, schooling or
       accommodation for minors.

    iv) Any care proceedings or appeal therefrom under Section 1
       of the 1969 Children and Young Persons Act (England and
       Wales); or in any proceedings relating to the variation
       or discharge of an order made under that Section.

    v) Any proceedings before a Children's Hearing, or any appeal
      therefrom.

The intention of the Act is that, notwithstanding its primary purpose, there should
be no obstacle to justice being seen to be done, especially in such situations
where the public interest or rights of an individual are at stake.

If the rehabilitated person is a party or witness in such proceedings, he can
consent to the revelation of any spent conviction(s); but equally a judicial
authority has power to order disclosure if it is considered necessary to the
justice of the proceedings - the emphasis is on the 'has power', not on any automatic ordering of such disclosure. Finally, subsection 5 states "no order made by
a Court otherwise than on conviction shall be included in any list of convictions
given or made to any court which is considering how to deal with him in respect
of any offence".

APPENDIX

Section 27 of the Social Work (Scotland) Act, 1968

Section 27 of the Social Work (Scotland) Act was designed to give legal effect to the integration of the former Scottish probation service into the newly created local authority social work departments.

Previously the framework and organisation of the probation service had been the creation of criminal justice legislation, and immediately prior to 1968 the arrangements were set out in schedule 3 of the 1949 Criminal Justice (Scotland) Act. It is instructive to set out, if only for purposes of comparison, the substantive parts of that schedule:-

Clause 1. provided for the definition of probation areas

Clause 2. defined the constitution of probation committees

Clause 3. set out the duties of probation committees:-

(1) It shall be the duty of every probation committee -

    (a) to appoint sufficient salaried probation officers for their probation area, subject, in the case of such classes or descriptions of probation officers as may be prescribed, to the approval of the appointment by the Secretary of State;

    (b) to pay to the probation officers appointed for their area such remuneration, allowances and expenses as may be prescribed;

    (c) to provide for the efficient carrying out of the work of probation officers and to supervise such work and to receive reports by such officers.

    (d) to make such payments and to such persons as may be prescribed in respect of persons under the supervision of probation officers, being persons required by a probation order or supervision order to reside in any place otherwise than for the purpose of their submitting to treatment of their mental condition as voluntary or resident patients; and their mental condition as voluntary or resident patients; and

(e) to perform such other duties in connection with the work of
    probation officers as may be prescribed.

Clause 4 said the duties of probation officers were:-

It shall be the duty of probation officers to supervise the
probationers and other persons placed under their supervision
and to advise, assist and befriend them; to inquire, in accordance with any directions of the court, into the circumstances
or home surroundings of any person with a view to assisting
the court in determining the most suitable method of dealing
with his case; to advise and befriend in such cases and in
such manner as may be prescribed, persons who have been released from custody; and to perform such other duties as may
be prescribed or may be imposed by any enactment.

Clause 5 referred to the selection of officers for particular types
of cases.

Clause 6 organised any sharing of expenses between probation areas, and,

Clause 7 gave the Secretary of State powers to make rules:-

(a) regulating the constitution, procedure, powers and duties of
    probation committees and case committees and the appointment
    and tenure of office of the members thereof;

(b) regulating the qualifications, manner of appointment, condit-
    ions of service and duties of probation officers;

(c) fixing scales of salaries and remuneration of salaried probation
    officers, and of expenses to be allowed to salaried and volun-
    tary probation officers;

(d) regulating the expenditure which may be incurred by probation
    and case committees and the manner in which such expenditure
    is to be defrayed;

(e) requiring probation committees to furnish reports with respect
    to the work or duties of their probation officers;

(f) empowering local authorities to appoint the clerk and other
    officers (other than probation officers) of probation com-
    mittees;

(g) for the auditing of the accounts of probation committees; and

(h) for prescribing anything else which under the provisions of
    this Schedule may be prescribed.

As against the fairly specific and even detailed arrangements of schedule 3 of the
1949 Act, section 27 of the Social Work Act goes for a broader opening "it shall be
a function of every local authority ... to provide a service for the following
purposes ..." and it leaves much of the detail to be worked out in a "probation
scheme" which each authority must have, and whose concepts the Secretary of State
must approve. Whilst subsection 7 of section 27 repeals the third schedule of the
1949 Act, subsection 6 previously required that "any function required by any

enactment to be performed by a probation officer shall . . . be performed by an
officer of the . . . local authority."

The contents of most probation schemes do not appear to include the wealth and
variety of detailed arrangments that were the subject of the rules previously
made by the Secretary of State under the 1949 Act. This means that everything from
conditions of service to the minutiae of social work practice, which had featured
in the "Probation Rules" which were previously made by the Secretary of State, no
longer are controlled or defined with the degree of close attention which previously
obtained, and that as a result, local authorities are much more the master of their
own affairs, particularly in relation to standards and methods of professional
practice.

It is an interesting comment that the duty on individual probation officers in the
1949 Act to advise, assist and <u>befriend</u> their charges has been replaced in section
27 of the 1968 Act by an obligation on the collectivity of a local authority to
"provide a service for . . . the supervision, and the provision of advice and
assistance" to such people: it seems as if the notion of "befriending" has been
removed from the social work task in this area of work.

Section 27 of the 1968 Act reads in full:-

(1) It shall be a function of every local authority under this part of this Act
to provide a service for the following purposes, that is to say:-

    (a) making available to any Court such Social Background Reports and
        other reports relating to persons appearing before the Court which
        the Court may require for the disposal of a case;

    (b) the supervision, and the provision of advice, guidance and
        assistance for:-

        (i) persons in their area who are under supervision by order
            of a Court made in the exercise of its criminal jurisdiction
            by virtue of any enactment, and

        (ii) persons in their area who, following on release from prison
            or any other form of detention, are required to be under
            supervision under any enactment or by the terms of an Order
            or licence of the Secretary of State or of a condition or
            requirement imposed in pursuance of any enactment.

(2) For the purposes of the foregoing subsection every local authority shall,
after consultation with the Sheriffs having jurisdiction in their area, prepare
a scheme (hereinafter referred to as a probation scheme) and submit it by such
date, as he may require, to the Secretary of State for his approval.

(3) A probation scheme shall make provision with regard to the following matters:-

    (a) the manner in which any report requested by the Court from the
        local authority is to be prepared and submitted to the Court;

    (b) arrangements for the attendance of officers of the local authority
        at the Court:

    (c) arrangements for the co-operation of the local authorities with
        the Courts, and such arrangements may include the appointment of
        one or more Sheriffs having jurisdiction of their areas to the

Social Work Committee and to any Sub-Committee thereof;

(d) arrangements for the keeping of adequate records and statistics regarding the performance of functions under this Section; and

(e) such matters as the local authority considers relevant to the service to be provided.

(4) The Secretary of State may approve a probation scheme with or without modifications.

(5) A local authority may apply to the Secretary of State for the revision of a probation scheme and, if the Secretary of State so requires, shall prepare and submit to the Secretary of State for his approval a revised scheme or a modification of an existing scheme.

(6) Any function required by any enactment to be performed by a probation officer shall, after the coming into operation of this Part of this Act, be performed by an officer of the appropriate local authority.

(7) Section 11 of and Schedule 3 to the Criminal Justice (Scotland) Act 1949 (administrative provisions as to probation) shall cease to have effect.

BIBLIOGRAPHY

Acts of Parliament;

        1948 Criminal Justice Act (England and Wales).
        1949 Criminal Justice (Scotland) Act.
        1960 Mental Health (Scotland) Act.
        1963 Criminal Justice (Scotland) Act.
        1967 Criminal Justice Act.
        1968 Social Work (Scotland) Act.
        1969 Children and Young Persons Act (England and Wales).
        1972 Criminal Justice Act (England and Wales).
        1973 Powers of Criminal Courts Act (England and Wales).
        1974 Rehabilitation of Offenders Act.
        1975 Criminal Procedure (Scotland) Act.
        1975 Children Act.
        1977 Criminal Law Amendment Act.
        1978 Community Service by Offenders (Scotland) Act.
        1980 Criminal Justice (Scotland) Act.
        1980 Bail (Scotland) Act.

H.M.S.O.

        1961 Report of the Interdepartmental Committee on the
             Business of the Higher Criminal Courts. Cmnd. 1289
             (The Steatfeild Report).
        1962 Report of the Interdepartmental Committee on the
             Probation Service. Cmnd. 1650.
             (The Morison Report).
        1963 Report of the Advisory Council on the Treatment of
             Offenders: the Organisation of After-Care.
        1969 The Sentence of the Court: a Handbook for Courts on
             the Treatment of Offenders.
        1970 Report of the Advisory Council on the Penal System:
             Non- and semi-custodial penalties.
             (The Wootton Report).
        1974 Report of the Advisory Council on the Penal System:
             Young Adult Offenders.
             (The Younger Report).
        1974 Crime and the Prevention of Crime:
             Memorandum by the Scottish Council on Crime.
        1974 Guide to the Rehabilitation of Offenders Act.
        1975 The Legal System of Scotland.
        1975 Second Report of the Committee on Criminal Procedure;
             (The Thomson Report).
        1976 Reparation by Offenders;
             (The Dunpark Report).

Also;   Annual reports of the Parole Board for Scotland,
              "   "   Prisons in Scotland.
         The Prison Rules.

Other References:

Davies M. and Knopf A. "Social Enquiry Reports and
     the Probation Service"   H.O.R.U. 1973

Ford P. "Advising Sentencers"   O.U.Penal Research Unit   1972

Hiddleston V. "Reports to Childrens Hearings" in:-
     "Childrens Hearings" (Ed) Martin F.M. and Murray K.   1976

Howard League for Scotland "Taken In" and   1975
     "Probation in Scotland-the case for revival"   1976

Jarvis F.F. "Probation Officers' Manual"   Butterworth   1969

Perry F.G. "Information for the Courts"   Cambridge   1974

Renton and Brown. "Criminal Procedure" (4th ed.)   Green   1974

S.W.S.G. "The Social Worker Reports"   Edinburgh   1974

S.W.S.G./S.H.H.D. "Guidance for Social Workers in
     relation to the Administrative Provisions for
     the Supervision of Persons released on Licence of
     Parole from Penal Establishments."   Edinburgh   1976

Sheehan A.V. "Criminal Procedures in Scotland
     and France"   H.M.S.O.   1975

INDEX

P

R